Phyllis Katz (1997–2000)
Daniel Perlman (1993–1996)
Stuart Oskamp (1988–1992)
George Levinger (1984–1987)
Joseph E. McGrath (1979–1983)
Jacqueline D. Goodchilds (1974–1978)
Bertram H. Raven (1970–1973)
Joshua A. Fishman (1966–1969)
Leonard Solomon (1963)
Robert Chin (1960–1965)
John Harding (1956–1959)
M. Brewster Smith (1951–1955)
Harold H. Kelley (1949)
Ronald Lippitt (1944–1950)

*Journal of Social Issues, Vol. 72, No. 3, 2016, pp. 419–431*
doi: 10.1111/josi.12174

# The Psychological Study of Positive Behavior Across Group Boundaries: An Overview

**Birte Siem**[*] **and Stefan Stürmer**
*FernUniversität in Hagen*

**Todd L. Pittinsky**
*Stony Brook University*

*Negative intergroup processes such as prejudice and conflict have been a traditional focus of social psychological research, while work that explicitly focuses on the determinants of positive intergroup processes is still in its infancy. Reflecting these relatively recent developments in the social and behavioral sciences, this volume's contributions represent current directions in psychological theorizing and research on positive and proactive behavior across group boundaries. One intriguing feature of positive cross-group behaviors is that they can be conceived, at one and the same time, as individual, interpersonal, and collective phenomena. Accordingly, this volume is organized into three sections that represent these different levels of analysis. This multilevel approach represents a distinctive perspective that extends contemporary work on positive intergroup behavior. At a more general level, then, one important future outcome of this work could be a more nuanced picture of human social behavior in the context of groups.*

Throughout the history of humanity, there are devastating examples of intergroup aggression and, in societies worldwide, manifestations of intergroup animosity and conflict pose grave social and political problems. However, most civilizations also provide pervasive proof of the opposite phenomenon—positive

---

*Correspondence concerning this article should be addressed to Birte Siem, Department of Psychology, FernUniversität in Hagen, Universitätsstraße 33, 58084 Hagen, Germany. [e-mail: birte.siem@fernuni-hagen.de].

The issue editors would like to thank the Society for the Psychological Study of Social Issues and the European Association of Social Psychology who jointly sponsored a small group meeting at Stony Brook University on Proactive Behavior Across Group Boundaries (organized by the issue editors). Most contributions of this volume were selected from a wider group of papers presented at this meeting.

behaviors across group boundaries—that manifests itself in multiple peaceful forms: intercultural exchange (as reflected in the arts and sciences, international trade, and the travel industry), efforts to explore and understand foreign cultures (as reflected in historic interest in extinct cultures and endeavors to uncover and explore "new" cultures), and a sense of curiosity and hospitality toward strangers (as reflected, for instance, in norms of providing assistance to travelers).

Psychological science (along with related disciplines) has contributed a lot more to our understanding of the angry segregationist than to our understanding of the traveler who cannot wait to immerse herself in a foreign way of life. Negative intergroup processes such as prejudice, ingroup favoritism, outgroup discrimination, and intergroup conflict have been a traditional focus of social psychological research on intergroup relations (e.g., Dovidio, Hewstone, Glick, & Esses, 2010). Research that explicitly focuses on the determinants of positive intergroup processes, in contrast, is still in its infancy (e.g., Jonas & Mummendey, 2008; Nagda, Tropp, & Paluck, 2006; Tropp & Mallett, 2011). The contributions to this volume represent current directions in psychological theorizing and research on positive and proactive behavior across group boundaries. The focus on positive (rather than negative) behaviors between groups and their members reflects relatively recent developments in the social and behavioral sciences. This volume, therefore, presents a new and distinctive perspective that differs in many respects from that found in contemporary treatments of group processes and intergroup relations.

## Traditional and Emerging Perspectives on Positive Behavior Across Group Boundaries

Historic explanations for psychology's focus on negative intergroup processes, especially prejudice and intergroup conflict, can be found in the specific social, historical, and political influences that shaped the development of modern social psychology in its founding phase: the Second World War, the Holocaust, and American racial segregation. Against this background, research on the origins of prejudice and intergroup hostility, as well as on possible ways of reducing them through psychological prevention and intervention, became the prime topics of intergroup research that still define the field today (Adorno, Frenkel-Brunswik, Levinson, & Sanford, 1950; Allport, 1954; Jones, 1998). Perhaps one of the most influential approaches in this domain is Gordon Allport's contact hypothesis (1954; i.e., the hypothesis that, under some specific conditions, intergroup contact has the potential to reduce prejudice). The contact hypothesis has stimulated a great deal of theoretical and empirical analysis that has tested and extended its basic assumptions in a variety of intergroup contexts (e.g., defined by race or ethnicity, age, or sexual orientation) and has focused on different forms of contact, such as direct, indirect, or extended contact and cross-group friendship (e.g., Davies, Tropp, Aron, Pettigrew, & Wright, 2011; Paolini, Hewstone, & Cairns, 2007;

Pettigrew, 1998; Pettigrew & Tropp, 2006, 2011; Wright, Aron, McLaughlin-Volpe, & Ropp, 1997). Still, the majority of this work has focused on contact as a means of reducing negative intergroup processes, such as prejudice or discrimination (e.g., Pettigrew & Tropp, 2011). Therefore, this research only provides rather indirect or limited answers to the questions of when and why people develop curiosity for other cultures or why they engage in cross-cultural exploration, travel, and contact seeking. Just as the occurrence of prosocial behavior cannot simply be explained by the absence or reduction of determinants causing aggression (Penner, Dovidio, Piliavin, & Schroeder, 2005), forms of positive intergroup attitudes and behaviors cannot simply be extrapolated from reduced levels of prejudice, anxiety, or hostility (Stürmer et al., 2013). Not hating is not the same as liking and not avoiding is not the same as approaching (e.g., Pittinsky, Rosenthal, & Montoya, 2011a; Tropp & Mallett, 2011). While the absence of prejudice may be sufficient to explain tolerance or indulgence of the culturally different, explaining positive and proactive behavior across group boundaries requires a perspective that goes beyond the negative intergroup behavior paradigm, one that takes into account the specific psychological and social processes that prompt people to deliberately and actively seek out cross-cultural contact. In recent years, an increasing number of intergroup researchers have started to look at positive behavior across group boundaries as a unique phenomenon requiring unique theoretical explanations (Morris, Chiu, & Liu, 2015; Pittinsky et al., 2011a; Stürmer et al., 2013).

One intriguing feature of positive behavior across group boundaries, such as travel, contact seeking, and exploration, is that it can be conceived, at one and the same time, as an individual, an interpersonal, and a collective phenomenon. This is because it involves the motives and activities of the individual, the experiences of interpersonal contact between members of different groups, and the collective context in which these activities and experiences occur (i.e., the social and political contexts structured by social groups and intergroup relations). Accordingly, a growing body of theoretical and empirical work has emerged, starting at different levels of social scientific inquiry. For instance, in line with a resurgence of interest in the role of personality in the study of intergroup attitudes and behavior (see Sibley & Duckitt, 2008), research starting at the individual (or micro) level has explored the contributions of personality structure (Stürmer et al., 2013) or of individual differences in motives (Dys-Steenbergen, Wright, & Aron, 2015), attitudes (Pittinsky, Rosenthal, & Montoya, 2011b), and beliefs (Rosenthal & Levy, 2010; Ryan, Casas, & Thompson, 2010) to contact seeking and cross-cultural engagement. Research focusing on the interpersonal (or meso) level, especially research in the tradition of Allport's (1954) contact hypothesis, has started to systematically investigate personal contact across group boundaries, especially cross-group friendships, as a means of directly promoting positive intergroup processes such as empathy, trust, forgiveness, outgroup knowledge acquisition, or willingness to approach members of the outgroup (e.g., Davies et al., 2011; Hewstone et al.,

2014; Mazziotta, Mummendey, & Wright, 2011; Pettigrew & Tropp, 2011; Swart, Hewstone, Christ, & Voci, 2010). Approaches on the group (or macro) level have started to investigate the role of collectively shared beliefs, ideologies, or norms such as shared beliefs about the values of inclusion and diversity (e.g., Tropp & Bianchi, 2006; Tropp, O'Brien, & Migacheva, 2014) that foster positive rather than negative intergroup processes.

Allport (1954) has proposed that even though humans may be thought of as "tribal," their preferential attachment to the ingroup does not necessarily imply negativity or hostility toward outgroups, but rather a general concern for the ingroup's well-being (see also Brewer, 1999). In fact, from an anthropological perspective, it seems reasonable to argue that the success of the human species substantially depended upon its fascinating capacity to establish relatively enduring and mutually beneficial relationships with culturally diverse groups outside the ingroup (rather than upon the capacity to fight and exterminate other groups). The research on positive intergroup behavior presented here may therefore provide fertile ground for a more general reconsideration of the forces governing intergroup relations, acknowledging that intergroup competition and conflict is but one of many means to foster the ingroup's well-being, with intergroup helping and reciprocal cooperation also being potent means.

## The Current *Journal of Social Issues* Volume

The major objective of this volume of the *Journal of Social Issues* is to provide examinations of representative lines of current theory and research on positive behavior across group boundaries. To this end, it brings together original contributions selected from a wider group of papers presented at a small group meeting at Stony Brook University in November/December 2012 on "Proactive Behavior Across Group Boundaries: Seeking and Maintaining Positive Interactions with Outgroup Members," organized by the issue editors. The meeting was jointly sponsored by the Society for the Psychological Study of Social Issues and the European Association of Social Psychology and received generous support from Stony Brook University. The issue comprises nine articles by scholars from eight countries who approach the topic from a wide range of theoretical backgrounds and with diverse research methodologies and designs, including correlational, experimental, and qualitative studies, laboratory and field research, and cross-sectional and longitudinal designs. The present volume combines these different approaches into a coherent and compelling theme. Specifically, it is organized into three sections that represent different levels of analysis of positive intergroup processes. The contributions in the first section center on the role of personal-level variables as determinants of positive intergroup processes. The second section focuses on interpersonal-level factors that shape the quality and the outcomes of one-on-one interactions with outgroup members. The third section deals with group-level determinants of positive intergroup processes. This multilevel approach to positive intergroup behavior represents a distinctive perspective that extends contemporary work on positive intergroup behavior. At a more general level, one important potential future outcome of this research, we suspect, could be a more nuanced picture of humans' social nature; specifically, of our social behavior in the context of groups.

*Personal Level: Personality Traits, Individual Motives, and Beliefs*

While an increasing number of studies have investigated the role of major personality traits in prejudice and discrimination (e.g., Sibley & Duckitt, 2008), the relations between personality characteristics and manifestations of positive behavior across group boundaries have received less attention (for exceptions, however, see van der Zee & van Oudenhoven, 2001; also Ponterotto, 2010). The four contributions in the first section seek to address this issue by emphasizing three distinct classes of personal-level determinants: major personality traits, individual motivations, and ideological beliefs.

Building on an integration of research findings on intergroup behavior from multiple fields of inquiry (biology, paleoanthropology, and social psychology) as well as research on the HEXACO personality framework, Barbarino and Stürmer (2016) present a prospective study among adolescents investigating the relations between major personality traits and their xenophile and xenophobic orientations. They hypothesized and found that xenophilia and xenophobia can be traced back to two distinct subsets of major personality traits. High levels of endeavor-related traits (i.e., Openness to Experience, Extraversion, and Conscientiousness) predicted greater xenophile orientation, whereas low levels of altruism-/cooperation-related traits (i.e., Honesty–Humility, Agreeableness, and Emotionality) predicted greater xenophobic orientation. Conclusions on the different personality origins were complemented through a distinct pattern of gender effects suggesting higher levels of xenophobic orientations among male and higher levels of xenophile orientations among female adolescents. The theoretical and practical implications of these findings, especially for designing tailored interventions to promote cross-cultural exploration, are discussed.

The contribution by Paolini, Wright, Dys-Steenbergen, and Favara (2016) addresses the question of how individuals' motivations for self-expansion prepare and motivate them to develop positive relationships across group boundaries. While there is evidence that self-expansion processes, like the inclusion of the other in the self, play an important role in cross-group relationships' ability to improve intergroup attitudes (e.g., Davies et al., 2011), the role of self-expansion motivation as an inspiration for cross-group contact and for seeking meaningful relationships with outgroup members has been largely untested. Paolini et al. present data from two studies, one correlational and the other experimental, demonstrating that self-expansion expectancies and a desire for self-expansion increase one's appetite for intergroup dissimilarity and thus inspire the formation of more and closer relationships with outgroup members. From an applied perspective, their research encourages the development of institutional cultures that assign positive value to self-expansion motivations, while providing reasons for confidence that these motivations can be satisfied through contact with outgroup members.

Rosenthal and Levy's (2016) contribution centers on polyculturalism, an individual-difference belief that different racial and ethnic groups have throughout history interacted and exchanged with each other, and thereby have influenced each other's cultures over time and into present day. Past work showing that greater endorsement of polyculturalism is positively associated with various indicators of positive intergroup attitudes employed mostly cross-sectional designs. The present contribution extends this work by examining the role of polyculturalism via a longitudinal investigation of undergraduates at a diverse university in the U.S. The authors found that greater endorsement of polyculturalism before the start of college prospectively predicted increases in intergroup contact and friendship from the spring of freshman year to the fall of sophomore year, after controlling for other potentially relevant predictors such as egalitarianism. Findings suggest that it may be fruitful to explore how polyculturalism could be implemented in interventions, programs, and policies at universities and colleges, as well as in other diverse settings.

*Interpersonal Level: One-on-One Interactions with Outgroup Members*

The second section brings together work that centers on interpersonal-level determinants of positive intergroup interactions. Specifically, the contributions identify interpersonal factors that shape the quality and outcomes of one-on-one interactions with outgroup members in various settings, such as teacher–student interactions at school or traveler–local interactions during travel. In doing so, they contribute to an emerging body of work focusing on the role of positive processes in personal contact across group boundaries (e.g., Davies et al., 2011). Most studies presented in this section use longitudinal designs, thus adding to relatively rare but much-needed longitudinal research on intergroup contact and friendship (e.g., Christ & Wagner, 2013; Hodson, Hewstone, & Swart, 2013).

The contribution by Davies and Aron (2016) centers on cross-group friendship as a specific form of intergroup contact. Although there is a growing body of work concerning cross-group friendship and intergroup attitudes, it typically focuses on a limited number of interpersonal processes among established friendships. In addition, little is known about the role of group-related processes within such friendships. Two studies were conducted to address this gap by investigating a variety of interpersonal- and intergroup-friendship variables at earlier and later stages of the friendship-development process. Results from a retrospective online survey and a longitudinal study reveal that both interpersonal friendship processes (e.g., affection, self-disclosure) and intergroup friendship processes (e.g., belief that an outgroup friend respects one's own group) are associated with positive intergroup attitudes. Specifically, the current findings suggest that interpersonal-friendship processes are vital to fostering positive outgroup attitudes early in the relationship, but that intergroup friendship processes become more strongly linked to attitudes once the relationship progresses. The authors discuss how their findings may be used to inform individuals who are in a position to encourage meaningful one-on-one interactions between members of different groups (e.g., community group leaders, public administrators, and educators).

Pittinsky and Montoya (2016) introduce empathic joy as an important predictor of allophilia, a positive personal attitude toward outgroup members. Empathy is one of the core emotions that regulate interpersonal interactions (e.g., Batson, 2011). Research on empathy, however, has focused almost exclusively on empathic sorrow, either defining empathy as a negative emotion or theoretically allowing it to be positive but then confining the actual study to the negative. Pittinsky and Montoya investigate the role of empathic joy in intergroup relations. Specifically, they test a model in which empathic joy affects allophilia, which, in turn, affects intergroup behavior, which, in turn, results in better outcomes for an outgroup. The setting is urban education; the subjects are mostly White teachers working in underperforming, largely non-White schools. Consistent with expectations, the authors find that empathic joy leads to better student outcomes and that it does so by leading to more positive attitudes (i.e., allophilia) of the teachers toward their students, which lead to more effecting teaching. The authors discuss the implications of their findings for and beyond the domain of education.

Livert (2016) focuses on the short- and long-term effects of positive one-on-one interactions with outgroup members. Specifically, he presents a mixed-methods longitudinal study documenting the short- and long-term impacts of a tour of Vietnam by 14 U.S. culinary students. Over 3 weeks, the travelers engaged in myriad intergroup interactions to experience Vietnam's cuisine and culture, exemplifying a positive intergroup orientation consistent with allophilia (Pittinsky & Montoya, 2016) and xenophilia (Stürmer et al., 2013). Measures included a pre-trip questionnaire, daily journal, and post-trip questionnaire, as well as participant observation. Short-term attitude change included significant increases in positive affect toward the Vietnamese, intergroup understanding, and a decrease in negative stereotypes. Nearly 10 years later, the author interviewed 10 of the original trip participants. Consistent with allophilia theory, participants expressed continued affection, kinship, and enthusiasm toward the Vietnamese people and remained motivated to engage the Vietnamese culture and cuisine. Given that longitudinal studies of the long-term effects of intergroup contact represent a notable lacuna in the literature (e.g., Lemmer & Wagner, 2015), the present study makes an important contribution.

*Group Level: Group-Based Beliefs, Needs, and Norms*

The previous two sections focused on personal and interpersonal determinants of positive intergroup processes that are not necessarily collectively shared or influenced by the nature of the intergroup context. Complementing these perspectives, the third section of this special issue turns to research on group-based determinants of positive intergroup processes and deals with the influence of challenges, needs, and norms that are directly defined by the groups' different positions in society and their relationships to each other.

Burhan and van Leeuwen (2016) present two experiments that address the relationships between immigrants and members of the host society and center on the question of how altering perceived cultural and economic challenges can increase helping and hospitality toward immigrants. Results from the first study showed that people who perceived immigrants as less of a threat to the society's economy were more willing to provide immigrants with empowerment help and less likely to expect immigrants to solve their own problems. Study 2 manipulated immigrants' perceived cultural adaptation and found that high cultural adaptation was seen as less of a threat than low cultural adaptation among the low and moderate nationalists, but not among high nationalists, who viewed immigrants as threatening regardless of their cultural adaptation. Participants who perceived immigrants as nonthreatening to the host society's cultural values were subsequently more willing to provide help in the form of direct assistance and less likely to expect immigrants to solve their own problems. In addition to addressing the ironic finding that the people who are most threatened by a perceived lack of adaptation by immigrants are also the least willing to help them in their adjustment process, Burhan and van Leeuwen offer several suggestions to increase willingness to help immigrants, especially among high nationalists.

Shnabel, SimanTov-Nachlieli, and Halabi (2016) focus on the role of group-based needs in promoting positive intergroup relations in a context of (seemingly) intractable conflict. Based on the framework of the needs-based model of reconciliation, they argue that in conflicts characterized by mutual transgressions, such as the Israeli–Palestinian conflict, group members prioritize their agency-related over morality-related needs. Optimistically, however, two studies conducted among Israeli Jews and West Bank Palestinians found that addressing group members' pressing need for agency through affirming their ingroup's strength, competence, and self-determination allowed their otherwise unprioritized moral considerations to come to the fore, leading to stronger prosocial tendencies across group boundaries. These studies suggest that group members need to feel secure and agentic in order to allow their moral needs to come into play. Practically, the insights regarding the positive effects of agency affirmation can be used in planning interventions by dialogue group facilitators, mediators, or group leaders who wish to encourage positive intergroup relations. The present contribution not only emphasizes the relatively neglected role of morality-related processes in the promotion of positive intergroup relations (e.g., Leach, Ellemers, & Barreto, 2007), but also addresses the pressing issue of finding peaceful solutions to seemingly intractable conflicts (e.g., Halperin & Sharvit, 2015).

In the final contribution of this section, Montoya and Pinter (2016) present a model of intergroup relations focused on the role of the ingroup-favoring norm in facilitating positive intergroup relations. The ingroup-favoring norm is a group-level norm that motivates and orients behavior in the intragroup and intergroup contexts by directing group members to first consider the interests of the ingroup. Despite the apparent contradiction that an orientation toward one's own group members can be beneficial to intergroup relations, Montoya and Pinter present different pathways by which the norm can result in more positive intergroup relations, including emphasizing the value of interactions with the outgroup, establishing cooperative intergroup norms, and establishing superordinate goals. In so doing, they discuss how classic moderators of intergroup relations—including leadership, guilt, and ingroup norms—facilitate positive intergroup relations once ingroup interests are considered.

## Societal Relevance

Societies worldwide are characterized by phenomena such as globalization, the opening of national borders, rising migration rates, and the explosive growth of new communication technologies. For most of us, meeting and dealing with people of diverse cultural backgrounds, ethnicities, and religions is already a part of everyday life and will become even more so in the future. Hence, one of the central questions of our time is how we can promote qualities such as tolerance and acceptance of "the other" and openness toward other social groups in an increasingly diverse society (e.g., Chiu, Gries, Torelli, & Cheng, 2011). This question becomes even more important as recent research suggests that the positive effects of (ethnic) diversity on intergroup relations might actually decrease with increasing levels of diversity (e.g., Thijs & Verkuyten, 2014; Vervoort, Scholte, & Scheepers, 2011). In line with the *Journal of Social Issue*'s mission, a major aim of the present volume is therefore to discuss how the work it presents can be used to inform theoretically and empirically well-grounded intervention strategies aimed at promoting qualities such as interest in and openness toward other groups. Accordingly, the closing paper by Nadler (2016) as well as a considerable part of each of the other contributions will be dedicated to a discussion of how the authors' work can be applied to social issues or social policy.

Given the different foci of the contributions, these suggestions should be of great interest to many practitioners working in settings where people of diverse backgrounds meet, including community planners, school or university administrators, online group leaders, volunteer program coordinators, and mediators. The contributions cover a wide array of intergroup contexts ranging from rather benevolent ones (e.g., contact between college students of different ethnic/racial backgrounds) to highly fraught intergroup contexts (e.g., the Israeli–Palestinian conflict), thus providing practical guidance on how to promote intergroup relations in everyday situations but also in extreme situations characterized by open hostility and violence. Moreover, the present volume has the potential to contribute to the development of multilevel intervention-based policies that address the issue of positive intergroup relations on the personal, the interpersonal, and the group level (see also Pettigrew, 1996; Pettigrew & Tropp, 2011). These might range from profiling the xenophile individual (based on a person's specific constellation of major personality traits, individual motivations, attitudes, and ideological beliefs) to creating optimal conditions for genuinely positive one-on-one interactions (e.g., through promoting empathic joy and intimate interpersonal processes) and strengthening the group-based needs and norms relevant for positive intergroup behavior.

In closing, we would like to note that, even though our view on positive intergroup processes is manifold and comprehensive, it still has a clear social psychological focus. To be sure, the articles collected in this special issue provide impressive examples of the myriad ways that social psychology is contributing to the investigation of positive behavior across group boundaries and make a variety of important conceptual, empirical, and methodological contributions. Still, our collection is also illustrative in highlighting some gaps in the current literature. Specifically, there is a relative scarcity of research endeavors conducted by scholars from different academic disciplines (e.g., anthropology, economics, psychology, and social neuroscience). Also, focusing more closely on psychology itself, social neuroscience research might help to integrate biological and behavioral levels of analysis in the social psychological perspective and thus provide a more detailed picture of the processes underlying positive intergroup relations and the policies that help promote them (e.g., Dovidio, Pearson, & Orr, 2008; Kang, Inzlicht, & Derks, 2010). Similarly, research on the developmental origins of xenophile behavior such as cross-group exploration or outgroup helping would provide valuable contributions to the design of intervention-based policies, especially since intergroup attitudes are not yet fully formed in early childhood, making interventions uniquely influential at that age (e.g., Abrams & Killen, 2014). Promoting work in these (and other) related areas and integrating it with social psychological approaches will advance our understanding of the processes contributing to positive intergroup behavior and contribute to the design of more powerful intervention-based policies to increase the prevalence of such behavior.

For the time being, the articles presented in this special issue provide promising starting points for future endeavors along these lines. We are hopeful and optimistic that, with the passage of time, these efforts will be successful and thus contribute meaningfully to a more comprehensive understanding of the benevolent and kinder side of human social nature.

# References


Abrams, D., & Killen, M. (2014). Social exclusion of children: Developmental origins of prejudice. *Journal of Social Issues*, *70*, 1–11. doi: 10.1111/josi.12043

Adorno, T. W., Frenkel-Brunswik, E., Levinson, D. J., & Sanford, R. N. (1950). *The authoritarian personality*. Oxford, United Kingdom: Harpers.

Allport, G. (1954). *The nature of prejudice*. Reading, MA: Addison Wesley.

Barbarino, M.-L., & Stürmer, S. (2016). Different origins of xenophile and xenophobic orientations in human personality structure: A theoretical perspective and some preliminary findings. *Journal of Social Issues*, *72*, 432–449.

Brewer, M. B. (1999). The psychology of prejudice: Ingroup love or outgroup hate? *Journal of Social Issues*, *55*, 429–444. doi:10.1111/0022-4537.00126

Batson, C. D. (2011). *Altruism in humans*. New York: Oxford University Press.

Burhan, O. K., & van Leeuwen, E. (2016). Altering perceived cultural and economic threats can increase immigrant helping. *Journal of Social Issues*, *72*, 548–565.

Chiu, C.-Y., Gries, P., Torelli, C. J., & Cheng, S. Y. Y. (2011). Toward a social psychology of globalization. *Journal of Social Issues*, *67*, 663–676. doi: 10.1111/j.1540-4560.2011.01721.x

Christ, O., & Wagner, U. (2013). Methodological issues in the study of intergroup contact: Towards a new wave of research. In G. Hodson & M. Hewstone (Eds.), *Advances in intergroup contact* (pp. 233–261). New York: Psychology Press.

Davies, K., & Aron, A. (2016). Friendship development and intergroup attitudes: The role of interpersonal and intergroup friendship processes. *Journal of Social Issues*, *72*, 489–510.

Davies, K., Tropp, L. R., Aron, A., Pettigrew, T. F., & Wright, S. C. (2011). Cross-group friendships and intergroup attitudes: A meta-analytic review. *Personality and Social Psychology Review*, *15*, 332–351. doi: 10.1177/1088868311411103

Dovidio, J. F., Hewstone, M., Glick, P., & Esses, V. M. (Eds.). (2010). *The SAGE handbook of prejudice, stereotyping, and discrimination*. London: Sage Publications.

Dovidio, J. F., Pearson, A. R., & Orr, P. (2008). Social psychology and neuroscience: Strange bedfellows or a healthy marriage? *Group Processes & Intergroup Relations*, *11*, 247–263.

Dys-Steenbergen, O., Wright, S. C., & Aron, A. (2015). Self-expansion motivation improves cross-group interactions and enhances self-growth. *Group Processes & Intergroup Relations*. Advance online publication. doi: 10.1177/1368430215583517

Halperin, E., & Sharvit, K. (Eds.). (2015). *The social psychology of intractable conflict: Celebrating the legacy of Daniel Bar-Tal*. Cham, Switzerland: Springer International.

Hewstone, M., Lolliot, S., Swart, H., Myers, E., Voci, A., Al Ramiah, A., & Cairns, E. (2014). Intergroup contact and intergroup conflict. *Peace and Conflict: Journal of Peace Psychology*, *20*, 39–53. doi: 10.1037/a0035582

Hodson, G., Hewstone, M., & Swart, H. (2013). Advances in intergroup contact: Epilogue and future directions. In G. Hodson & M. Hewstone (Eds.), *Advances in intergroup contact* (pp. 262–305). New York: Psychology Press.

Jonas, K. J., & Mummendey, A. (2008). Positive intergroup relations: From reduced outgroup rejection to outgroup support. In U. Wagner, L. R. Tropp, G. Finchilescu, & C. Tredoux (Eds.), *Improving intergroup relations: Building on the legacy of Thomas F. Pettigrew* (pp. 210–224). Oxford, United Kingdom: Blackwell.

Jones, E. E. (1998). Major developments in five decades of social psychology. In D. T. Gilbert, S. T. Fiske, & G. Lindzey (Eds.), *The hand-book of social psychology* (4th ed., Vol. 1, pp. 3–57). Boston, MA: McGraw-Hill.

Kang, S. K., Inzlicht, M., & Derks, B. (2010). Social neuroscience and public policy on intergroup relations: A Hegelian analysis. *Journal of Social Issues*, *66*, 585–601. doi: 10.1111/j.1540-4560.2010.01664.x

Leach, C. W., Ellemers, N., & Barreto, M. (2007). Group virtue: The importance of morality (vs. competence and sociability) in the positive evaluation of in-groups. *Journal of Personality and Social Psychology, 93*, 234–249. doi: 10.1037/0022-3514.93.2.234

Lemmer, G., & Wagner, U. (2015). Can we really reduce ethnic prejudice outside the lab? A meta-analysis of direct and indirect contact interventions. *European Journal of Social Psychology, 45*, 152–168.

Livert, D. (2016). A cook's tour abroad: Long term effects of intergroup contact on positive outgroup attitudes. *Journal of Social Issues, 72*, 524–547.

Mazziotta, A., Mummendey, A., & Wright, S. C. (2011). Vicarious intergroup contact effects: Applying social-cognitive theory to intergroup contact research. *Group Processes & Intergroup Relations, 14*, 255–274. doi: 10.1177/1368430210390533

Montoya, R. M., & Pinter, B. (2016). A model for understanding positive intergroup relations using the ingroup-favoring norm. *Journal of Social Issues, 72*, 584–600.

Morris, M. W., Chiu, C.-Y., & Liu, Z. (2015). Polycultural psychology. *Annual Review of Psychology, 66*, 631–659. doi: 10.1146/annurev-psych-010814-015001

Nadler, A. (2016). The historical and relational contexts of the study of positive behaviors across group boundaries. *Journal of Social Issues, 72*, 601–613.

Nagda, B. A., Tropp, L. R., & Paluck, E. L. (2006). Looking back as we look ahead: Integrating research, theory, and practice on intergroup relations. *Journal of Social Issues, 62*, 439–451. doi: 10.1111/j.1540-4560.2006.00467.x

Paolini, S., Hewstone, M., & Cairns, E. (2007). Direct and indirect intergroup friendship effects: Testing the moderating role of the affective-cognitive bases of prejudice. *Personality and Social Psychology Bulletin, 33*, 1406–1420. doi: 10.1177/0146167207304788

Paolini, S., Wright, S., Dys-Steenbergen, O., & Favara, I. (2016). Self-expansion and intergroup contact: Expectancies and motives to self-expand lead to greater interest in outgroup contact and more positive intergroup relations. *Journal of Social Issues, 72*, 450–471.

Penner, L. A., Dovidio, J. F., Piliavin, J. A., & Schroeder, D. A. (2005). Prosocial behavior: Multilevel perspectives. *Annual Review of Psychology, 56*, 365–392. doi: 10.1146/annurev.psych.56.091103.070141

Pettigrew, T. F. (1996). *How to think like a social scientist.* New York: Harper Collins.

Pettigrew, T. F. (1998). Intergroup contact theory. *Annual Review of Psychology, 49*, 65–68.

Pettigrew, T. F., & Tropp, L. R. (2006). A meta-analytic test of intergroup contact theory. *Journal of Personality and Social Psychology, 90*, 751–783. doi: 10.1037/0022-3514.90.5.751

Pettigrew, T. F., & Tropp, L. R. (2011). *When groups meet: The dynamics of intergroup contact.* New York, NY: Psychology Press.

Pittinsky, T. L., & Montoya, M. (2016). Empathic joy in positive intergroup relations. *Journal of Social Issues, 72*, 511–523.

Pittinsky, T. L., Rosenthal, S. A., & Montoya, R. M. (2011a). Liking is not the opposite of disliking: The functional separability of positive and negative attitudes toward minority groups. *Cultural Diversity And Ethnic Minority Psychology, 17*, 134–143. doi: 10.1037/a0023806

Pittinsky, T. L., Rosenthal, S. A., & Montoya, R. M. (2011b). Measuring positive attitudes toward outgroups: Development and validation of the Allophilia Scale. In L. R. Tropp & R. K. Mallett (Eds.), *Beyond prejudice reduction: Pathways to positive intergroup relations* (pp. 41–60). Washington, DC: American Psychological Association.

Ponterotto, J. G. (2010). Multicultural personality: An evolving theory of optimal functioning in culturally heterogeneous societies. *Counselling Psychologist, 38*, 714–758. doi: 10.1177/0011000009359203

Rosenthal, L., & Levy, S. R. (2010). The colorblind, multicultural, and polycultural ideological approaches to improving intergroup attitudes and relations. *Social Issues and Policy Review, 4*, 215–246. doi: 10.1111/j.1751-2409.2010.01022.x

Rosenthal, L., & Levy, S. R. (2016). Endorsement of polyculturalism predicts increased positive intergroup contact and friendship across the beginning of college. *Journal of Social Issues, 72*, 472–488.

Ryan, C. S., Casas, J. F., & Thompson, B. K. (2010). Interethnic ideology, intergroup perceptions, and cultural orientation. *Journal of Social Issues, 66*, 29–44. doi: 10.1111/j.1540-4560.2009.01631.x

Shnabel, N., SimanTov-Nachlieli, I., & Halabi, S. (2016). The power to be moral: Affirming Israelis' and Palestinians' agency promotes prosocial tendencies across group boundaries. *Journal of Social Issues, 72*, 566–583.

Sibley, C. G., & Duckitt, J. (2008). Personality and prejudice: A meta-analysis and theoretical review. *Personality and Social Psychology Review, 12*, 248–279. doi: 10.1177/1088868308319226

Stürmer, S., Benbow, A. E. F., Siem, B., Barth, M., Bodansky, A. N., & Lotz-Schmitt, K. (2013). Psychological foundations of xenophilia: The role of major personality traits in predicting favorable attitudes toward cross-cultural contact and exploration. *Journal of Personality and Social Psychology, 105*, 832–851. doi: 10.1037/a0033488

Swart, H., Hewstone, M., Christ, O., & Voci, A. (2010). The impact of crossgroup friendships in South Africa: Affective mediators and multigroup comparisons. *Journal of Social Issues, 66*, 309–333. doi: 10.1111/j.1540-4560.2010.01647.x

Thijs, J., & Verkuyten, M. (2014). School ethnic diversity and students' interethnic relations. *British Journal of Educational Psychology, 84*, 1–21. doi: 10.1111/bjep.12032

Tropp, L. R., & Bianchi, R. (2006). Valuing diversity and interest in intergroup contact. *Journal of Social Issues, 62*, 533–551. doi: 10.1111/j.1540-4560.2006.00472.x

Tropp, L. R., & Mallett, R. K. (Eds.). (2011). *Moving beyond prejudice reduction: Pathways to positive intergroup relations*. Washington, DC: American Psychological Association.

Tropp, L. R., O'Brien, T. C., & Migacheva, K. (2014). How peer norms of inclusion and exclusion predict children's interest in cross-ethnic friendships. *Journal of Social Issues, 70*, 151–166. doi: 10.1111/josi.12052

Van der Zee, K., & Van Oudenhoven, J. P. (2001). The Multicultural Personality Questionnaire: Reliability and validitiy of self- and other ratings of multicultural effectiveness. *Journal of Research in Personality, 35*, 278–288. doi: 10.1006/jrpe.2001.2320

Vervoort, M. H. M., Scholte, R. H. J., & Scheepers, P. L. H. (2011). Ethnic composition of school classes, majority-minority friendships, and adolescents' intergroup attitudes in the Netherlands. *Journal of Adolescence, 34*, 257–267. doi: 10.1016/j.adolescence.2010.05.005

Wright, S. C., Aron, A., McLaughlin-Volpe, T., & Ropp, S. A. (1997). The extended contact effect: Knowledge of cross-group friendships and prejudice. *Journal of Personality and Social Psychology, 73*, 73–90. doi: 10.1037/0022-3514.73.1.73

BIRTE SIEM is a research associate and lecturer at FernUniversität in Hagen. She received her PhD in psychology from that university and completed a postdoctoral fellowship at the International Graduate College on Conflict and Cooperation between Social Groups at the Friedrich-Schiller-University in Jena. Her research interests include empathy, prosocial behavior between social groups, and perceptions of inequality in intergroup relations.

STEFAN STÜRMER is Professor of Psychology at FernUniversität in Hagen. In his research, he investigates inter- and intragroup processes, with a particular emphasis on the role of group processes in social movement participation, cooperation, helping, and altruism. He is co-editor of The Psychology of Prosocial Behavior: Group Processes, Intergroup Relations, and Helping.

TODD L. PITTINSKY is Professor at Stony Brook University (SUNY). He was previously associate professor at the Harvard Kennedy School, where he served as research director for Harvard's Center for Public Leadership. His recent projects include Us Plus Them: Tapping the Positive Power of Difference (Harvard Business Publishing). He received his BA in psychology from Yale and his PhD jointly from Harvard's Graduate School of Arts and Science and Harvard Business School.

*Journal of Social Issues, Vol. 72, No. 3, 2016, pp. 432–449*
*doi: 10.1111/josi.12175*

# Different Origins of Xenophile and Xenophobic Orientations in Human Personality Structure: A Theoretical Perspective and Some Preliminary Findings

**Maria-Luisa Barbarino**[*] **and Stefan Stürmer**
*FernUniversität in Hagen*

*Building on an integration of research findings on proactive intergroup behavior from multiple fields of inquiry (biology, paleoanthropology, social psychology) as well as research on the HEXACO personality framework, a prospective study among adolescents investigated the relations between personality traits and xenophile and xenophobic orientations (Total N = 455, 219 males, $M_{age}$ = 17.66 years). Path models corroborate that xenophile orientations and xenophobic orientations were predicted by two distinct subsets of major personality traits: High scores in endeavor-related traits (i.e., Openness to Experience, Extraversion, and Conscientiousness) predicted greater xenophile orientations, whereas low scores in altruism/cooperation-related traits (i.e., Honesty-Humility, Agreeableness, and Emotionality) predicted greater xenophobic orientations. Conclusions on the effects of personality traits were complemented by a distinct pattern of gender effects suggesting higher levels of xenophobic orientations among male adolescents and higher levels of xenophile orientations among females. Theoretical and practical implications of these findings are discussed.*

In times featuring near daily news of wars and genocide all around the globe, xenophobia seems a human universal. Still, there is also a brighter side of human nature that is frequently overlooked: xenophilia—an attraction to foreign cultures or people that manifests itself in curiosity and benevolent cross-cultural

---

[*]Correspondence concerning this article should be addressed to Maria-Luisa Barbarino or Stefan Stürmer, Department of Psychology, FernUniversität in Hagen, Universitätsstr. 33, 58084 Hagen, Germany [e-mail: maria-luisa.barbarino@fernuni-hagen.de or stefan.stuermer@fernuni-hagen.de]

The study was conducted by Maria-Luisa Barbarino under Stefan Stürmer's supervision in partial fulfillment of the requirements of a doctoral degree. This research was made possible by a grant from the Deutsche Forschungsgemeinschaft to Stefan Stürmer (STU 250/5-1).

432

exploration (Antweiler, 2009). Psychological science has extensively studied the social and psychological roots of xenophobia. However, just as the occurrence of altruism cannot be explained by the absence (or reduction) of determinants causing aggression (Krueger, Hicks, & McGue, 2001), forms of positive intergroup behaviors cannot simply be extrapolated from the absence of processes causing intergroup hostility (Pittinsky, Rosenthal, & Montoya, 2011; Stürmer & Snyder, 2010; Tropp & Mallett, 2011). Some researchers have thus started to look at human attraction to other cultural groups as a unique phenomenon with a unique evolutionary, cultural and psychological etiology (Davies & Aron, 2016; Morris, Chiu, & Liu, 2015; Paolini, Wright, Dys-Steenbergen, & Favara, 2016; Pittinsky et al., 2011; Rosenthal & Levy, 2016; Stürmer, Benbow, Siem, Barth, Bodansky, & Lotz-Schmitt, 2013).

Like individual differences in general, interindividual variations in xenophile (or xenophobic) orientations are likely to be produced through a complex interplay of multiple factors (e.g., personality traits, individual experiences, social influence from in-group members, cultural values). The present research investigates the personality foundations of these phenomena—a focus that is consistent with increasing interest in the role of personality in cross-cultural relations (e.g., Benet-Martínez & Haritatos, 2005; Van der Zee & Van Oudenhoven, 2000, 2001). In particular, we suggest that xenophile orientations on the one hand and xenophobic orientations on the other represent two related though distinct phenomena which can be, at least partially, traced back to two distinct subsets of major personality traits. Our hypotheses are grounded in a recent personality perspective on xenophilia integrating findings on intergroup behavior from multiple fields of scientific inquiry (biological and cultural paleoanthropology, social psychology) with research on the HEXACO personality framework (Stürmer et al., 2013). The HEXACO personality framework (e.g., Ashton & Lee, 2007) suggests that, in contrast to the traditional "Big-Five" model of personality structure (e.g., Costa & McCrae, 1992; Goldberg, 1993), personality is better represented by a six-factor structure (facet-level trait subdomains according to Ashton and Lee, 2007, are given in parentheses): Honesty-Humility (fairness, sincerity, greed avoidance, modesty), Emotionality (sentimentality, anxiety, fearfulness, emotional dependence), Extraversion (social self-esteem, social boldness, sociability, liveliness), Agreeableness (forgiveness, gentleness, flexibility, patience), Conscientiousness (organization, diligence, perfectionism, prudence), and Openness to experience (aesthetic appreciation, inquisitiveness, creativity, unconventionality). One particularly interesting aspect of the HEXACO framework for the purposes of the analyses presented here is the distinction between endeavor-related and altruism/cooperation-related personality traits derived from theoretical biology (see Ashton & Lee, 2007; also Ashton & Lee, 2001). According to this classification, endeavor-related traits (Extraversion, Openness, and Conscientiousness) represent conceptually parallel dimensions geared toward investing individual resources in distinct types of endeavors that will bring about distinct benefits for the self (e.g., social gains such as new friends, mates, and allies, ideational or material gains resulting from discovery, economic gains through the improved use of resources). By contrast, altruism/cooperation-related traits (Honesty-Humility, Emotionality, and Agreeableness) represent (biologically anchored) tendencies to contribute to some mutual or collective benefit (e.g., through helping kin or friends, see Ashton & Lee, 2007, p. 156).

The distinction between endeavor-related traits and altruism/cooperation-related traits points directly to a potential differential role of HEXACO personality traits in stimulating xenophile or xenophobic orientations. An accumulating body of empirical research in biological and cultural anthropology suggests that cross-group contact with conspecifics outside the immediate in-group circle brings about distinct benefits for the group and its members that cannot be obtained through in-group interaction (in biological terms, for instance, genetic variability through offering new mating opportunities, e.g., Charlesworth & Willis, 2009; Glémin, Ronfort, & Bataillon, 2003; Moore & Ali, 1984; in more general social-cultural terms gains in artifacts, people and knowledge through exchange and trade, e.g., Bar-Yosef, 2002; Klein, 1999; Stringer, 2001). Nevertheless, leaving the in-group is also a potentially dangerous undertaking as it entails the risk of hostile intergroup encounters or exploitation (e.g., Manson & Wrangham, 1991; Schaller & Neuberg, 2012). A main premise of the personality perspective presented here is that the ambiguous nature of interactions with culturally different and unfamiliar out-groups critically shapes the relationships between personality traits and xenophile or xenophobic orientations. Following the HEXACO framework, people with high scores in endeavor-related traits are particularly disposed to invest individual resources in the exploration of new opportunities to obtain social, ideational, or material gains despite potential risks. Accordingly, individuals high in endeavor-related traits should also be particularly disposed to investing their time and energy in benevolent exploration of other cultural groups. Altruism and cooperation, on the other hand, require mutual trust and the certainty that one's contribution to the cooperation will not be exploited (which is, in fact, one of the key reasons why, from a biological perspective, altruism and cooperation take place within relatively stable and secure social relationships, such as the ones provided by the family or in-groups; see, for instance, Axelrod, 1984). By integrating the HEXACO framework with the research findings outlined above, it therefore seems likely that people high in altruism/cooperation-related traits may be rather reluctant to actively seek out cross-group contact as long as the nature of the intergroup interaction appears ambiguous. Altruism/cooperation-related traits may play a more prominent role in the etiology of humans' xenophobic orientations, however. According to the HEXACO framework, high levels in altruism/cooperation-related traits stimulate a tendency to cooperate and share *and* a tendency to avoid aggression and hostility in social relations (Ashton & Lee, 2007, p. 156). One can thus expect that individuals low in altruism/cooperation-related traits (i.e., individuals who generally prefer cooperation over antagonism) should show significantly higher inclinations toward intergroup dominance and hostility (i.e., xenophobia) than individuals high in altruism/cooperation-related traits.

Empirical support for our hypotheses about the relative primacy of endeavor-related over altruism/cooperation-related traits in stimulating xenophile orientations comes from a series of three independent studies (total $N = 1,007$) employing different operationalizations of major personality traits (the HEXACO-PI-R inventory and the BFI-10; Stürmer et al., 2013). Specifically, our analyses confirmed that individual differences in levels of Extraversion, Openness and Conscientiousness explained significantly more variance in xenophile orientations than individual differences in levels of altruism/cooperation-related traits (i.e., Honest-Humility, Emotionality, and Agreeableness). There was also some evidence for positive relationships between altruism/cooperation-related traits and xenophile orientations in each study. Importantly, however, in line with our theory and in contrast to the links involving endeavor-related traits, these positive relationships were exclusively indirect relationships, suggesting that high levels of altruism/cooperation-related traits predispose individuals to adopting favorable attitudes toward cross-cultural exploration only to the extent that this disposition translates into reduced preference toward intergroup dominance and hostility.

Our hypotheses about the primacy of endeavor-related traits in stimulating xenophile orientations are in line with studies exploring the role of the Big Five personality factors in multicultural engagement (e.g., Van der Zee & Van Oudenhoven, 2000; Zimmermann & Neyer, 2013; also Mak & Tran, 2001). Our hypotheses about the primacy of altruism/cooperation-related traits in stimulating xenophobic orientations, on the other hand, resonate with findings that competitiveness and hostility, including prejudice and discrimination against out-group members, are generally facilitated by *low* levels of Agreeableness, Emotionality and/or Honesty-Humility (e.g., Lee & Ashton, 2012; Leone, Desimoni, & Chirumbolo, 2012; Sibley, Harding, Perry, Asbrock, & Duckitt, 2010). Although there is also evidence that low levels of Openness predict greater prejudice (e.g., Sibley & Duckitt, 2008), the preponderance of findings seem consistent with our idea that individual differences in levels of altruism/cooperation-related traits have greater power to predict xenophobic orientations than individual differences in levels of endeavor-related traits.

Even though the findings reported above suggest that xenophile and xenophobic orientations can be, at least partially, traced back to two distinct subsets of major personality traits, we are not aware of any study directly testing this hypothesis. The main aim of the present research was thus to fill this gap in the research literature. Investigating the role of personality in positive (and negative) behaviors across group boundaries not only engages fundamental questions about human sociality in the contexts of groups, but also relates to practical social goals and societal problems. If we are able to better understand which personality traits stimulate xenophilia (and which, by contrast, stimulate xenophobic reactions), we might also be able to devise more tailored interventions that strengthen individual curiosity about other cultures and interest in benevolent cross-cultural exploration.

We tested our specific personality hypotheses in the context of a larger scale project on the social and psychological aspects of adolescents' intergroup orientations (Stürmer & Barbarino, 2013). We focused on this particular age group for two reasons. First, previous research on the personality foundations of intergroup attitudes has almost exclusively focused on adults (e.g., Sibley & Duckitt, 2008; Stürmer et al., 2013). Replicating previous findings among a sample of adolescents would provide some evidence for the generalizability of our and other researchers' findings across different age groups. Second, from the point of our theory, adolescence also presents a particularly interesting life phase because, as parental influences decrease and individual autonomy increases, there is also increasing room for personality factors to influence the development of new social relationships, including relationships spanning across cultural boundaries.

## Method

*Respondents and Procedure*

Measures for this report and informed consent were obtained from 455 final-year high school students (219 males, 236 females, $M_{age} = 17.66$ years, $SD = 0.74$ years) with a German cultural background from three co-educational public high schools in Germany who participated in two time-lagged testing sessions (total sample at Time 1 = 635, response rate at Time 2 = 72%). The main predictor variables of the present analyses (HEXACO personality traits) were measured in the first half of the final school year (Time 1), while the main criterion variables (indicators of xenophile and xenophobic orientations) were measured in the second half of the school year, up to six months later (Time 2). Data were collected in a paper-and-pencil based format in group sessions. Students with non-German cultural background who also participated in the study were not included in the analyses because of the ambiguity of their responses to the cross-cultural contact items. An additional follow-up among 130 respondents from the original panel sample (response rate = 29%) allowed us to obtain further information about adolescents' xenophile orientations up to six month after graduation (and twelve months after the completion of the Time 1 personality questionnaire).

*Measures*

*Personality traits (measured at Time 1).* To measure respondents' personality traits, we used an established German version of the 96-item

HEXACO-Personality Inventory-Revised (HEXACO-PI-R; Lee & Ashton, 2004). In line with the English version, each of the six higher-order personality dimensions were measured with four 4-item subscales pertaining to more narrow facets of the corresponding dimension. Response scales ranged from 1 (*strong disagreement*) to 5 (*strong agreement*).

   *Xenophobia-related measures (measured at Time 2).*   Xenophobia is a multifaceted construct involving a sense of dominance and superiority with regard to one's own cultural group, feelings of fear of other cultural groups, and a readiness to show open hostility toward members of other cultural groups (see, for instance, Watts, 1996). To assess these aspects of xenophobia, we used three separate multi-item scales: First, to tap respondents' general preference for group-based dominance, we used an established German version of Pratto, Sidanius, Stallworth, and Malle's (1994) 10-item Social Dominance Orientation scale (hereafter: SDO) with response scales ranging from 1 (*very negative*) to 7 (*very positive*). Second, to tap respondents' fear and disapproval of other cultural groups, we used a German version of Arends-Tóth and van de Vijver's (2003) 10-item Multicultural Ideology scale (hereafter: MI) with response scales ranging from 1 (*strongly disagree*) to 7 (*strongly agree*). Third, to tap respondents' unwillingness to control hostile reactions toward foreigners we used a reverse coded version of Banse and Gawronski's (2003) 16-item motivation to control prejudice scale (hereafter: MTCP-R) with response scales ranging from 1 (*not true at all*) to 5 (*completely true*). For each of the three separate composite scales, items were coded such that higher scores indicate higher levels of social dominance orientation, higher fear and disapproval of other cultural groups, and lower motivation to control hostility and prejudice.

   *Xenophilia-related measures (measured at Time 2).*   In a very basic psychological sense, xenophilia can be conceptualized as a favorable attitude toward exploratory contact with individuals from cultural groups perceived as unfamiliar or strange (Stürmer et al., 2013). To assess cognitive, affective and conative aspects of this orientation, we used three separate composite scales: First, to tap respondents' sense of *knowledge and understanding of other cultures,* we employed the 6-item Intergroup Understanding subscale of Stephan's (1999) Intergroup Dialogue Programs Evaluation Questionnaire (e.g., "I believe that I have a good understanding of how members of other cultural groups view the world,"). Respondents rated each item on separate five-point ratings scales ranging from 1 (*strongly disagree*) to 5 (*strongly agree*). Second, we measured respondents' *feelings in cross-cultural interactions* by way of seven pairs of adjectives derived from the Intergroup Anxiety subscale of Stephan's (1999) evaluation instrument (e.g., *not at all comfortable – extremely comfortable, not at all confident – extremely confident*). Ratings were made on 5-point scales ranging from 1 to 5. Third, to measure respondents' behavioral tendencies, and following Stürmer et al.'s (2013,

Study 2) procedure, respondents were asked to indicate how much time they had previously spent on the following pastimes: (a) reading travel magazines or reports about long distance travel, (b) learning a foreign language in their leisure time, (c) watching or listening to radio and TV programs in a foreign language, (d) consuming exotic fruits, dishes and beverages from foreign cultures, (e) visiting intercultural festivals and events, (f) listening to music from foreign cultures, (g) studying philosophical or religious ideas of foreign cultures, (h) engaging with foreign ways of life, and (i) making contact with people from other countries and cultures. Respondents rated each item on separate seven-point ratings scales ranging from 1 (*no time at all*) to 7 (*very much time*). For each subscale, we computed separate composite scores.

## Results

Descriptive statistics, scale reliabilities and scale intercorrelations for the total sample ($n = 455$) are presented in Table 1. To recall, we have three xenophilia-related and three xenophobia-related composite measures (see methods section). In order to create separate overall measures for respondents' xenophobic orientations and xenophile orientations respectively, we first subjected the three xenophobia-related composite measures (SDO, MI, MTCP-R) and the three xenophilia-related composite measures (i.e., knowledge and understanding, feelings, behavioral tendencies) to a principal component analysis with subsequent oblimin rotation. This analysis revealed two moderately correlated factors ($r = -.33, p < .001$) with Eigenvalues exceeding 1 that accounted for 63.41% of the total common variance. The three xenophobia-related composite measures showed loadings of .84 or greater on the first factor, whereas the three xenophilia-related composites showed loadings of .66 or greater on the second factor. We saved the factor scores obtained from this analysis for each factor and then used these scores as two separate and overall measures of respondents' xenophobic and xenophile orientations, respectively, in our statistical analyses.

To test our specific hypotheses, we specified path models in which the scale scores of the six HEXACO traits served as predictor variables and the factor scores for xenophile and xenophobic orientations served as the criterion variables. The first model that we tested allowed only for paths from altruism/cooperation-related traits to xenophobic orientations, from endeavor-related traits to xenophile orientations, and for intercorrelation between xenophobic and xenophile orientations. Although this restrictive model fit the data reasonably well, $\chi^2(6, N = 455) = 22.58, p = .001$, CFI = .944, RMSEA = .078, SRMR = .037, analyses on the six omitted paths (i.e., the three paths from endeavor-related traits to xenophobic orientations and the three paths from altruism/cooperation to xenophile orientations) revealed that adding a path from Openness to xenophobic orientations significantly improved model fit. We therefore included this path in the model.

**Table 1.** Descriptive Statistics, Scale Reliabilities, and Scale Intercorrelations for All Theoretically Relevant Variables (Time 2 Panel Sample)

| | | $\alpha$ | 1 | 2 | 3 | 4 | 5 | 6 | 7 | 8 | 9 | 10 | 11 | 12 | 13 | 14 | 15 |
|---|---|---|---|---|---|---|---|---|---|---|---|---|---|---|---|---|---|
| 1 | Gender | — | — | .36*** | .56*** | −.02 | −.05 | .01 | .08 | −.33*** | −.38*** | −.26*** | .11* | .16** | .06 | −.37*** | .14** |
| 2 | Honesty-Humility | .83 | | — | .27*** | .35*** | −.15** | .12* | .12* | −.51*** | −.45*** | −.44*** | .07 | .11* | .07 | −.53*** | .11* |
| 3 | Emotionality | .81 | | | — | .04 | −.01 | .01 | .06 | −.26*** | −.41*** | −.20*** | .08 | .14** | −.04 | −.34*** | .07 |
| 4 | Agreeableness | .82 | | | | — | −.11* | −.03 | .00 | −.25*** | −.26*** | −.25*** | .03 | .08 | .01 | −.29*** | .05 |
| 5 | Extraversion | .85 | | | | | — | .03 | .10* | .06 | .09 | .07 | .13** | .14** | .31*** | .08 | .27*** |
| 6 | Openness | .74 | | | | | | — | −.01 | −.19*** | −.11* | −.19*** | .34*** | .20*** | .14** | −.18*** | .33*** |
| 7 | Conscientiousness | .84 | | | | | | | — | .09 | −.05 | .02 | .06 | .05 | .10* | .03 | .09* |
| 8 | SDO | .87 | | | | | | | | — | .60*** | .68*** | −.14** | −.26*** | −.24*** | .88*** | −.27*** |
| 9 | MTCP-R | .83 | | | | | | | | | — | .59*** | −.15** | −.32*** | −.13** | .85*** | −.24*** |
| 10 | MI | .81 | | | | | | | | | | — | −.22*** | −.31*** | −.26*** | .87*** | −.37*** |
| 11 | Cross-Cultural Engagement | .76 | | | | | | | | | | | — | .31*** | .25*** | −.15** | .79*** |
| 12 | Understanding | .81 | | | | | | | | | | | | — | .22*** | −.40*** | .66*** |
| 13 | Positive Feelings | .81 | | | | | | | | | | | | | — | −.23*** | .67*** |
| 14 | Xenophobic Orientations | — | | | | | | | | | | | | | | — | −.33*** |
| 15 | Xenophile Orientations | — | | | | | | | | | | | | | | | — |
| $M$ | | | — | 3.39 | 3.14 | 3.02 | 3.62 | 3.08 | 3.33 | 2.61 | 2.54 | 3.72 | 3.66 | 3.18 | 3.54 | 0.00 | 0.00 |
| $SD$ | | | — | .65 | .59 | .56 | .57 | .58 | .60 | 1.00 | .54 | .90 | 1.07 | .67 | .62 | 1.00 | 1.00 |

*Note.* n = 455. Gender: 0 = male 1 = female, SDO = Social dominance orientation, MTCP-R = Reduced motivation to control prejudice, MI = Rejection of multiculturalism. Personality traits were measured at Time 1. SDO, MTCP-R, MI, Cross-Cultural Exploration, Intergroup Understanding, Intergroup Anxiety were measured at Time 2 (up to 6 months later)
*p < .05; **p < .01; ***p < .001 (two-tailed).

The resulting model is presented in Figure 1, $\chi^2(5, N = 455) = 11.61, p = .041$, CFI $= .978$, RMSEA $= .054$, sRMR $= .027$.

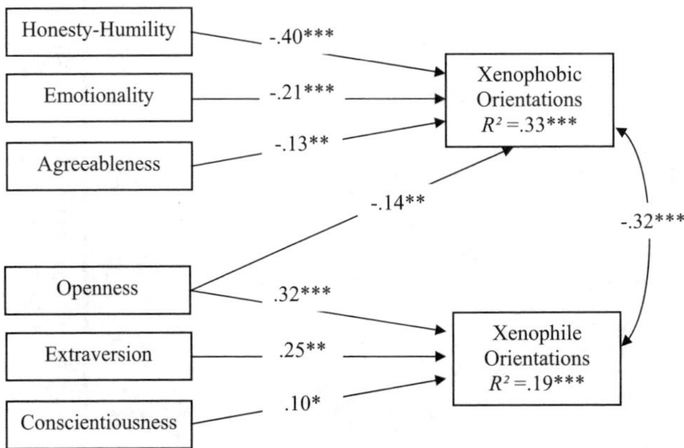


**Fig. 1.** Path model with altruism/cooperation-related traits as predictors for *Xenophobia* (Time 2) and endeavor-related traits as predictors for *Xenophilia* (Time 2).
$\chi^2$ (5, $N = 455$) $= 11.61, p = .041$, CFI $= .978$, RMSEA $= .054$, SRMR $= .027$.
$*p < .05; **p < .01; ***p < .001$ (two-tailed).

As can be seen, in line with our assumptions, xenophobic orientations (overall $R^2 = .33, z = 9.05, p < .001$) were consistently predicted by low levels of the three altruism/cooperation-related traits—Honesty-Humility ($\beta = -.40, z = -9.34, p < .001$), Emotionality ($\beta = -.21, z = -5.08, p < .001$) and Agreeableness ($\beta = -.13, z = -3.09, p = .002$). In addition, low Openness was a significant predictor of xenophobic orientations ($\beta = -.14, z = -3.10, p = .002$). Xenophile orientations (overall $R^2 = .19, z = 5.50, p < .001$), on the other hand, were significantly predicted by high levels of the three endeavor-related traits, Openness ($\beta = .32, z = 7.57, p < .001$), Extraversion ($\beta = .25, z = 6.16, p < .001$), and Conscientiousness ($\beta = .10, z = 2.45, p = .014$).

To estimate the unique proportions of variance explained by altruism/cooperation-related (or endeavor-related) traits in xenophobic (or xenophile) orientations, we also performed hierarchical multiple regression analyses. We used factor scores derived from the confirmatory factor analysis reported above as measures of xenophobic or xenophile orientations, and in a second step, we entered either the three endeavor-related traits (Extraversion, Openness, Conscientiousness) or the three altruism/cooperation-related traits (Honesty-Humility, Emotionality, Agreeableness) as predictors, after having controlled for the scores of xenophobic (or xenophile) orientations and the alternative sets of personality traits in a first step. As expected, the unique proportion of variance in xenophobic orientations explained through altruism/cooperation-related traits, $\Delta R^2 = .28, f^2 = .51, \Delta F(3, 447) = 73.99, p < .001$, was several times higher than the unique proportion of the variance in this variable explained through endeavor-related traits, $\Delta R^2 =$ .02, $f^2 = .03$, $\Delta F(3, 447) = 4.79$, $p = .003$. Conversely, but also as expected, the unique proportion of variance in xenophile orientations explained through endeavor-related traits, $\Delta R^2 = .16$, $f^2 = .22$, $\Delta F(3, 447) = 32.50$, $p < .001$, was several times higher than the unique proportion of the variance in this variable explained through altruism/cooperation-related traits, $\Delta R^2 = .01$, $f^2 = .01$, $\Delta F$ $(3, 447) = 1.20$, $p = .310$.

As shown in Table 1, respondents' gender ($0 =$ male $1 =$ female) was significantly correlated with their xenophobic and xenophile orientations. We thus set up an analogous path model to the one depicted in Figure 1, but included respondents' gender as an additional predictor variable of their xenophile or xenophobic orientations, $\chi^2$ $(5, N = 455) = 9.55$, $p = .089$; CFI $= .985$; RMSEA $= .045$, SRMR $= .019$. Importantly, including gender in the model left the path parameters for the personality traits reported in Figure 1 virtually unchanged. Gender had a significant negative effect on xenophobic orientations ($\beta = -.16$, $z = -3.52$, $p < .001$), suggesting higher levels of this orientation among males than among females. Moreover, gender had a significant positive effect on xenophile orientations ($\beta = .14$, $z = 3.45$, $p = .001$), suggesting higher levels in this tendency among females than among males. We also conducted separate moderated regression analyses using either the xenophile orientation or xenophobic orientation measures as criterion variables while gender, traits and gender x trait two-way interactions served as predictors. These analyses yielded one marginally significant gender x trait interaction effect ($\beta = .10$, $z = 1.81$, $p = .072$): low Honesty-Humility had a somewhat stronger effect on xenophobic orientations among male ($\beta = -.40$, $z = -6.82$, $p < .001$) than among female adolescents ($\beta = -.31$, $z = -4.94$, $p < .001$), for the remaining gender x trait interactions all associated $ps \geq .250$.

## Follow-Up Analyses

Six months after graduation (and twelve month after the measurement of personality traits at Time 1), 130 respondents (41 males, 89 females, $M_{\text{age}} = 17.63$ years, $SD = 0.72$) who provided their email addresses at Time 2 consented to completing an online questionnaire which included identical versions of the three xenophilia-related measures used at Time 2 (i.e., the understanding, positive feelings, and past cross-cultural engagement scales). In addition, the questionnaire included a German translation of Pittinsky et al.'s (2011) 17-item Allophilia scale measuring five different aspects of respondents' attitudes toward members of foreign cultural groups: (a) affection (e.g., "I like people from foreign cultures,") (b) comfort (e.g., "I am at ease around people from foreign cultures,") (c) engagement (e.g., "I am truly interested in understanding the points of view of people from foreign cultures,") (d) enthusiasm (e.g., "I am enthusiastic about people from foreign cultures,") and (e) kinship (e.g., "I feel a kinship with people from foreign cultures"). Respondents rated each item on separate six-point rating scales ranging from 1 (*strong disagreement*) to 6 (*strong agreement*). Relative to the sample at Time 2 ($n = 455$), the follow-up sample included a higher percentage of female respondents, $\chi^2(1, N = 585) = 11.28, p < .001$. Further, the follow-up respondents scored higher on Emotionality, on Honesty-Humility, and on Openness than the respondents who did not continue their participation in the study, all $ts \geq |-2.20|, ps \leq .028$. For the between-sample-comparisons on Agreeableness, Extraversion, and Conscientiousness, all associated $ps \geq .159$.

To substantiate the validity and generalizability of our findings obtained at Time 2, we pursued the following analytical strategies. First, and following a similar procedure to the one described above, we created factor scores for respondents' xenophobic and xenophile orientations, respectively, and then used these factor scores in a set of path analyses as the main criterion variables. Second, we also replicated our findings in an analogous set of path analyses in which we used respondents' scale scores on Pittinsky et al.'s (2011) Allophilia scale rather than the factor scores as an indicator of xenophile orientations. Converging evidence from analyses using either factor scores derived from three different composite scales or scale scores of an overall attitude measure (i.e., the Allophilia scale) would significantly strengthen our confidence in the validity and generalizability of our findings.

Descriptive statistics, reliabilities and intercorrelations for the follow-up sample ($n = 130$) are presented in Table 2.

Figure 2 presents the path model using factor scores for respondents' xenophile orientations after graduation as the criterion variable. Since the

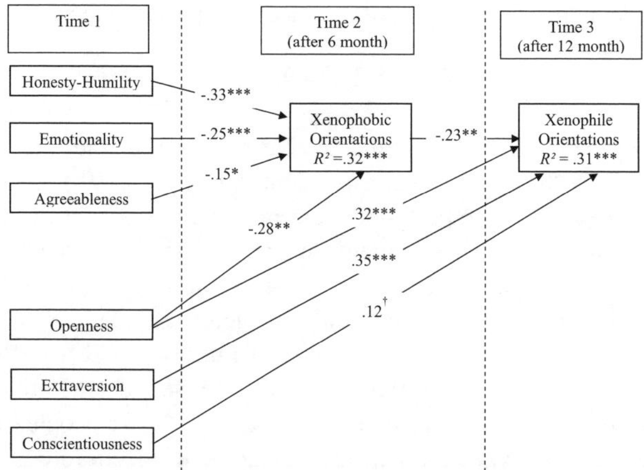


**Fig. 2.** Path model predicting *Xenophobia* (Time 2) and *Xenophilia* (Time 3). $\chi^2 (5, N = 130) = 1.59, p = .903$, CFI $= 1.00$, RMSEA $= .000$, SRMR $= .014$.
†$p < .10$; *$p < .05$; **$p < .01$; ***$p < .001$ (two-tailed).

**Table 2.** Descriptive Statistics, Scale Reliabilities, and Scale Intercorrelations for All Theoretically Relevant Variables (Follow-Up Sample)

| | | $\alpha$ | 1 | 2 | 3 | 4 | 5 | 6 | 7 | 8 | 9 | 10 | 11 | 12 | 13 | 14 | 15 | 16 |
|---|---|---|---|---|---|---|---|---|---|---|---|---|---|---|---|---|---|---|
| 1 | Gender | — | — | .34*** | .56*** | −.08 | .17 | −.06 | .14 | −.18* | −.21* | −.11 | .25** | .05 | .04 | −.19* | .14 | .14 |
| 2 | Honesty-Humility | .84 | | — | .21* | .28** | −.09 | .15 | .16 | −.42*** | −.43*** | −.41*** | .13 | .20* | .13 | −.47*** | .18* | .29** |
| 3 | Emotionality | .82 | | | — | −.08 | .19* | −.22* | .04 | −.20* | −.34*** | −.12 | −.19* | .02 | −.03 | −.25** | .07 | .14 |
| 4 | Agreeableness | .81 | | | | — | −.08 | −.05 | .05 | −.10 | −.24** | −.22** | −.04 | .15 | .09 | −.21* | .08 | .09 |
| 5 | Extraversion | .84 | | | | | — | −.07 | .01 | .05 | .07 | −.02 | .22* | .12 | .36*** | .05 | .32*** | .11 |
| 6 | Openness | .79 | | | | | | — | −.01 | −.23*** | −.15 | −.30** | .35*** | .34*** | .15 | −.27** | .35*** | .37*** |
| 7 | Conscientiousness | .87 | | | | | | | — | −.07 | −.13 | −.01 | .14 | .15 | .05 | −.08 | .14 | .12 |
| 8 | SDO | .85 | | | | | | | | — | .68*** | .73*** | −.29** | −.32*** | −.16 | .90*** | −.31*** | −.52*** |
| 9 | MTCP-R | .82 | | | | | | | | | — | .63*** | −.26** | −.35*** | −.09 | .87*** | −.26** | −.52*** |
| 10 | MI | .81 | | | | | | | | | | — | −.25** | −.31*** | −.12 | .88*** | −.26** | −.43*** |
| 11 | Cross-Cultural Engagement | .83 | | | | | | | | | | | — | .43*** | .35*** | −.31*** | .76*** | .59*** |
| 12 | Understanding | .84 | | | | | | | | | | | | — | .36*** | −.41*** | .75*** | .49*** |
| 13 | Positive Feelings | .79 | | | | | | | | | | | | | — | −.08 | .78*** | .33*** |
| 14 | Xenophobic Orientations | — | | | | | | | | | | | | | | — | −.30*** | −.56*** |
| 15 | Xenophile Orientations | — | | | | | | | | | | | | | | | — | .60*** |
| 16 | Allophilia | .94 | | | | | | | | | | | | | | | | — |
| $M$ | | | — | 3.54 | 3.29 | 3.07 | 3.60 | 3.18 | 3.32 | 2.40 | 2.37 | 3.55 | 3.77 | 3.32 | 3.57 | 0.00 | 0.00 | 4.20 |
| $SD$ | | | — | .63 | .59 | .54 | .56 | .61 | .66 | .83 | .49 | .87 | 1.21 | .70 | .54 | 1.00 | 1.00 | .80 |

*Note.* $n = 130$. Gender: 0 = male 1 = female  SDO = Social dominance orientation, MTCP-R = Reduced motivation to control prejudice, MI = Rejection of multiculturalism. Personality traits were measured at Time 1. SDO, MTCP-R, MI were measured at Time 2. Cross-Cultural Exploration, Intergroup Understanding, Intergroup Anxiety were measured at Time 3 (up to 6 months later).
*$p < .05$; **$p < .01$; ***$p < .001$ (two-tailed).

indicators of xenophile orientations were measured after the indicators of xenophobic orientations, we modeled xenophobic orientations at Time 2 as a predictor of xenophile orientations at Time 3 (rather than merely as a correlate). As can be seen in Figure 2, predicting xenophile orientations after graduation generally replicated the analyses reported in Figure 1, $\chi^2(5, N = 130) = 1.59, p = .903$, CFI $= 1.00$, RMSEA $= .000$, SRMR $= .014$.

Specifically, xenophobic orientations at Time 2 (overall $R^2 = .32, z = 4.59$, $p < .001$) were significantly predicted by low levels of Honesty-Humility ($\beta = -.33, z = -4.44, p < .001$), Emotionality ($\beta = -.25, z = -3.51, p < .001$), and Agreeableness ($\beta = -.15, z = -1.98, p = .047$). In addition, low Openness was a significant predictor of xenophobic orientations at Time 2 ($\beta = -.28, z = -3.38, p = .001$). Xenophile orientations after graduation, on the other hand, were significantly predicted by high levels of Openness ($\beta = .32, z = 4.72, p < .001$) and Extraversion ($\beta = .35, z = 5.41, p < .001$). The predictive value of Conscientiousness ($\beta = .12, z = 1.73, p = .083$) was marginally significant. Low levels of xenophobic orientations at Time 2 also predicted xenophile orientations after graduation ($\beta = -.23, z = -3.24, p < .001$, overall $R^2 = .31, z = 4.56, p < .001$). Subsequent hierarchical multiple regression analyses confirmed that the unique proportion of variance in xenophile orientations after graduation explained through endeavor-related traits, $\Delta R^2 = .22, f^2 = .34, \Delta F(3, 122) = 13.19, p < .001$, was several times higher than the unique proportion of the variance in this variable explained through altruism/cooperation-related traits. In fact, the unique proportion of variance explained by altruism/cooperation related traits in xenophile orientations after graduation was negligible, $\Delta R^2 = .01, f^2 = .01, \Delta F (3, 122) = .39$, $p = .758$.

Using respondents' scale scores of Pittinsky et al.'s (2011) Allophilia scale (instead of factor scores) as the indicator of xenophile orientations at Time 3 generally replicated these findings, $\chi^2(5, N = 130) = .72, p = .982$, CFI $= 1.00$, RMSEA $= .000$, SRMR $= .009$. Specifically, Allophilia measured after graduation was significantly predicted by high levels of Openness ($\beta = .25, z = 4.17, p < .001$) and Extraversion ($\beta = .15, z = 2.43, p = .015$). The predictive value of Time 1 Conscientiousness was nonsignificant, however ($\beta = .08, z = 1.19, p = .234$). Low levels of xenophobic orientations at Time 2 also predicted Allophilia after graduation ($\beta = -.49, z = -7.64, p < .001$, overall $R^2 = .39$, $z = 6.31, p < .001$). Hierarchical multiple regression analyses confirmed that the unique proportion of variance in Allophilia after graduation explained through endeavor-related traits, $\Delta R^2 = .08, f^2 = .13, \Delta F(3, 122) = 5.53, p = .001$, was several times higher than the unique proportion of the variance in this variable explained through altruism/cooperation-related traits. Again, the unique proportion of variance explained by altruism/cooperation related traits in Allophilia after graduation was negligible, $\Delta R^2 = .00, f^2 = .00, \Delta F(3, 122) = .13, p = .940$.

## Discussion and Conclusions

The present study among a sample of adolescents provides consistent support for our theoretical perspective on the different personality foundations of xenophile and xenophobic orientations in humans. In line with this perspective, high levels of endeavor-related traits (i.e., Openness to Experience, Extraversion, and, somewhat less consistently, Conscientiousness) predicted greater xenophile orientations among adolescents, and this even over a period of up to twelve months. Low levels of altruism/cooperation-related traits (i.e., low Honesty-Humility, Agreeableness and Emotionality), on the other hand, predicted greater xenophobic orientations among respondents in this age group. Consistent with previous research (e.g., Sibley & Duckitt, 2008), there were also indications that low levels of Openness predicted stronger xenophobic orientations. Still, on the whole, altruism/cooperation-related traits explained several times more variance in xenophobic orientations than endeavor-related traits, while with regard to explaining xenophile orientations, the opposite was true. Our results on the differing personality origins of xenophile and xenophobic orientations were complemented through a distinct pattern of gender effects suggesting higher levels of xenophobic orientations among male adolescents and higher levels of xenophile orientations among female adolescents. Addition analyses suggest that higher levels of xenophobic orientations in males can at least partially be explained through a gender x trait interaction involving Honesty-Humility (i.e., the trait stimulating interest in special entitlement and elevated social status, see Lee and Ashton, 2012). Although not predicted *a priori*, the specific relations between gender, traits and xenophobia fit well with evolutionary perspectives on intergroup behavior, suggesting that men's psychology may be particularly designed in ways that facilitate competitiveness and aggression in encounters with members of other cultural groups (e.g., McDonald, Navarrete, & Van Vugt, 2012; Van Vugt, De Cremer, & Janssen, 2007).

Our findings extend previous research in several important ways. First, while previous studies on the personality foundations of intergroup orientations focused either on the prediction of xenophobic tendencies (for a review, see Sibley & Duckitt, 2008) or, more recently, on the prediction of xenophile tendencies (Stürmer et al., 2013), the present study is among the first to show that xenophilia and xenophobia can be conceived as two related though distinct phenomena, each with distinct antecedents in human personality structure. Second, previous studies on the links between personality and intergroup orientations have focused almost exclusively on adults. The present replication of the differential role of altruism/cooperation-related traits and endeavor-related traits in stimulating xenophile or xenophobic orientations among adolescents suggests that these relationship patterns are rather robust phenomena that may consistently emerge in adolescence and adulthood. Third, our findings offer also promising venues for future research at the intersection of personality and developmental psychology.

While there is a large body of research investigating social, psychological and developmental factors in the etiology of prejudice in childhood (for a meta-analytic review, see Raabe & Beelmann, 2011), at present, comparably less is known about the emergence of xenophile orientations among adolescents. Finding that high levels of Openness, Extraversion and Conscientiousness are important dispositions in this respect (while high levels of Emotionality, Agreeableness, Honesty-Humility are apparently less relevant), suggest that the role of these traits and their interactions with social and developmental factors should be devoted specific attention in future research.

Nevertheless, some limitations must be kept in mind when interpreting our findings. First, our data are limited to self-report measures. Analyses employing peer or adult assessments of adolescents' xenophile or xenophobic orientations would provide a very valuable validation of the work presented here. Second, our findings are limited to specific operationalizations of the xenophilia and xeno-phobia concepts. Follow-up analyses in which we replicated our findings using Pittinsky et al.'s (2011) Allophilia scale rather than factor scores derived from three distinct composites as the criterion measure of xenophile orientations pro-vide some evidence for the robustness of our results. Still, future studies using different operationalizations than the ones employed in the present research are needed to further substantiate the validity and generalizability of our conclusions. Likewise, even though previous research demonstrates that major personality traits in the HEXACO personality framework (Ashton & Lee, 2007) and major person-ality traits in the Big Five framework (e.g., Costa & McCrae, 1992; Goldberg, 1993) show a relatively similar relationship pattern when it comes to predicting xenophile orientations (see, for instance, Stürmer et al., 2013, Study 2), future research is needed to substantiate the validity of the findings reported here using different operationalizations of major personality traits.

Despite these limitations, we believe our findings contribute to answering some fundamental questions about human sociality and underscore the potential of structural models of personality in understanding the psychological bases and origins of intergroup orientations. Specifically, the conceptualization of xenophilia and xenophobia as two related though distinct dimensions of intergroup behav-ior, each with distinct antecedents in human personality structure, helps us to better understand the often ambiguous nature of cross-cultural contact (i.e., the co-occurrence of positive *and* negative reactions toward members of other cul-tural groups). In addition, our findings also have some practical implications. A traditional focus of practical applications of intergroup research is on reducing stereotypes and prejudice toward other cultural groups (see Pettigrew & Tropp, 2006, for a meta-analytical review). From the theoretical perspective presented here, however, a reduction of prejudice or stereotypes is not sufficient (and some-times not even necessary) for individuals to develop xenophile orientations. Our re-search highlights that some universal aspects of human personality (i.e., Openness,

Extraversion, Conscientiousness) render individuals more likely to seek contact with and to explore other groups compared to other aspects (Honesty-Humility, Agreeableness, Emotionality). Hence, if one's goal is to promote cross-cultural engagement through active interventions, it seems a promising strategy to enrich intercultural encounters such that participants come to perceive contact as an opportunity to engage in idea-related endeavors (e.g., learning, imagining, and thinking about different cultures, generating ideational and material gains resulting from cross-cultural discovery), social endeavors (e.g., socializing, leading or entertaining in different cultural groups, leading to social gains such as new cross-cultural friends, mates, and allies) and/or task-related endeavors (e.g., working, planning, and organizing in cross-cultural teams, creating material and economic gains through the exchange of resources across cultural boundaries). From the personality perspective presented here, this should maximize the chance that individual characteristics such as Openness, Extraversion and Conscientiousness will have a stimulating effect. We note that many educational training programs promoting cross-cultural engagement include some elements of this strategy—although perhaps often on a less systematic and careful basis that might be necessary to create an optimal fit between participants' personality and cross-cultural interventions. Further investigations along the lines of the research reported here have thus strong potential to produce more practical knowledge about how to foster benevolent cross-cultural exploration.

# References


Antweiler, C. (2009). Was ist den Menschen gemeinsam? Über Kultur und Kulturen [What do humans have in common? About culture and cultures] (2nd ed.). Darmstadt, Germany: Wissenschaftliche Buchgesellschaft.

Arends-Tóth, J. R., & van de Vijver, F. J. S. (2003). Multiculturalism and acculturation: Views of Dutch and Turkish–Dutch. *European Journal of Social Psychology, 33*, 249–266. doi: 10.1002/ejsp.143

Ashton, M. C., & Lee, K. (2001). A theoretical basis for the major dimensions of personality. *European Journal of Personality, 15*, 327–353. doi: 10.1002/per.417

Ashton, M. C., & Lee, K. (2007). Empirical, theoretical, and practical advantages of the HEXACO model of personality structure. *Personality and Social Psychology Review, 11*, 150–166. doi: 10.1177/1088868306294907

Axelrod, R. M. (1984). *The evolution of cooperation.* New York: Basic Books.

Banse, R., & Gawronski, B. (2003). Die Skala Motivation zu vorurteilsfreiem Verhalten: Skaleneigenschaften und Validierung [The "Motivation to Act without Prejudice Scale": Psychometric properties and validity]. *Diagnostica, 49*, 4–13. doi: 10.1026//0012-1924.49.1.4

Benet-Martínez, V., & Haritatos, J. (2005). Bicultural Identity Integration (BII): Components and psychosocial antecedents. *Journal of Personality, 73*, 1015–1050. doi: 10.1111/j.1467-6494.2005.00337.x.

Bar-Yosef, O. (2002). The upper paleolithic revolution. *Annual Review of Anthropology, 31*, 363–393. doi: 10.1146/annurev.anthro.31.040402.085416

Charlesworth, D., & Willis, J. H. (2009). The genetics of inbreeding depression. *Nature Reviews Genetics, 10*, 783–793. doi: 10.1038/nrg2664

Costa, P. T., Jr., & McCrae, R. R. (1992). *Revised NEO Personality Inventory (NEO-PI-R) and NEO Five-Factor Inventory (NEO-FFI) professional manual*. Odessa, FL: Psychological Assessment Resources.

Davies, K., & Aron, A. (2016). Friendship development and intergroup attitudes: The role of interpersonal and intergroup friendship processes. *Journal of Social Issues, 72*, 489–510.

Glémin, S., Ronfort, J., & Bataillon, T. (2003). Patterns of inbreeding depression and architecture of the load in subdivided populations. *Genetics, 165*, 2193–2212.

Goldberg, L. R. (1993). The structure of phenotypic personality traits. *American Psychologist, 48*, 26–34. doi: 10.1037/0003-066X.48.1.26

Klein, R. (1999). *The human career: Human biological and cultural origins* (2nd ed.). Chicago: University of Chicago Press.

Krueger, R. F., Hicks, B. M., & McGue, M. (2001). Altruism and antisocial behavior: Independent tendencies, unique personality correlates, distinct etiologies. *Psychological Science, 12*, 397–402. doi: 10.1111/1467-9280.00373.

Lee, K., & Ashton, M. C. (2012). *The H factor of personality: Why some people are manipulative, self-entitled, materialistic, and exploitive – and why it matters for everyone*. Waterloo, ON: Wilfrid Laurier University Press.

Leone, L., Desimono, M., & Chirumbolo, A. (2012). HEXACO, social worldviews and socio-political attitudes: A mediation analysis. *Personality and Individual Differences, 53*, 995–1001. doi: 10.1016/j.paid.2012.07.016

Mak, A. S., & Tran, C. (2001). Big five personality and cultural relocation factors in Vietnamese Australian students' intercultural social self-efficacy. *International Journal of Intercultural Relations, 25*, 181–201. doi: 10.1016/S0147-1767(00)00050-X

Manson, J. H., & Wrangham, R. W. (1991). Intergroup aggression in chimpanzees and humans. *Current Anthropology, 32*, 369–390. doi: 10.1086/203974

McDonald, M. M., Navarrete, C. D., & Van Vugt, M. (2012). Evolution and the psychology of intergroup conflict: The male warrior hypothesis. *Philosophical Transaction of the Royal Society B, 367*, 670–679. doi: 10.1098/rstb.2011.0301

Moore, J., & Ali, R. (1984). Are dispersal and inbreeding avoidance related? *Animal Behaviour, 32*, 94–112. doi: 10.1016/S0003-3472(84)80328-0

Morris, M. W., Chiu, C.-Y., & Liu, Z. (2015). Polycultural psychology. *Annual Review of Psychology, 66*, 631—659. doi: 10.1146/annurev-psych-010814-015001

Paolini, S., Wright, S., Dys-Steenbergen, O., & Favara, I. (2016). Self-expansion and intergroup contact: Expectancies and motives to self-expand lead to greater interest in outgroup contact and more positive intergroup relations. *Journal of Social Issues, 72*, 450–471.

Pettigrew, T. F., & Tropp, L. R. (2006). A meta-analytic test of intergroup contact theory. *Journal of Personality and Social Psychology, 90*, 751–783. doi: 10.1037/0022-3514.90.5.751

Pittinsky, T. L., Rosenthal, S. A., & Montoya, R. (2011). Measuring positive attitudes toward outgroups: Development and validation of the Allophilia Scale. In L. R. Tropp, R. K. Mallett, & K. Robyn (Eds.), *Moving beyond prejudice reduction: Pathways to positive intergroup relations* (pp. 41–60). Washington, DC: American Psychological Association. doi: 10.1037/12319-000

Pratto, F. S., Sidanius, J., Stallworth, L. M., & Malle, B. F. (1994). Social dominance orientation: A personality variable predicting social and political attitudes. *Journal of Personality and Social Psychology, 67*, 741–763. doi: 10.1037/0022-3514.67.4.741

Raabe, T., & Beelmann, A. (2011). Development of ethnic, racial, and national prejudice in childhood and adolescence: A multinational meta-analysis of age differences. *Child Development, 82*, 1715–1737. doi: 10.1111/j.1467-8624.2011.01668.x

Rosenthal, L., & Levy, S. R. (2016). Endorsement of polyculturalism increased positive intergroup contact and friendship across the beginning of college. *Journal of Social Issues, 72*, 472–488.

Schaller, M., & Neuberg, S. L. (2012). Danger, disease, and the nature of prejudice(s). *Advances in Experimental Social Psychology, 46*, 1–54. doi: 10.1016/B978-0-12-394281-4.00001-5

Sibley, C. G., & Duckitt, J. (2008). Personality and prejudice: A meta-analysis and theoretical review. *Personality and Social Psychology Review, 12*, 248–279. doi: 10.1177/1088868308319226

Sibley, C. G., Harding, J. F., Perry, R., Asbrock, F., & Duckitt, J. (2010). Personality and prejudice: Extension to the HEXACO personality model. *European Journal of Personality, 24*, 515–534. doi: 10.1002/per.750

Stephan, W. G. (1999). A survey for use in Evaluating Dialogue Programs. As presented by Western Justice Center. Retrieved from http://ncdd.org/exchange/files/docs/walter_stephan.pdf. Accessed at June 28, 2016.

Stringer, C. (2001). The evolution of modern humans: Where are we now? *General Anthropology, 7,* 1–5.

Stürmer, S., & Barbarino, M.-L. (2013). *Unpublished panel data.* Hagen: FernUniversität in Hagen.

Stürmer, S., Benbow, A. E. F., Siem, B., Barth, M., Bodansky, A. N., & Lotz-Schmitt, K. (2013). Psychological foundations of xenophilia: The role of major personality traits in predicting favorable attitudes towards cross-cultural contact and exploration. *Journal of Personality and Social Psychology, 105,* 832–851. doi: 10.1037/a0033488

Stürmer, S., & Snyder, M. (2010). Helping "Us" versus "Them": Towards a group-level theory of helping and altruism within and across group boundaries. In S. Stürmer & M. Snyder (Eds.), *The psychology of prosocial behavior: Group processes, intergroup relations, and helping* (pp. 33–58). Oxford: Wiley & Blackwell.

Tropp, L. R., & Mallett, R. K. (2011). *Moving beyond prejudice reduction: Pathways to positive intergroup relations.* Washington, DC: American Psychological Association. doi: 10.1037/12319-000

Van der Zee, K., & Van Oudenhoven, J. P. (2000). The Multicultural Personality Questionnaire: A multidimensional instrument of multicultural effectiveness. *European Journal of Personality, 14,* 291–309. doi: 10.1002/1099-0984

Van der Zee, K., & Van Oudenhoven, J. P. (2001). The Multicultural Personality Questionnaire: Reliability and validitiy of self- and other ratings of multicultural effectiveness. *Journal of Research in Personality, 35,* 278–288. doi: 10.1006/jrpe.2001.2320

Van Vugt, M., De Cremer, D., & Janssen, D. (2007). Gender differences in competition and cooperation: The male warrior hypothesis. *Psychological Science, 18,* 19–23. doi: 10.1111/j.1467-9280.2007.01842.x

Watts, M. W. (1996). Political xenophobia in the transition from socialism: Threat, racism and ideology among East German youth. *Political Psychology, 17,* 97–126. doi: 10.2307/3791945

Zimmermann, J., & Neyer, F. J. (2013). Do we become a different person when hitting the road? Personality development of sojourners. *Journal of Personality and Social Psychology, 105,* 515–530. doi: 10.1037/a0033019

MARIA-LUISA BARBARINO is a doctoral student in Social Psychology at the FernUniversität in Hagen (Germany). Her research focuses on cultural diversity, socialization, and xenophilia.

STEFAN STÜRMER, Ph.D., is Professor of Social Psychology at the FernUniversität in Hagen (Germany). A particular emphasis of his research is on positive intergroup behavior, helping, and altruism. He is co-editor of The Psychology of Prosocial Behavior: Group Processes, Intergroup Relations, and Helping.

*Journal of Social Issues, Vol. 72, No. 3, 2016, pp. 450–471*
*doi: 10.1111/josi.12176*

# Self-Expansion and Intergroup Contact: Expectancies and Motives to Self-Expand Lead to Greater Interest in Outgroup Contact and More Positive Intergroup Relations

**Stefania Paolini**[*]
*The University of Newcastle*

**Stephen C. Wright and Odilia Dys-Steenbergen**
*Simon Fraser University*

**Irene Favara**
*University of Padova*

*Sixty years of research on intergroup contact demonstrates that positive interactions across group boundaries can improve intergroup attitudes and can contribute to forging tolerant, integrated, multicultural societies. However, to fully realize the benefits of growing diversity around the globe, individuals need to exploit opportunities for intergroup contact that are available to them. Yet, it is relatively unknown why people might deliberately engage in cross-group interactions and how individuals' expectations and motives prepare them to develop positive interpersonal relationships with outgroup members. In this article, we begin to address these research gaps. We discuss the self-expansion model and present new evidence that is consistent with this model. Two studies, one correlational in a cross-cultural setting and the other experimental, show the value of high*

---

[*]Correspondence concerning this article should be addressed to Stefania Paolini, School of Psychology, the University of Newcastle, Behavioral science building, Callaghan NSW 2308, Australia [e-mail: Stefania.Paolini@newcastle.edu.au].

This research was part supported by an Australian Research Council grant awarded to the first author (DP150102210) and a Social Science and Research Council of Canada grant (41020110864) held by the second author.

We thank Punvadee Somkittikanon and Milen Milanov for assistance with Study 1 data collection, Songwut Burimjit and Lilly Bltghen for help with Thai-English back-translation, Antonio Di Bernardo for help with data modeling, Ruchi Sharma, Mehnaz Thawer, Marcel Koller, Amanda Hall, and Moncia Toews for their assistance with Study 2 data collection.

*self-expansion expectancies and motivation in promoting interest in and producing more and higher quality interactions across group boundaries. We discuss implications of these findings for policy and intervention.*

> *"He who is different from me does not impoverish me - he enriches me . . . For no man seeks to hear his own echo, or to find his reflection in the glass."*
> — Antoine de Saint-Exupéry (1900–1944)

Many contemporary societies are becoming increasingly diverse, and the large intergroup contact literature describes the potential for cross-group interactions to improve intergroup attitudes (see Pettigrew & Tropp, 2006; see Livert, 2016). In order to reap the benefits of this growing diversity, individuals however need to be interested in exploiting opportunities for contact. Yet, most social psychological research has focused on contact avoidance motives (e.g., anxiety, Stephan, 2014; or homophile; Stürmer et al., 2013), and on contact's negative self-relevant outcomes (e.g., depletion of affective and cognitive resources; see Paolini, Harris, & Griffin, 2016 for a review; cf. Pittinsky & Montoya, 2016). As a result, relatively little is known about *why* people might deliberately engage in cross-group interactions with interest and positive anticipation (see Pittinsky, 2012). In addition, although it is well-established that feelings of closeness and friendship across the group boundaries afford largest positive changes in intergroup attitudes (e.g., Paolini, Hewstone, Cairns, & Voci, 2004; for reviews, Davies, Tropp, Aron, Pettigrew, & Wright, 2011; Turner, Hewstone, Voci, Paolini, & Christ, 2007; see Davies & Aron, 2016), there has been limited discussion of *how individuals' expectations and motives* prepare and propel them to develop these close relationships. In this article, we discuss theory and present evidence from two studies, one correlational and the other experimental, that begin to address these gaps by showing the value of high self-expansion expectancies and motivation in promoting interest in, and producing more and higher quality, interactions across group boundaries.

## The Self-Expansion Model and People's Appetite for "Different" Others

Although Aron and Aron's (1986) self-expansion model was initially inspired by ancient Indian traditions (Vedic philosophies and the Upanishads), the inspiring outlook on human diversity expressed by the French poet Saint Exupéry in the quotation we used to open this article speaks to the core idea of the model: that hearing one's own echo, or finding one's own reflection is not nearly as motivating as engaging *dissimilar others* who can serve as a source of personal enrichment or *self-expansion*. According to the self-expansion model, this positive orientation toward "otherness" stems from a fundamental human motivation to expand the self in order to increase one's general self-efficacy. We engage and create relationships with others as one means of acquiring new resources, perspectives and identities that facilitate the achievement of present and future goals, while keeping boredom low and life engagement high (Aron & Aron, 1986; Aron, Aron, & Norman, 2001). Twenty years of research has shown this model to be exceptionally generative and integrative. It has advanced specific and related predictions for human behaviors at a number of different levels of analysis (e.g., Aron et al., 2001; Mattingly & Lewandowski, 2014).

At the *intrapersonal* level, one can satisfy this motive for self-expansion by engaging in challenging and novel activities, like trying new food, traveling to novel destinations, or taking up new hobbies or sports (Mattingly & Lewandowski, 2013a; 2014) presumably because these activities require the individual to take on new perspectives and/or develop new skills. Thus, Mattingly and Lewandowski (2013a) found that the number of novel activities participants engaged during the last six months correlated positively with the size of their self-concept, and this larger self-concept was in turn associated with greater general self-efficacy (Mattingly & Lewandowski, 2013b).

A second, perhaps more fundamental way of meeting one's self-expansion motive, is to form meaningful, close *interpersonal* relationships with others. Thus, potential friends and romantic partners are attractive *because* they offer resources, perspectives, and identities that the individual currently does not possess. As friendships or romantic partnerships grow, the partners engage in a process of including-the-other-in-the-self (Aron et al., 2004), whereby the other progressively comes to be seen as part of one's own self-concept. Aron and colleagues offer compelling and consistent evidence of this kind of self-expansion through close interpersonal relationships. For example, Aron, Paris, and Aron (1995) found that young adults who had recently fallen in love described their self-concept as having more diverse attributes, and reported increased self-efficacy. Also, consistent with the proposed centrality of self-other overlaps and intimacy, personal traits that had been rated as descriptive of "self" *and* "spouse" were found to be confused during speeded me/not me decisions (i.e., "does this trait belong to me?" decisions). Further, this pattern of response latencies predicted self-report relationship quality, including subjective closeness over a 3-month period (see, Aron et al., 2001).

One unique feature of the self-expansion model is that it places a premium on forming close relationships with *dissimilar* others (e.g., Aron, Steele, Kashdan, & Perez, 2006), thus offering an alternative to the dominant view in the study of interpersonal relations that similarity breeds attractiveness. Similar others, by definition, offer little in terms of novel resources, perspective, and identities, while dissimilar others offer resources, perspectives, and identities not currently available to the self. Thus, a motivation to self-expand through social relationships should naturally draw people toward dissimilar others. Yet, according to Aron et al. (2006), similarity *and* differences play unique roles in interpersonal attraction. Similarity is attractive because it increases the prospect of intimacy with others (aka the possibility of including the other in the self). Differences, on the other hand, enhance the value that closeness can afford the self, by offering a variety of valued self-relevant outcomes, including self-growth and increased self-efficacy. Thus, to the degree that one has confidence in the possibility of relationship development and growing intimacy, dissimilarity becomes increasingly attractive.

Importantly for this Special Issue, dissimilarity need not only involve interpersonal differences between individuals, but can also involve group-based differences. Thus, we suggest that self-expansion motives and expectancies can also propel *intergroup behavior*. Wright, Aron, and Tropp (2002) proposed an intergroup extension of the self-expansion model, claiming that people should be motivated to actively seek out relationships with outgroup members because they recognize—at least unconsciously—that a relationship with an outgroup member offers an especially good opportunity to enrich the self and augment self-efficacy (see also Pittinsky, 2012)

Curiously, a focus on the outcomes of cross-group contact (e.g., in terms of prejudice reduction and improved intergroup relations), rather than on the processes that might lead one to engage in cross-group contact in the first place, underpins both intergroup contact research more broadly, and the application of self-expansion theory. While, there is evidence that the self-expansion processes, like the inclusion of the other in the self, play an important role in cross-group relationships' ability to improve intergroup attitudes (e.g., Davies, Wright, & Aron, 2011; Turner, Hewstone, Voci, Paolini, & Christ, 2008; Wright, Aron, & Brody, 2008; Wright, Brody, & Aron, 2005), the role of self-expansion motivation as a predictor and an inspiration for cross-group contact and for seeking meaningful relationship with outgroup members has been largely untested. We present data from two studies, one correlational and the other experimental, that demonstrate that self-expansion expectancies and a motive for self-expansion increase one's appetite for *intergroup* dissimilarity and thus inspires the formation of more and closer interpersonal relationships with outgroup members.

## Study 1: Self-Expansion Expectancies Pave the Way for More and More Positive Intergroup Relations across Cultures

Expectations that social relationships afford self-expansion opportunities should encourage an interest in, and improve the quality of, cross-group interactions. We tested these predictions cross-sectionally in a study of young adults from city and rural background transitioning to university—a context and time in life with high potential for self-expansion. By collecting data in both Australia and Thailand, we tested the generalizability of our findings across individualistic and collectivistic societies, thus responding to a gap in extant self-expansion research (see Aron et al., 2004).

*Method*

*Sample and settings.*    Young adults studying psychology at an Australian ($N = 443$; 335 female; 108 male; $M = 22.76$ years, $SD = 7.87$) and Thai university ($N = 161$; 145 female, 16 male; $M = 21.23$ years, $SD = 2.33$) completed a questionnaire for a "study on students' lifestyle and personality" in their first language. We focused on a distinction that is meaningful in both countries: participants' "city" versus "rural" background (Australian city $n = 267$; rural $n = 176$; Thai city $n = 67$; rural $n = 94$) and addressed their experience of contact with their city/rural student outgroup. In Australia, the city/rural divide shapes government policies, statistics, and public debates due to wide geographical variations in infrastructures, climate, and population density. Many rural students leave home for the first time to go to a regional university, and there have their first meaningful interactions with people from different backgrounds—the Australian data collection site was the largest regional university in the country. In the Thai context, the city/rural distinction underpins strong urbanization forces taking large sections of rural communities to the city for study and work. At the Thai data collection site, these broad social pressures have led to the rural minority in the broader Thai society becoming the *numerical* majority (see Hewstone et al., 2006) in this university in the capital Bangkok.

*Procedure*

*Self-expansion measure and validation checks.*    To measure participants' expectations of self-expansion through (nonromantic) social relationships, we adapted Lewandowski and Aron's (2002) (SEQ) self-expansion scale. This new 12-item scale (SEQ-BSRV: see Appendix A) is consistent with contemporary conceptualizations of self-expansion (Lewandowski, Aron, Bassis, & Kunak, 2006); however, to offer fresh validity checks, we included cross-culturally validated measures of the Big-5 personality factors (i.e., measures of extraversion, agreeableness, openness to experiences, emotional stability, and conscientiousness; Goldberg, 1992), and interdependent self-construal (Cross, Bacon, & Morris, 2000) and assessed theoretically meaningful co-variations with our new self-expansion scale. Details of the new self-expansion scale are in Appendix A.

*Interest in and experiences of intergroup contact.*    Participants reported on the amount and quality of cross-group contact with students from the rural/city outgroup on global measures of *quality of contact* and *quantity of contact* (Voci & Hewstone, 2003) and number of *direct* and *indirect cross-group friendships* (Paolini et al., 2004). Participants also indicated their interest in contact with the outgroup on two measures: *willingness to approach contact*, "If you were free to choose, would you like to have more contact with rural/city people?"; *desire to avoid contact*, "to what extent do you feel you try to avoid contact with rural/city people?; 1 = *not at all; 7 = very much*).

*Meaningfulness of the intergroup context and controls.* A set of ancillary measures were included to assess the psychological meaningfulness of the city/rural divider for our participants and as control variables. These were measures of *ingroup identification, intergroup category salience, intergroup anxiety, outgroup prejudice* (Voci & Hewstone, 2003), self-reported family income, and academic proficiency.[1]

## Results and Discussion

*Preliminary Analyses*

*Checking the meaningfulness of the intergroup context.* The focal city/rural intergroup distinction was moderately and equally meaningful for Australians and Thai (ingroup identification, $M_{Au} = 4.26$ $SD = 1.34$; $M_{Thai} = 4.46$; $SD = 1.58$ on a 1–7 scale, *ns*) and uncorrelated with family income and students' academic proficiency ($rs = -.018$ and .041, respectively). Some cross-cultural differences did signal unique social and political factors. Although not openly acrimonious, the city/rural distinction was reported as being *more* chronically accessible and polarizing among Thai than Australian participants (intergroup category salience, $M_{Au} = 3.15$ $SD = 1.46$ vs. $M_{Thai} = 4.24$; $SD = 1.35$; outgroup prejudice, $M_{Au} = 2.87$ $SD = 1.02$ vs. $M_{Thai} = 3.66$; $SD = 1.12$; $ps < .001$).

*Cross-cultural validation of the self-expansion measure.* Among both Australian and Thai participants, the 12 items in the new SEQ-BSRV self-expansion scale loaded on a single factor in a principal components analysis with Oblimin rotation, explained satisfactory variance, and demonstrated good internal consistency (see Appendix A). When assessing correlations with conceptually related individual differences (see bottom pane), we found that self-expansion expectancies were positively and significantly correlated with positive and cooperative engagement with others (Big-5's extraversion and agreeableness), with intellectual curiosity, and with interest in novelty (openness), and with a propensity to structure one's self-view around social relationships (interdependent self-construal). These results are indicative of satisfactory convergent validity and confirm the suitability of our new self-expansion measure for cross-cultural investigations.

---

[1] Maximum likelihood (ML) imputation procedures were used to replace scatter missing responses across variables (0.4% of the total responses; Schafer & Graham, 2002).

**Table 1.** Reliabilities, Descriptives, Zero-Order Correlations between Self-Expansion and Outgroup Contact Variables, Partial Correlations Controlling for Intergroup Anxiety (Cross-Cultural Study 1)

| | Australians ($N = 443$) | | | Thai ($N = 161$) | | |
|---|---|---|---|---|---|---|
| Outcome and control variables | Alpha (no. of items) | $M$ *(SD)* | zero-order $r$ (partial $r$) | Alpha (no. of items) | $M$ *(SD)* | zero-order $r$ (partial $r$) |
| Willingness to approach contact | – | 4.53 | .208[***] | – | 4.80 | .207[**] |
| | (1) | (1.30) | (.194[***]) | (1) | (1.43) | (.225[*]) |
| Willingness to avoid contact | – | 1.73 | .030 | – | 2.55 | .010 |
| | (1) | (1.29) | (.057) | (1) | (1.57) | (.056) |
| Quality of contact | .74 | 5.01 | .317[***] | .67 | 4.56 | .189[*] |
| | (6) | (.89) | (.192[***]) | (6) | (.93) | (.190[*]) |
| Quantity of contact[a] | .92 | 3.99 | .073 | .85 | 4.71 | .098 |
| | (3) | (1.66) | (.060) | (3) | (1.47) | (.086) |
| Number of direct friendships[b] | .91 | 4.23 | .077[*] | .87 | 5.59 | .040 |
| | (2) | (2.17) | (.103[*]) | (2) | (2.05) | (.041) |
| Number of indirect friendships[b] | – | 4.95 | .142[**] | – | 4.45 | −.065 |
| | (1) | (2.25) | (.151[**]) | (1) | (2.31) | (−.062) |
| Intergroup anxiety (covariate) | .87 | 2.77 | – | .75 | 3.89 | – |
| | (7) | (.73) | | (7) | (1.08) | – |

*Note.* Partial $r$ = controls for intergroup anxiety. No. of items = number of items included in composite index.
[a]index that was standardized to equate metrics (descriptives from a 7-point item as indicative benchmark).
[b]denotes indices ranging from 1 to 9; all other indices range from 1 to 7. Items/sample items: If you were free to choose, would you like to have more contact with rural/city people? (willingness to approach contact); to what extent do you feel you try to avoid contact with rural/city people? (willingness to avoid contact); when you meet rural/city people, in general do you find the experience . . . . . . enjoyable (quality of contact); overall, how much contact do you have with rural/city people? (quantity of contact); how many rural/city people are you friend with? (number of direct friends); indicate the number of friends of your background who have close friends with people of the other background (number of indirect friends).
*$p < .05$; **$p < .01$; ***$p < .001$.

## *Self-expansion predicts interest in and experiences of intergroup contact*

We performed correlational (see Table 1) and path analysis (see Figure 1) to test whether self-expansion expectancies predicted individuals' willingness to approach contact and desire to avoid contact with the outgroup, and their experiences with outgroup contact. Inspecting the zero-order correlations, we see that self-expansion expectations were associated with greater willingness to approach contact, but were unrelated to participants' desire to avoid contact with the outgroup among both Australians and Thai. This pattern confirms that self-expansion taps a motive to actively approach dissimilar others, rather than reducing active avoidance (see also Mattingly, McIntyre, & Lewandowski, 2012).

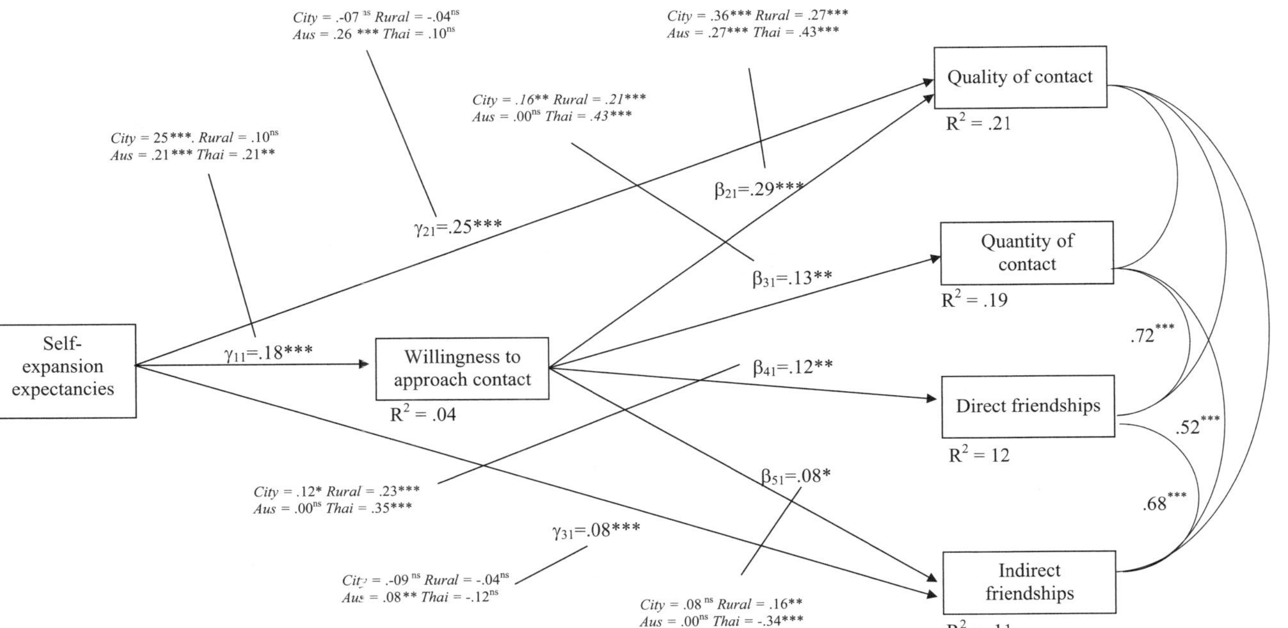


**Fig. 1.** Estimated structural equation model (SEM) testing self-expansion expectancies predicting more and better quality intergroup relations through increased interest in outgroup contact in cross-cultural Study 1.
Values are standardized beta weights. Coefficients on path diagram are for whole sample ($N = 604$). Coefficients off the diagram are for the two subsamples (Australian $n = 443$; Thai $n = 161$; City background $n = 334$; Rural background $n = 270$).
*$p < .05$; **$p < .01$; ***$p < .001$.

Self-expansion expectancies were also associated with participants' *actual* experience of contact. However, these relationships were more evident in path analyses considering both direct and indirect effects on experiences of contact of willingness to approach contact.[2] In zero-order correlations, higher self-expansion expectancies were associated with higher quality of contact (but not more frequent contact), and more direct and indirect cross-group friendships among Australians. It was also associated with higher quality of contact in the smaller Thai sample. These relationships were substantially unaffected when controlling for intergroup anxiety (cf. zero-order and partial correlations in Table 1), suggesting that they reflect unique contributions of self-expansion, rather than representing contact avoidance effects documented in previous research (see, e.g., Paolini et al., 2016).

A richer net of relationships emerged when willingness to approach contact was treated as the mediator of the self-expansion/contact relationships. A structural equation model with observed variables was estimated using the maximum likelihood estimation method (LISRELv8.70; Joreskog & Sorbom, 2004). See Figure 1 for the estimated path model. The model had a good fit to the data, as indicated by a nonsignificant chi-square, $\chi^2(2, N = 604) = 0.96, p = .62$, a CFI of 1.00 (should be equal or greater than .95), small RMSEA and SRMR indices (RMSEA = .00 and SRMR = .005; should be equal or less than .08; see Hu & Bentler, 1999). Estimated coefficients for the Australian/Thai and city/rural subsamples were also computed and are also reported in Figure 1. As anticipated, participants' self-expansion expectancies predicted higher quality and frequency of contact, and more direct and indirect cross-group friendships and did *so through* increased willingness to approach contact with the outgroup. Interestingly, this pattern of results was substantially invariant across city and rural participants (cf. "City" and "Rural" beta coefficients in Figure 1), suggesting that self-expansion expectancies are equally consequential for majority and minority individuals (see Dys-Steenbergen, Wright, & Aron, 2016). Some cross-cultural differences were however observed (cf. "Aus" and "Thai" coefficients): The indirect links between self-expansion expectancies and the four indices of intergroup contact were driven by the Thai participants; whereas the direct link between self-expansion expectancies and contact quality was driven by Australians. These cross-cultural differences suggest that the process whereby self-expansion affects actual outgroup contact is context specific (see Aron et al., 2004).

In summary, this first correlational study involving two cultural groups suggests some enticing possibilities for the intergroup self-expansion model. It confirms that one's level of self-expansion—indexed by individual differences in

---

[2]This pattern is indicative of willingness to approach contact acting as a suppressor variable and mediating the self-expansion-contact relationships (MacKinnon, Lockwood, Hoffman, West, & Sheets, 2002).

self-expansion expectancies—during a time of important life transitions can influence interest in interacting with outgroup members, which in turn, increases the quality and (to some extent) the quantity of cross-group contact. While effective for both majority and minority groups (Dys-Steenbergen et al., 2016), these positive links do display some culture/context-specific features.

Nonetheless, being correlational, these findings do not unequivocally establish that self-expansion has a causal influence on intergroup contact. Also, being field research, the self-expansion/contact relationships may be influenced or constrained by a host of (uncontrolled) structural and dynamic factors. In natural settings, even when wishing to engage in more contact with dissimilar others, people may be unable to do so because of formal and informal group segregation (e.g., Alexander & Tredoux, 2010; Dixon & Durrheim, 2003), or unfamiliarity with and uncertainty in novel settings, like university for our study participants (Aron et al., 2001). We expect these factors to chronically or temporarily skew self-expansion effects (and possibly underpin the context variations in self-expansion effects we detected here between the Australian and Thai institutional contexts) by interfering with the relationship between one's *interest* in cross-group contact and one's *ability* to engage in and establish such relationships. It is evident that a more conclusive test requires self-expansion to be experimentally manipulated, and requires a controlled research setting that removes common and uncontrolled barriers to intergroup contact.

## Study 2: Self-Expansion Motivation Inspires Interest in Novel Cross-group Interactions

While individual differences in self-expansion expectations should orient and sustain one's *general* motivation to self-expand, a key element of the model is that self-expansion motivation is also malleable and influenced by one's current and recent circumstances and experiences (i.e., the model implies person x situation interactions). Thus, self-expansion motivation waxes and wanes as periods of high self-expansion are followed by periods of self-integration. In addition, current levels of self-expansion motivation will be influenced by competition with other motives and concerns that encourage one to maintain one's current sense of self (i.e., needs for stability, self-coherence, and self-consistency). Thus, changing social contexts, recent experiences, and local environmental cues (including experimental primes) should have the capacity to increase (or decrease) current self-expansion motivation and, in so doing, influence interest in and the quality of subsequent cross-group interactions.

An experiment by Dys-Steenbergen et al. (2016) provides initial evidence of this. Prior to interacting, cross-ethnic pairs of incoming first year undergraduates at a Canadian institution were primed with one of two self-expansion motivation messages describing how university students should focus on either:

(1) the benefits of being open to new challenges, seeking novelty, and expanding oneself (high self-expansion motivation), or (2) the benefits of sticking to well-defined personal goals, knowing "who you are," and being consistent with one's true self (low self-expansion motivation). The cross-ethnic partners then completed the Fast Friends Activity (Aron, Melinat, Aron, Vaollone, & Bator, 1997), followed by measures of perceived quality of the interaction, feelings of interpersonal closeness, and feelings of self-growth. Two weeks later, after engaging in additional friendship-making activities, the partners completed a measure of social self-efficacy. Consistent with the self-expansion model, compared to the low self-expansion prime, the high self-expansion motivation prime resulted in higher quality interactions, greater interpersonal closeness, stronger feelings of self-growth and, following a second interaction 2 weeks later, stronger feelings of social self-efficacy. In addition, these outcomes showed predicted patterns of mediation: The reported quality of the interaction and felt closeness mediated the relationship between the manipulation of self-expansion motivation and feelings of self-growth and self-efficacy.

Although, Dys-Steenbergen and colleagues demonstrated that self-expansion motivation can be successfully manipulated and that it can influence the quality of subsequent cross-group interactions, because all participants engaged in a cross-group interaction, this experiment is unable to answer the question of whether self-expansion motivation can *inspire interest in* cross-group interactions. What is needed is an experiment that manipulates self-expansion motivation and measures interest in subsequent cross-group interactions. Our second study provides this experimental test. We first manipulated participants' current self-expansion motivation using a bogus personality measure that primed feelings associated with low or high need for self-expansion (and a no prime control). Participants then rated their interest in a number of ethnic ingroup and ethnic outgroup members as potential interaction partners for a second part of the study. We predicted that those exposed to the high self-expansion motivation prime would be more interested in cross-group interactions than those exposed to the low self-expansion motivation prime.

*Method*

*Participants.*     Four participants failed to report their ethnicity, and eight expressed suspicion about the purpose of the study during the debriefing, and were excluded from analyses. The final sample included 57 White students (43 female; *M*age = 19.34) and 58 students (39 female; *M*age = 19.96) from a variety of other ethnic groups (East Asian = 21; South Asian = 12; Middle Eastern = 5; mixed heritage = 8; other = 12). All participants signed up for a study on "Personality and Interactions" and received course credit for their participation.

*Procedure.*     Participants were run in groups and were aware that others were in the lab. However, immediately upon arrival they were placed in separate cubicle rooms so that no one saw any other participant. This was to ensure that they believed that they would be interacting with another participant later in the study, but we could control the information they received about the other participants. Participants were told that they would complete a personality measure and that they would then engage in a friendship-building interaction with a same-gender partner who was completing the study in another cubicle.

*Self-expansion motivation manipulation.*     Participants first completed a 70-item "personality/personal life questionnaire" including items collected from existing personality inventories and attitude measures. This questionnaire formed the basis of the cover story used to manipulate self-expansion. When the participant finished the questionnaire, the experimenter returned to their cubicle with an elaborate color-coded scoring key and 16 different colored folders. She explained that this scientifically validated scoring procedure would produce one of 16 different personal profiles. While the participant completed the second task—a brief description of themselves—the experimenter sat across from them apparently scoring their questionnaire. With some elaboration about the validity of the test, the experimenter then gave the participant one of three written "profiles" that contained the self-expansion primes.

All profiles began with a paragraph containing broad Barnum statements. For the low self-expansion prime, the second paragraph stated that his/her responses showed that (s)he was "somewhat overwhelmed," desired greater "control and calmness in [his/her] life," was feeling "unusually pulled in too many directions and working hard to try to integrate the many parts of their life," and showed "concern about [his/her] ability to meet challenges that will require coherence and clarity of character" (i.e., the message made it clear that their need for self-expansion was *over*-satisfied). The high self-expansion prime stated that the participant's responses showed (s)he was "bored," wished to be "a more complex and multidimensional person," was feeling "unusually simple, small, even unidimensional" and showed "concern about [his/her] ability to meet challenges that will require breadth of character." (i.e., the message made it clear that their need for self-expansion was *under*-satisfied). The control condition included only the initial Barnum statements (no second paragraph).

*Measure of interest in cross-group and ingroup interactions.*     After the participant was given time to read and digest their profile, the experimenter returned with a package of 6 brief self-descriptions (similar to the participant had written) and explained that these were from the other six people currently in the lab and that they would be interacting with one of them in the next part of the study. Before the interaction, they would first rate each of them on a number of dimensions. The hand-written self-descriptions were created to reflect average first-year undergraduates and all were the same gender as the participant (this was not unexpected as participants signed up for male or female-only sessions). In addition, clearly printed at the top of each description was the person's name. The set included two Caucasian names (e.g., Ryan Wells, Nicole Windsor), two East Asian names (e.g., Tang Leung, TseMei Chang), and two East Indian names (e.g., Amarjit Johal, Harpreet Sindu). The six names were counterbalanced so they appeared equally on each of the six descriptions across the three conditions. Participants were encourage to carefully read each name "to be absolutely sure that you do not know any of the other participants as you are not allowed to interact with someone you know."

Participants rated each of the six targets on three items using a 5-point scale ($1 = $ *not at all*, $5 = $ *extremely*): "How interesting does this person seem to you?", "How excited would you be about having a chance to meet this person?", "How likely is it that you could become friends with this person?" ($\alpha = .81$).

*Final questionnaire.*     When participants completed their ratings of the six potential interaction partners, the experimenter indicated that she needed a few minutes to tabulate the ratings of all participants and asked the participant to complete a short questionnaire. All rating were provided on a 5-point scale ($1 = $ *not at all*, $5 = $ *extremely*).

A *manipulation check* was designed for this study and included a set of self-relevant statements reflecting a need for self-expansion. Based on the stem "How true is each of the following statements about you at the moment?" participants rated three statements ($\alpha = .74$)[3]: "Right now, I need a change in my life," "I feel like I am in a bit of a rut," and "At this moment, my life is full and complete" (reverse coded).

The *perceived accuracy of the personality profile* was assessed using a 2-item measure ($r = .63$). This asked participants the degree to which they felt the personality profile that was given to them was "accurate" and "reflected their current feelings and views".

Finally participant reported *demographics*—their age, gender, and ethnic heritage, and whether they were an international student.

## Results and Discussion

*Preliminary Analyses*

*Perceived accuracy of the personality profile.*     A significant one-way ANOVA comparing the three self-expansion conditions (low self-expansion, high

---

[3] A fourth item, "Right now, I feel like I couldn't add one more thing to my life," was removed as it substantially reduced the reliability of the scale.

self-expansion, and control), $F(2, 110) = 3.98$, $p = .04$, $\eta^2 = .05$, followed by post hoc comparisons (Tukey HSD) indicated that participants in the control condition perceived their profile to be significantly less accurate ($M = 3.61$, $SD = 1.12$) than participants in both the low ($M = 4.02$, $SD = 0.97$; $p = .02$) and high ($M = 3.87$, $SD = 0.91$; $p = .04$) self-expansion conditions, and these groups were not significantly different from each other. However, all scores were above the midpoint, indicating that all three groups perceived the profile to be reasonably accurate. The lower ratings in the control condition may be due to this profile being shorter and containing less specific information.

*Manipulation check.* A significant one-way ANOVA comparing the three self-expansion conditions (low self-expansion, high self-expansion, and control), $F (2, 112) = 5.70$, $p = .004$, $\eta^2 = .09$ followed by post hoc comparisons (Tukey HSD) indicated that participants in the low ($M = 2.64$, $SD = 0.81$), compared to the high ($M = 3.31$, $SD = 0.93$), self-expansion condition reported lower self-expansion motivation ($p < .01$). Scores for participants in the control condition ($M = 2.98$, $SD = 0.90$) fell in between these two and were not significantly different from either.

*Key analyses*

For our primary analyses of the impact of the self-expansion manipulation on interest in engaging in a friendship building interaction with ingroup and outgroup members, the data from White participants and minority participants were analyzed separately. This was necessary as many of the ethnic minority participants did not have members of their specific ethnic ingroup among the six potential partners. Thus, a full analysis contrasting preference for ingroup members and outgroup members was not possible for this group. For White participants, the ratings of the two East Asian and two East Indian targets were combined to produce a single *Outgroup Targets* score which was contrasted with the combined ratings for the two *Ingroup* (White) *Targets*.

*Interest in cross-group and ingroup interactions: White participants.* A 3 self-expansion condition (low, high, control) by 2 target group (ingroup vs. outgroup) mixed ANOVA with target group as within-subject factor, yielded a significant main effect of self-expansion condition, $F(2,54) = 3.83$, $p = .03$, $\eta^2 = .13$, a main effect of target group, $F (1, 54) = 12.67$, $p < .001$, $\eta^2 = .19$, and a self-expansion by target group interaction, $F (2, 54) = 3.84$, $p = .03$, $\eta^2 = .13$ (see Figure 2). Although there appears to be a small effect of condition on interest in interacting with ingroup members, this effect was not statistically significant ($p = .89$). However, the self-expansion manipulation did have a significant effect

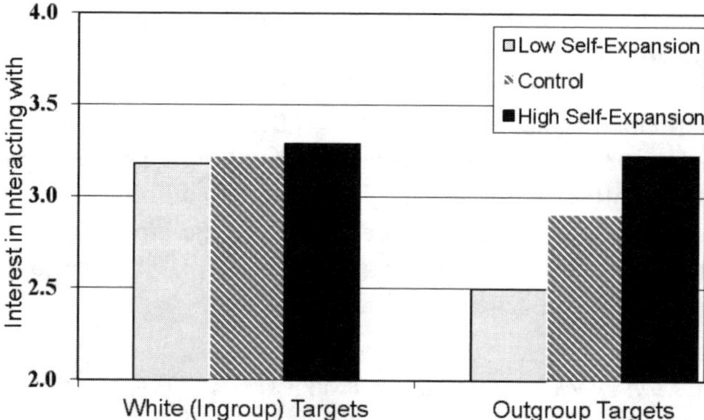



**Fig. 2.** Interest in cross-group and ingroup interactions in each of three self-expansion conditions (White participants).

on interest in interacting with outgroup targets, $F(2,54) = 11.28, p < .001, \eta^2 = .28$. Pairwise comparisons (Tukey HSD) indicated that compared to White participants in the low self-expansion condition ($M = 2.50$, $SD = .51$), those in the high self-expansion condition ($M = 3.23$, $SD = .45$) showed significantly greater interest in engaging in a friendship building activity with an ethnic outgroup member ($p < .001$). In addition, those in the control condition ($M = 2.91$, $SD = .48$) reported significantly higher interest in cross-group interactions than those in the low self-expansion condition ($p = .03$).

In addition, comparisons of the relative interest in interactions with ingroup versus outgroup targets revealed a significant preference for ingroup targets in the low self-expansion condition, $F(1,54) = 18.32, p < .001$. However, in the control conditions, $F(1,54) = 2.67, p = .11$, and in the high self-expansion condition, $F(1,54) = .15, p = .70$, this difference was not significant

*Interest in cross-group interactions: Ethnic-minority participants.*    As many ethnic minority participants did not have members of their specific ethnic ingroup among the six targets, we were unable to contrast interest in cross-group interactions with interested in ingroup interactions among these participants. However, as the White targets were outgroup members for all of the ethnic minority participants, we tested the effect of the self-expansion primes on interest in interacting with Whites (outgroup members). A one-way ANOVA comparing the three self-expansion conditions (low, high, control) yielded a significant effect of condition, $F(2,55) = 3.27 \ p = .04, \eta^2 = .11$. Post hoc comparison (Tukey HSD) revealed that, compared to ethnic minority participants in the low self-expansion condition ($M = 2.57$, $SD = .88$), those in the high self-expansion condition ($M = 3.14$, $SD = .67$) reported significantly greater interest in engaging in a friendship building activity with a White partner ($p = .04$), and the ratings for those in the control condition ($M = 2.62$, $SD = .74$) fell between these two conditions.

In summary, the findings from our manipulation check are consistent with work by Dys-Steenbergen et al. (2016) showing that self-expansion motivation can be manipulated by providing specific self-relevant information. However, this study used a somewhat different procedure. More importantly, to our knowledge this study provides the first experimental evidence that raising self-expansion motivation among both ethnic majority group members (Whites) and ethnic minority group members can lead to greater interest in engaging in a meaningful interaction with an outgroup members, while lowering self-expansion motivation can reduce interest in cross-group interactions.

Of course, measuring expressed *interest* does not necessarily equate with actual *engagement* in cross-group interactions. However, in this particular case, participants clearly believed that the interaction was imminent: All but the eight participants who were dropped from the analyses indicated in the debriefing that they expected an interaction. In addition, they believed that their expressed interest would influence who their interaction partner would be. Thus, we feel that these ratings of interest are in no way hypothetical and represent participants' honest desires for an interaction they expected to engage in. There are also legitimate concerns with the generalizability of results that emerge in the rather artificial environment of a laboratory, but again when combined with the highly ecologically valid research in Study 1, we believe that this concern is greatly reduced. Finally, for all of our results, while the high and low self-expansion conditions consistently differed significantly, in some cases they were not significantly different from the control condition. Visual inspection of the means (e.g., Figure 2) show that the control consistently fell relatively close to midway between the two experimental conditions. However, it remains a reasonable question (especially for the ethnic minority group) whether increasing and decreasing self-expansion motivation can be expected to have equivalent (but opposite) effects on interest in cross-group interactions. Nonetheless, we can confidently claim that the current results support the hypothesis that the relative level of self-expansion motivation that a person has at a given time will play a role in their interest in pursuing meaningful social interaction across group boundaries.

## Conclusions

Social psychology's dominant focus on the difficulties and perils of cross-group interactions (e.g., anxiety, Stephan, 2014; or homophile; Stürmer et al., 2013), and negative self-relevant outcomes (e.g., depletion of affective and cognitive resources; see Paolini et al., 2016 for a review) paints a surprisingly pessimistic picture (cf. Page-Gould, Mendes, & Major, 2010). We believe that the self-expansion model with its focus on the motivating quality of "otherness" offers one potential counter to this pessimistic view.

The research we reported in his article provides both correlational/cross-cultural and experimental support for the important role of self-expansion motivation—operationalized here in terms of self-expansion expectations and motives—in motivating interest in cross-group interactions (Study 1 and 2) and in influencing the subsequent quality of the resulting relationships (Study 1; Dys-Steenbergen et al., 2016). Thus, this research is directly relevant to the critical question of why people might actively seek to engage in cross-group interaction and to form meaningful interpersonal relationships with members of outgroups.

It is our contention that we should consider interest in cross-group interaction as involving a competition between opponent processes. On one side, driven by security concerns and perhaps laziness (Legault, Green-Demers, Grant, & Chung, 2007), people may be motivated to avoid potentially problematic and more difficult interactions with outgroup members in favor of the more familiar and perhaps safer ingroup members. However, driven by motives like curiosity and the need for growth and self-expansion, outgroup members may also become appealing opportunities and exciting alternatives to the more mundane ingroup. The challenge that remains is to develop a fuller understanding of when and why each of these two opposing sets of motives will win out, and thus when we will avoid or seek outgroup members.

We believe that these findings also have important practical implications. Study 1 demonstrates that there may be real benefits to nurturing the development of higher general expectations for self-expansion. Parents, teachers and other institutions of socialization might be wise to reinforce the view that interpersonal relationships across the group boundaries offer a clear opportunity for self-growth. Based on Study 1, it would appear that this higher degree of general self-expansion expectations can serve to increase interest in cross-group interaction and to the development of a more diverse and positive network of close friends. Study 2 points out that independent of the individual's general level of self-expansion expectancies, the motivation to expand the self can be influenced by information in the local environment. Thus, it would be wise for those who control these kinds of messages (e.g., parents, teachers, the media, leaders in the workplace or other social institutions) to provide people with a general sense that they could benefit from self-growth and exposure to novel opportunities and interactions. Similarly, messages that exaggerate the demands, difficulties and requirements of our current relationships or activities may undermine self-expansion motivation and reduce interest in interactions and relationship development across group boundaries.

More generally, this line of research encourages a shift away from the dominant focus on the problematic aspects of intergroup relations. It shows the value of seeing "the other" not as a target of distrust, trepidation and avoidance, but rather as one that is an appealing source of potential self-growth. As such, our research reinforces the relevance of social interventions and social policies that highlight the unique merits of seeking contact with otherness (e.g., Dunne, 2013; see Rosenthal & Levy, 2016). It also encourages a social climate and the development of institutional cultures that assign positive value to self-expansion motivations, while providing confidence that self-expansion expectations can be met and self-expansion desires satisfied through contact with outgroup members. It encourages us to contemplate the truth of the claim made in Saint-Exupéry's quote with which we began—that those who are different from us do not impoverish us—they enrich us.

## Appendix A

Psychometrics for the Self-Expansion Questionnaire: Broader Social Relationships Version (SEQ-BSRV) Scale for Australians ($N = 443$) and Thai ($N = 161$)

| Items | Australians loading | Thai loading |
|---|---|---|
| Having social relationships makes me learn new things | .901 | .888 |
| Engaging socially with other people results in me having new experiences | .888 | .905 |
| Social relationships offer opportunities for exciting experiences | .855 | .832 |
| Having social relationships gives me the chance to meet new people | .844 | .865 |
| I gain knowledge through my relationships with others | .829 | .791 |
| Social relationships are important because they expose me to people with different interests | .804 | .839 |
| Social interactions allow me to explore the ideas of other people | .769 | .836 |
| Through my social relationships with others, I can become a better person | .711 | .474 |
| Having social relationships allows me to make new friends | .528 | .600 |
| My social relationships do not help me accomplishing new things (r) | .528 | .208 |
| I would go to a party even if I did not know many of the people that would be there | .454 | .570 |
| I dislike being part of a group of people I don't know (r) | .327 | .297 |
| **Expl. variance in 1-factor solution** | 52.88 % | 50.97% |
| **Cronbach's alpha** | .88 | .89 |

Continued

| Predictor and Validity Checks | Australians | | | Thai[a] | | |
|---|---|---|---|---|---|---|
| | *M* | *SD* | *r* | *M* | *SD* | *r* |
| Self-expansion | 5.33 | .73 | – | 4.93 | .96 | – |
| Extraversion[b] | 3.28 | .75 | .463*** | 3.30 | .51 | .162* |
| Agreeableness[b] | 4.07 | .55 | .517*** | 3.95 | .52 | .358*** |
| Openness to exper.[b] | 3.80 | .56 | .244*** | 3.55 | .53 | .330*** |
| Emotional stability[b] | 2.95 | .78 | .186*** | 3.14 | .75 | .010 |
| Conscientiousness[b] | 3.23 | .65 | .109* | 3.35 | .55 | .074 |
| Interdependent self- | 2.79 | .83 | .349** | 3.40 | .80 | .395*** |

*Note.* (r) items reverse coded.
[a]Thai items were translated from English to Thai and back-translated by two independent bilinguals.
[b]denotes indices ranging from 1 to 5; all other indices range 1 to 7.
*$p < .05$; **$p < .01$; ***$p < .001$.

# References

Alexander, L., & Tredoux, C. (2010). The spaces between us: A spatial analysis of informal segregation at a South African university. *Journal of Social Issues, 66*, 367–386. doi: 10.1111/j.1540-4560.2010.01650.x

Aron, A., & Aron, E. N. (1986). *Love and the expansion of self: Understanding attraction and satisfaction.* New York: Hemisphere Publishing Corp/Harper & Row Publishers.

Aron, A., Aron, E. N., & Norman, C. (2001). The self expansion model of motivation and cognition in close relationships and beyond. In M. Clark & G. Fletcher (Eds.), *Blackwell handbook in social psychology: Vol. 2. Interpersonal processes* (pp. 478–501). Oxford: Blackwell.

Aron, A., McLaughlin-Volpe, T., Mahek, D., Lewandowski, G., Wright, S., & Aron, E. (2004). Inclusions of others in the self. *European Review of Social Psychology, 15*, 101–132.

Aron, A., Melinat, E., Aron, E. N., Vaollone, R., & Bator, R. (1997). The experimental generation of interpersonal closeness: A procedure and some preliminary findings. *Personality and Social Psychology Bulletin, 23*, 363–377. doi: 10.1177/0146167297234003

Aron, A., Paris, M., & Aron, E. N. (1995). Falling in love: Prospective studies of self-concept change. *Journal of Personality and Social Psychology, 69*, 1102. doi: 10.1037/0022-3514.69.6.1102

Aron, A., Steele, J. L., Kashdan, T. B., & Perez, M. (2006). When similars do not attract: Tests of a prediction from the self-expansion model. *Personal Relationships, 13*, 387–396.

Cross, S. E., Bacon, P. L., & Morris, M. L. (2000). The relational-interdependent self-construal and relationships. *Journal of Personality and Social Psychology, 78*, 791–808. doi: 10.1037/0022-3514.78.4.791

Davies, K., & Aron, A. (2016). Friendship development and intergroup attitudes: The role of interpersonal and intergroup friendship processes. *Journal of Social Issues, 72*, 489–510.

Davies, K., Tropp, L. R., Aron, A., Pettigrew, T. F., & Wright, S. C. (2011). Cross-group friendships and intergroup attitudes: A meta-analytic review. *Personality and Social Psychology Review, 15*, 332–351. doi: 10.1177/1088668311411103

Davies, K., Wright, S. C., & Aron, A. (2011). Cross-group friendships: How interpersonal connections encourage positive intergroup attitudes. In L. R. Tropp & R. K. Mallett (Eds.), *Moving beyond prejudice reduction: Pathways to positive intergroup relations* (pp. 119–138). Washington, DC: American Psychological Association.

Dixon, J., & Durrheim, K. (2003). Contact and the ecology of racial division: Some varieties of informal segregation. *British Journal of Social Psychology, 42*, 1–23. doi: 10.1348/014466603763276090

Dunne, C. (2013). Exploring motivations for intercultural contact among host country university students: An Irish case study. *International Journal of Intercultural Relations, 37*, 567–578. doi: 10.1016/j.ijintrel.2013.06.003

Dys-Steenbergen, O., Wright, S. C., & Aron, A. (2016). Self-expansion motivation improves cross-group interactions and enhances self-growth. *Group Processes & Intergroup Relations, 19*, 60–71. doi: 10.1177/1368430215583517.

Goldberg, L. R. (1992). The development of markers for the Big-Five factor structure. *Psychological Assessment, 4*, 26–42. doi: 10.1037/1040-3590.4.1.26

Hewstone, M., Crisp, R. J., Contarello, A., Voci, A., Conway, L., Marletta, G., & Willis, H. (2006). Tokens in the tower: Perceptual processes and interaction dynamics in academic settings with 'skewed', 'tilted' and 'balanced' sex ratios. *Group Processes & Intergroup Relations, 9*, 509–532. doi: 10.1177/1368430206067558

Hu, L. T., & Bentler, P. M. (1999). Cutoff criteria for fit indexes in covariance structure analysis: Conventional criteria versus new alternatives. *Structural Equation Modeling: A Multidisciplinary Journal, 6*, 1–55. doi: 10.1080/10705519909540118

Jöreskog, K., & Sörbom, D. (2004). LISREL 8.70. Chicago: Scientific Software International Inc.

Legault, L., Green-Demers, I., Grant, P., & Chung, J. (2007). On the self-regulation of implicit and explicit prejudice: A self -determination theory perspective. *Personality and Social Psychology Bulletin, 33*, 732–749. doi: 10.1177/0146167206298564

Lewandowski, G. W., Jr., & Aron, A. (2002, February). *The Self-Expansion Scale: Construction and validation*. Paper presented at the annual meeting of the Society of Personality and Social Psychology, Savannah, GA.

Lewandowski, G. W., Jr., Aron, A., Bassis, S., & Kunak, J. (2006). Losing a self-expanding relationship: Implications for the self-concept. *Personal Relationships, 13*, 317–331. doi: 10.1111/j.1475-6811.2006.00120.x

Livert, D. (2016). A cook's tour abroad: Long term effects of intergroup contact on positive outgroup attitudes. *Journal of Social Issues, 72*, 524–547.

MacKinnon, D. P., Lockwood, C. M., Hoffman, J. M., West, S. G., & Sheets, V. (2002). A comparison of methods to test mediation and other intervening variable effects. *Psychological Methods, 7*, 83–104. doi: 10.1037//1082-989X.7.1.83

Mattingly, B. A., & Lewandowski, G. W. (2013a). Expanding the self brick by brick: Nonrelational self-expansion and self-concept size. *Social Psychological and Personality Science, 5*, 484–490. doi: 10.1177/1948550613503886

Mattingly, B. A., & Lewandowski, G. W. (2013b). An expanded self is a more capable self: The association between self-concept size and self-efficacy. *Self & Identity, 12*, 621–634. doi: 10.1080/15298868.2012.718863

Mattingly, B. A., & Lewandowski, G. W. (2014). Broadening horizons: Self-expansion in relational and non-relational contexts. *Social & Personality Psychology Compass, 8*, 30–40. doi: 10.1111/spc3.12080

Mattingly, B. A., Mcintyre, K. P., & Lewandowski, G. W. (2012). Approach motivation and the expansion of self in close relationships. *Personal Relationships, 19*, 113–127. doi: 10.1111/j.1475-6811.2010.01343.x

Page-Gould, E., Mendes, W. B., & Major, B. (2010). Intergroup contact facilitates physiological recovery following stressful intergroup interactions. *Journal of Experimental Social Psychology, 46*, 854–858. doi: 10.1016/j.jesp.2010.04.006

Paolini, S., Harris, N. C., & Griffin, A. S. (2016). Learning anxiety in interactions with the outgroup: Towards a learning model of anxiety and stress in intergroup contact. *Group Processes & Intergroup Relations, 19*, 275–313. doi: 10.1177/1368430215572265

Paolini, S., Hewstone, M., Cairns, E., & Voci, A. (2004). Effects of direct and indirect cross-group friendships on judgments of Catholics and Protestants in Northern Ireland: The mediating role of an anxiety-reduction mechanism. *Personality and Social Psychology Bulletin, 30*, 770–786. doi: 10.1177/0146167203262848

Pettigrew, T. F., & Tropp, L. R. (2006). A meta-analytic test of intergroup contact theory. *Journal of Personality and Social Psychology, 90*, 751–783. doi: 10.1037/0022-3514.90.5.751

Pittinsky, T. L. (2012). *Us plus them: Tapping the positive power of difference.* Harvard Business Press.

Pittinsky, T. L., & Montoya, M. (2016). Empathic joy in positive intergroup relations. *Journal of Social Issues, 72*, 511–523.

Rosenthal, L., & Levy, S. R. (2016). Endorsement of polyculturalism predicts increased positive intergroup contact and friendship across the beginning of college. *Journal of Social Issues, 72*, 472–488.

Schafer, J. L., & Graham, J. W. (2002). Missing data: Our view of the state of the art. *Psychological Methods, 7*, 147. doi: 10.1037/1082-989X.7.2.147

Stephan, W. G. (2014). Intergroup anxiety theory, research, and practice. *Personality and Social Psychology Review, 18*, 239–255. DOI: 10.1177/1088868314530518

Stürmer, S., Benbow, A. E., Siem, B., Barth, M., Bodansky, A. N., & Lotz-Schmitt, K. (2013). Psychological foundations of xenophilia: the role of major personality traits in predicting favorable attitudes toward cross-cultural contact and exploration. *Journal of Personality and Social Psychology, 105*, 832–851. doi: 10.1037/a0033488

Turner, R. N., Hewstone, M., Voci, A., Paolini, S., & Christ, O. (2007). Reducing prejudice via direct and extended cross-group friendship. *European Review of Social Psychology, 18*, 212–255. doi: 10.1080/10463280701680297

Voci, A., & Hewstone, M. (2003). Intergroup contact and prejudice toward immigrants in Italy: The mediational role of anxiety and the moderational role of group salience. *Group Processes & Intergroup Relations, 6*, 37–54. doi: 10.1177/1368430203006001011

Wright, S. C., Aron, A., & Brody, S. M. (2008). Extended contact and including others in the self: Building on the Allport/Pettigrew legacy. In U. Wagner, L. R. Tropp, G. Fensheilescu, & C. Tredoux (Eds.), *Improving intergroup relations: Building on the legacy of Thomas F. Pettigrew* (pp. 143–159). Malden, MA: Wiley-Blackwell.

Wright, S. C., Aron, A., & Tropp, L. R. (2002). Including others (and groups) in the self: Self-expansion and intergroup relations. In J. P. Forgas & K. D. Williams (Eds.), *The social self: Cognitive, interpersonal and intergroup perspectives* (pp. 343–363). Philadelphia: Psychology Press.

Wright, S. C., Brody, S. M., & Aron, A. (2005). Intergroup contact: Still our best hope for improving intergroup relations. In C. S. Crandall & M. Schaller (Eds.), *Social psychology of prejudice: Historical and contemporary issues* (pp. 115–142). Seattle, WA: Lewinian Press.

STEFANIA PAOLINI is senior lecturer at the University of Newcastle, Australia. Stefania obtained her Laurea degree at the University of Padova, Italy, and her PhD from Cardiff University, UK. She uses models and methods of intergroup contact and social categorization research to explore intergroup emotions, affect, and cognitions in conflict-laden, as well as peaceful intergroup settings. She has published and is regularly invited to act as reviewer for journals and grant agencies on the topics of member-to-group generalization, intergroup contact, intergroup friendship, and intergroup emotions.

STEPHEN WRIGHT is Professor of Psychology at *Simon Fraser University*. He received his PhD from *McGill University* and was a faculty member at the *University of California, Santa Cruz* from 1991 to 2003. He held a *Canada Research Chair* in Social Psychology, is a fellow of the *Association of Psychological Sciences*, the *Society for the Psychological Study of Social Issues*, and the *Canadian Psychological Association*. His research focuses on intergroup relations, specifically collective action participation, prejudice and its reduction, and issues of minority languages and cultures.

ODILIA DYS-STEENBERGEN is a Masters student at *Simon Fraser University (SFU)*. Odilia received her Bachelor of Arts (Honors with Distinction) from *SFU* in 2013 and has been the recipient of SSHRC Canada Graduate Masters Scholarship, Provost's Prize of Distinction Award, Vice-President Research-Undergraduate Student Award and various Simon Fraser University Open Undergraduate Scholarships. Her research interests are motivation, identity, positive intergroup relations, social justice, and well-being.

IRENE FAVARA obtained her PhD in Social Psychology at the University of Padova (Italy) and is now a practicing clinical and social psychologist. She visited and worked with Stefania Paolini at the University of Newcastle, in Australia, as part of her research training. Irene's main research interests are in intergroup contact, social identity, and the self-expansion model.

*Journal of Social Issues, Vol. 72, No. 3, 2016, pp. 472–488*
*doi: 10.1111/josi.12177*

# Endorsement of Polyculturalism Predicts Increased Positive Intergroup Contact and Friendship across the Beginning of College

**Lisa Rosenthal**[*]
*Pace University*

**Sheri R. Levy**
*Stony Brook University*

*U.S. universities are increasingly racially/ethnically diverse, offering students opportunities for positive, proactive intergroup interactions. However, not all students take advantage of these opportunities, making it important to understand what factors contribute to intergroup contact and friendship. In the current longitudinal investigation with 329 undergraduates at a diverse, mid-sized, public university in the Northeastern U.S., we examined the role of polyculturalism, which is the belief that diverse racial/ethnic groups have throughout history interacted and exchanged with each other, thereby influencing each other's cultures over time. We found that greater endorsement of polyculturalism before the start of college prospectively predicted increases in intergroup contact and friendship from spring of first year to fall of second year, controlling for endorsement of multiculturalism, colorblindness, and egalitarianism before the start of college. Findings suggest polyculturalism deserves further attention in research and might be useful for interventions, programs, and policies aimed at fostering positive intergroup interactions.*

Given growing globalization, people all around the world are having increasing contact with diverse people and cultures, including in educational settings (e.g., Chiu, Gries, Torelli, & Cheng, 2011; Zirkel, 2008). In light of increasing racial/ethnic diversity at U.S. universities and colleges, and consistent with a movement among psychologists to understand and promote positive intergroup

---

[*]Correspondence concerning this article should be addressed to Lisa Rosenthal, Psychology Department, Pace University, 41 Park Row, New York, NY 10038 [e-mail: lrosenthal@pace.edu].

472

dynamics (e.g., Barbarino & Stürmer, 2016; Nagda, Tropp, & Paluck, 2006; Pittinsky & Montoya, 2016; Pittinsky, Rosenthal, & Montoya, 2011; Siem, Stürmer, & Pittinsky, 2016; Stürmer et al., 2013), researchers, educators, and policy makers have been considering what can be done to foster positive intergroup relations on campuses and ensure that students of all racial/ethnic backgrounds can feel welcome and succeed as undergraduates (Gurin, Dey, Hurtado, & Gurin, 2002; Hurtado, 2005; Sidanius, Levin, Van Laar, & Sears, 2010). This increasing diversity at universities offers undergraduates opportunities for positive intergroup contact and friendship, which for many students is a change from more racially/ethnically homogenous neighborhoods and schools they have experienced previously (Gurin et al., 2002). And, there are many positive consequences of increased intergroup contact for undergraduates, such as for sense of belonging and critical thinking skills (Bowman & Denson, 2012; Locks, Hurtado, Bowman, & Oseguera, 2008; Pascarella et al., 2014). However, some students do not take advantage of these opportunities for increased intergroup contact and instead self-segregate based on race/ethnicity (Grasmuck & Kim, 2010; Sidanius et al., 2010; Sidanius, Van Laar, Levin, & Sinclair, 2004).

Much past research has demonstrated that greater positive intergroup contact and friendship lead to improved intergroup attitudes, and some of this research has demonstrated the positive effects of interventions that foster or create instances of intergroup contact, including among undergraduates (Berryman-Fink, 2006; Bowman & Brandenberger, 2012; Davies & Aron, 2016; Lopez, 2004; Pettigrew & Tropp, 2006). It is also important to understand what factors, such as beliefs about racial and ethnic groups, might lead some people naturally to have greater intergroup contact and friendships. Understanding these factors may advance basic research on intergroup contact and friendship as well as inform additional new approaches to interventions, programs, and policies that can promote more positive intergroup contact and attitudes among undergraduates as well as others living, going to school, and working in diverse settings. Thus, in the current investigation, we examined the role of polyculturalism—the belief that different racial/ethnic groups interact and influence each other's cultures, which has been found to be associated with more positive intergroup attitudes—in predicting changes in the extent of undergraduates' intergroup contact and friendship across the beginning of college at a diverse university in the Northeastern U.S. Below, we review research to date on polyculturalism and its associations with intergroup attitudes, the importance of the transition to college and the role of racial/ethnic diversity during that transition, and then provide an overview of the current investigation.

## Polyculturalism

Throughout human history, diverse groups of people have interacted with each other, exchanged ideas, and influenced each other's cultures (Flint, 2006;

Kelley, 1999; Prashad, 2001, 2003). Historians Kelley (1999) and Prashad (2001) introduced the concept of polyculturalism, aptly noting that connections and influences across cultures are often not highlighted as much as they could be, although an abundance of examples throughout history and in contemporary culture exist, including from architecture, art, cuisine, dance, language, martial arts, music, and science. Building on these historians' insights, we developed a program of research studying polyculturalism from a psychological perspective as an individual difference belief that diverse racial and ethnic groups have throughout history interacted and exchanged with each other, and thereby have influenced each other's cultures over time and into present day (Bernardo, Rosenthal, & Levy, 2013; Rosenthal & Levy, 2010, 2012; 2013; Rosenthal, Levy, Katser, & Bazile, 2015; Rosenthal, Levy, London, & Lewis, 2016; Rosenthal, Levy, & Militano, 2014; Rosenthal, Levy, & Moss, 2012; Rosenthal, Ramírez, Bernardo, & Levy, under review). Therefore, endorsement of polyculturalism involves attending to mutual cross-cultural influences, viewing different racial/ethnic groups as interconnected, and understanding cultures as dynamic and constantly changing.

Polyculturalism, which uniquely focuses on cross-cultural connections and influences, is conceptually and empirically distinct from other beliefs and approaches related to addressing diversity, including colorblindness, assimilation, and multiculturalism (e.g., Rosenthal & Levy, 2010, 2012; Rosenthal et al., 2012, 2014). Colorblindness involves minimizing or ignoring social categories or differences between diverse groups (e.g., Ryan, Hunt, Weible, Peterson, & Casas, 2007; Wolsko, Park, Judd, & Wittenbrink, 2000), which can serve to justify inequality (see Bonilla-Silva, 2003), and relatedly assimilation involves minimizing group categories through the suggestion that all groups should integrate into or adopt the dominant culture (e.g., Verkuyten, 2005). In contrast, polyculturalism involves a recognition of all groups' identities and particularly how they are interconnected with one another. Multiculturalism also involves a recognition of all groups' identities, but generally focuses on recognizing and appreciating cultural differences between groups (e.g., Ryan et al., 2007; Wolsko et al., 2000), which is distinct from polyculturalism's focus on dynamic connections among groups.

Although polyculturalism is not a term that is familiar to most people, across many studies with community and college samples mostly in the United States but also in Colombia and the Philippines, we have found that participants tend to endorse items reflecting polyculturalism, scoring on average on the "Agree" side of the scale (Bernardo et al., 2013; Rosenthal & Levy, 2010, 2012, 2013; Rosenthal et al., 2012, 2014, 2015, 2016, under review). This growing body of research in psychology suggests that endorsement of polyculturalism may help to orient people toward appreciating, being interested, and being comfortable with diversity. Endorsement of polyculturalism has been associated with a range of both less negative as well as more positive intergroup attitudes and processes, including more positive attitudes toward social equality, people of other racial/ethnic backgrounds, and people from other countries, as well as less intergroup anxiety (Bernardo et al., 2013; Rosenthal & Levy, 2012; Rosenthal et al., 2015, 2016, under review); less sexual prejudice or less negative attitudes toward gay men and lesbian women (Rosenthal et al., 2012); and less sexist attitudes (Rosenthal et al., 2014). The findings of associations of polyculturalism with more positive intergroup attitudes have been consistent across gender and racial/ethnic groups, and have remained significant while controlling for many potentially confounding variables, such as other diversity-related beliefs (assimilation ideology, colorblindness, multiculturalism), beliefs relevant to intergroup relations and political perspectives (conservatism, egalitarianism, ethnic and gender essentialism, right-wing authoritarianism, social dominance orientation), forms of group identification (ethnic, gender, and national identification), individual difference factors (general social anxiety, grade point average, mood, self-esteem), and various sociodemographic variables. Because polyculturalism has been associated with more positive and less negative intergroup contact-related processes, including more interest in, appreciation for, and comfort with diversity, greater willingness for intergroup contact, and less intergroup anxiety among diverse undergraduates (Rosenthal & Levy, 2012; Rosenthal et al., 2015, under review), we suggest that greater endorsement of polyculturalism might lead undergraduates to be more open and likely to have positive intergroup contact and develop intergroup friendships in college.

## The Transition to College and Racial/Ethnic Diversity

Much research supports that the transition to college is a key developmental period, as students face a new environment and experience heightened stress, and during which students explore and change aspects of identities, beliefs, attitudes, goals, and behaviors (London, Rosenthal, Levy, & Lobel, 2011; Mendoza-Denton, Downey, Purdie, Davis, & Pietrzak, 2002; Rosenthal, London, Levy, Lobel, & Herrera-Alcazar, 2011). In addition, when students enter racially/ethnically diverse colleges and universities, many have the opportunity to interact with people who are more racially/ethnically diverse than their home communities and elementary and high schools because of continued issues of segregation across the United States and the increasing diversity of U.S. colleges and universities (Gurin et al., 2002). Thus, the transition to college along with the undergraduate period as a whole has been noted as a relevant and crucial time to examine intergroup contact (Hurtado, 2005; Sidanius et al., 2010). Indeed, much research has found that intergroup contact during college can have positive consequences for undergraduates' intergroup attitudes, as well as their sense of belonging and critical thinking skills, among other outcomes, and that these benefits exist for students of all racial and ethnic backgrounds (Berryman-Fink, 2006; Bowman & Brandenberger, 2012; Bowman & Denson, 2012; Chang, 1999; Hurtado, 2005; Locks et al., 2008; Lopez, 2004; Pascarella et al., 2014).

However, although the transition to a diverse college opens the door for increased positive intergroup contact and friendship, which can have positive consequences for undergraduates, some students continue to self-segregate based on race/ethnicity, and sometimes intergroup contact is not positive, including some instances of conflict (e.g., Grasmuck & Kim, 2010; Sidanius et al., 2004, 2010). This suggests that the transition to college represents a pivotal time to examine individual differences in intergroup contact and friendship and factors that drive those differences. Some research, such as that of Davies and Aron (2016) in this special issue, has examined the potential for interventions, curricula, or other policy or programs at universities that create instances of intergroup contact to improve students' intergroup attitudes. We also suggest that it is important to examine factors that contribute to already existing individual differences in the extent to which undergraduates have greater intergroup contact and friendship because this can help to inform new approaches to fostering more positive intergroup contact and attitudes on college campuses as well as other diverse settings. And, we suggest that polyculturalism might be one such factor.

## The Current Investigation

In the current investigation, we aimed to advance past research on polyculturalism by using a longitudinal design and examining the association of polyculturalism with changes across the beginning of college in intergroup contact and friendships among a sample of racially/ethnically diverse undergraduates, allowing us to examine changes over time during the critical period of the transition to college. We used data from a large, longitudinal, collaborative study of undergraduates at Stony Brook University, and specifically examined the association of undergraduates' endorsement of polyculturalism before the start of college with intergroup contact and friendship over 1 year later. Given the findings described above that polyculturalism has been associated with more interest in, appreciation for, and comfort with diversity, greater willingness for intergroup contact, and less intergroup anxiety among diverse undergraduates (Rosenthal & Levy, 2012; Rosenthal et al., 2015, 2016), we predicted that greater endorsement of polyculturalism before the start of college would prospectively predict greater increases in intergroup contact and friendship across the beginning of college, even while controlling for potentially confounding variables, such as endorsement of multiculturalism, colorblindness, and egalitarianism before the start of college. We used a composite measure of items assessing multiple aspects of positive intergroup contact and friendship (i.e., chatting or doing social things with students from other racial/ethnic backgrounds, as well as having friends or visiting in their homes friends from other racial/ethnic backgrounds; adapted from Schmid, Hewstone, Tausch, Cairns, & Hughes, 2009) to capture a range of positive intergroup experiences in which undergraduates may be engaged. We controlled for multiculturalism and colorblindness given much past research that has made comparisons between these diversity beliefs in terms of their implications for intergroup relations (see Rosenthal & Levy, 2010 for a review), and we controlled for egalitarianism given its relevance and use in studies of intergroup attitudes, including racial/ethnic attitudes (Katz & Hass, 1988; Levy, West, Ramirez, & Karafantis, 2006; Pratto, Sidanius, Stallworth, & Malle, 1994). We aimed to test whether polyculturalism has unique associations with intergroup contact and friendship while accounting for the influence of each of these relevant factors.

## Method

At Stony Brook University, a racially/ethnically diverse, mid-sized, public university in the Northeastern U.S., participants were recruited and data were first collected using paper and pencil surveys with incoming undergraduate students during their orientation visit to the university (a few weeks before beginning their first year as undergraduates) in summer of 2010. Participants were then contacted by email to complete follow-up surveys online toward the end of the spring semester of their first year of college and during the fall semester of their second year in college.

We use a regression analysis to examine whether endorsement of polyculturalism at baseline predicted amount of intergroup contact and friendship at fall of second year follow-up, while controlling for endorsement of multiculturalism, colorblindness, and egalitarianism at baseline as well as amount of intergroup contact and friendship at spring of first year follow-up. Because intergroup contact and friendship in the spring of first year is included as a control variable, with intergroup contact and friendship in the fall of second year as the outcome variable, this analysis models change over time in intergroup contact and friendship.

*Participants*

The current analyses were conducted with 329 undergraduates who completed surveys at all three time points (baseline orientation, Spring of 1st year follow-up, and Fall of 2nd year follow-up). The mean age of these 329 participants at baseline was 17.66 ($SD = 0.62$), 198 were women, and 131 were men. Participants were racially and ethnically diverse, with 158 identifying as Asian, 120 as White, 18 as Latino, 17 as Black, 23 as Other or Multiracial/ethnic, and 3 did not indicate race/ethnicity. The majority of participants were born in the United States (251 born in U.S., 75 outside of U.S., 3 did not indicate). The background survey was distributed during orientation sessions, and there was no monetary incentive. For the follow-up online surveys, participants received a small monetary incentive and were entered into a raffle to receive a larger cash award.

*Measures*

*Participant characteristics.*     Participants were asked to report characteristics including their age, gender, race/ethnicity, and whether they were born in the United States at the baseline survey.

*Polyculturalism.*     Participants completed the 5-item measure of polyculturalism on a scale of 1 (*Strongly Disagree*) to 6 (*Strongly Agree*), and a mean score was calculated (Rosenthal & Levy, 2012; e.g., "Different racial, ethnic, and cultural groups influence each other"; $\alpha = .89$ at baseline).

*Multiculturalism.*     Participants completed a 5-item measure of the form of multiculturalism that focuses on recognizing important differences between racial/ethnic groups on a scale of 1 (*Strongly Disagree*) to 6 (*Strongly Agree*), and a mean score was calculated (Rosenthal & Levy, 2012; e.g., "There are differences between racial and ethnic groups, which are important to recognize"; $\alpha = .78$ at baseline).

*Colorblindness.*     Participants completed a 5-item measure of the combined form of colorblindness that focuses on recognizing the unique qualities of individuals and commonalities across groups on a scale of 1 (*Strongly Disagree*) to 6 (*Strongly Agree*), and a mean score was calculated (Rosenthal & Levy, 2012; e.g., "At our core, all human beings are really all the same, so racial and ethnic categories do not matter"; $\alpha = .85$ at baseline).

*Egalitarianism.*     Participants completed a 6-item measure of egalitarianism on a scale of 1 (*Strongly Disagree*) to 6 (*Strongly Agree*), and a mean score was calculated (Levy et al., 2006, adapted from Katz & Hass, 1988; e.g., "Every person should be kind to all people"; $\alpha = .83$ at baseline).

*Intergroup contact and friendship.*     Participants completed a 4-item measure of intergroup contact and friendship on a scale of 1 (*Not At All*) to 7 (*A lot*) that assessed the amount of: chatting with students at their university from racial/ethnic groups other than their own, doing social things with students at their university from racial/ethnic groups other than their own, having friends from racial/ethnic groups other than their own, and visiting friends from racial/ethnic groups other than their own in those friends' homes (adapted from Schmid et al., 2009). A mean score was calculated ($\alpha = .85$ at spring of first year, $\alpha = .89$ at fall of second year).

**Table 1.** Bivariate Correlations, Means, and Standard Deviations ($N = 329$)

|  | 1 | 2 | 3 | 4 | 5 | 6 |
|---|---|---|---|---|---|---|
| 1. Polyculturalism baseline | ___ |  |  |  |  |  |
| 2. Multiculturalism baseline | .33** | ___ |  |  |  |  |
| 3. Colorblindness baseline | −.00 | −.18** | ___ |  |  |  |
| 4. Egalitarianism baseline | .26** | .12* | .25** | ___ |  |  |
| 5. Intergroup contact and friendship spring of first year | .21** | .01 | .11* | .02 | ___ |  |
| 6. Intergroup contact and friendship fall of second year | .23** | .03 | .07 | .13* | .51** | ___ |
| $M$ | 4.99 | 4.55 | 3.80 | 4.88 | 5.25 | 5.12 |
| $SD$ | 0.66 | 0.72 | 1.12 | 0.79 | 1.36 | 1.35 |

*Note.* *$p < .05$; **$p < .01$.

**Table 2.** Results of Regression Analysis ($N = 329$)

|  | Intergroup contact and friendship fall of second year | | |
|---|---|---|---|
|  | ß | $t$ | $p$ |
| Step 1 |  |  |  |
| Multiculturalism | .00 | 0.06 | .954 |
| Colorblindness | −.02 | −0.32 | .748 |
| Egalitarianism | .12 | 2.41 | .016* |
| Intergroup contact and friendship spring of second year | .51 | 10.60 | <.001** |
| Step 2 |  |  |  |
| Multiculturalism | −.03 | −0.64 | .524 |
| Colorblindness | −.01 | −0.25 | .801 |
| Egalitarianism | .09 | 1.81 | .071 |
| Intergroup contact and friendship spring of second year | .48 | 9.91 | <.001** |
| Polyculturalism | .12 | 2.30 | .022* |

*Note.* ß's are standardized regression coefficients. *$p < .05$; **$p < .01$. Step 1: $R^2 = .27, p < .001$; Step 2: $\Delta R^2 = .01, p = .022$.

## Results

Means, standard deviations, and bivariate correlations can be seen in Table 1, and the results of the regression analysis can be seen in Table 2. In the regression analysis, positive intergroup contact and friendship in fall of second year was the outcome variable, with multiculturalism, colorblindness, and egalitarianism at baseline and positive intergroup contact and friendship in spring of first year included as predictor variables in Step 1, and then polyculturalism at baseline included as a predictor in Step 2. In Step 1 of the analysis, endorsement of egalitarianism at baseline and positive intergroup contact and friendship in the spring of first year each significantly predicted greater positive intergroup contact and friendship in fall of second year, while endorsement of multiculturalism and colorblindness at baseline were not significant predictors. Consistent with hypotheses, in Step 2 of the analysis, endorsement of polyculturalism at baseline significantly predicted greater positive intergroup contact and friendship in fall of second year; positive intergroup contact and friendship at spring of first year remained a significant predictor, while endorsement of egalitarianism at baseline became a marginally significant predictor, and endorsement of multiculturalism and colorblindness at baseline remained nonsignificant predictors.

We also conducted follow-up analyses to test whether controlling for race/ethnicity (with two dummy-coded variables for the two largest racial/ethnic groups, Asian and White) would change the results for polyculturalism, and whether race/ethnicity would moderate the results for polyculturalism. The results did not change when controlling for race/ethnicity, and race/ethnicity did not moderate the results for polyculturalism. Finally, we conducted a correlation (for age), two t-tests (for gender and nativity), and an analysis of variance (for race/ethnicity) to test if there were any significant demographic differences in level of endorsement of polyculturalism, and there were none.

## Discussion

Numerous settings around the world, including universities and colleges, are becoming increasingly diverse, opening up avenues for increased intergroup contact and friendship. This study is part of an important area of research aiming to identify factors that foster positive intergroup contact. In a longitudinal study with undergraduates at a racially/ethnically diverse, mid-sized, public university in the Northeastern U.S., we found for the first time that greater endorsement of polyculturalism shortly before the beginning of college was associated with increases in the amount of intergroup contact and friendship students have from the spring of their first year to the fall of their second year. This association was above and beyond the contributions of endorsement of other beliefs including multiculturalism, colorblindness, and egalitarianism before the beginning of college. Egalitarianism also significantly predicted increases in intergroup contact and friendship before polyculturalism was included in the model, but then became marginally significant with polyculturalism included. This finding is consistent with our past work that has found polyculturalism to be negatively associated with social dominance orientation (e.g., Rosenthal & Levy, 2012). Low scores on the social dominance orientation scale (Pratto et al., 1994) represent support for egalitarianism, suggesting an important connection between polyculturalism and egalitarianism, which might be explored further in future research. The forms of colorblindness (recognizing the unique qualities of individuals and commonalities across groups) and multiculturalism (recognizing important differences between racial/ethnic groups) assessed in the current study did not predict changes in intergroup contact and friendship. Although these are beliefs that have been found to be relevant to intergroup attitudes, including prejudice and stereotyping (e.g., Ryan et al., 2007), it may be that they do not particularly promote students seeking out and maintaining intergroup contact and friendships across the transition to college. As multiculturalism and colorblindness can be defined in multiple ways or have different forms, results may have differed if different measures of multiculturalism and colorblindness were used (see Rosenthal & Levy, 2010 for a review). The findings for polyculturalism also remained consistent when considering the race/ethnicity of participants, suggesting the link between polyculturalism and positive intergroup contact is consistent across both dominant (White Americans) and nondominant (e.g., Asian Americans) racial/ethnic groups.

Polyculturalism, then, in drawing attention to the ways that different racial and ethnic groups have interacted and influenced each other's cultures throughout history and into present day, is a belief that seems to encourage and foster intergroup contact and friendship over time among undergraduates attending a diverse university. These findings are consistent with and notably extend past findings that endorsement of polyculturalism is associated with greater interest in, appreciation for, and comfort with diversity, lower intergroup anxiety, and greater willingness for intergroup contact (Rosenthal & Levy, 2012; Rosenthal et al., 2015, under review). The longitudinal design of this study, with polyculturalism prospectively predicting changes in intergroup contact and friendship over time, allows us to have greater confidence in the direction of effects, suggesting polyculturalism may promote positive intergroup contact.

*Limitations and Future Directions*

There are some limitations of the current study. At the baseline survey, there were no questions about prior intergroup contact and friendship before entering college, so we could not assess changes occurring from before the start of college or the role that those prior experiences might play over time. Past research has found that undergraduates' experiences with diversity prior to college can influence the amount of intergroup contact they have during college and the effects of that intergroup contact (e.g., Bowman & Denson, 2012; Locks et al., 2008). Future research, then, may want to examine the role of diversity experience prior to college for the association of polyculturalism with intergroup contact and friendship, as well as the changes that occur across all years of college in polyculturalism and intergroup contact and friendship. The measure of intergroup contact and friendship was also self-reported and so may be affected by bias, although obtaining objective measures of intergroup contact and friendship is quite difficult. Subsequent studies may collect more detailed information about ongoing and new friendships by asking participants to list initials of their new and ongoing friends and report the race/ethnicity of each friend (see Mendoza-Denton et al., 2002), or controlled laboratory studies could directly observe interactions with members of different racial/ethnic backgrounds.

Future studies might also consider other measures of polyculturalism. The measure of polyculturalism used in this study, which is the same as has been used in numerous past studies (Bernardo et al., 2013; Rosenthal & Levy, 2012; Rosenthal et al., 2012, 2014, 2015, 2016, under review), was developed purposefully to be a neutral measure and avoid confounds with valence. Therefore, the measure simply assesses people's endorsement of there being connections and influences between cultures, but does not assess whether people think those connections and influences are positive or negative, which may be an important direction for future research to explore. Further, the contexts in which intergroup contact and influence happen can be both positive and negative. Indeed, slavery, colonization, and imperialism have played important roles in the United States and around the world in creating contexts for cross-cultural contact and influence. Although we have found endorsement of polyculturalism to be associated consistently with more positive intergroup attitudes, future work might explore what the consequences of positive versus negative views of and contexts for intergroup influence are for intergroup attitudes and behaviors, as well as what types of examples of polyculturalism people are exposed to and thinking about when completing these items.

This study was conducted at one university in the Northeastern U.S. and thus the results may be limited to that one setting. In our past research, we have found that polyculturalism has positive associations with intergroup attitudes across samples in Colombia, the Philippines, and the United States (Bernardo et al., 2013; Rosenthal & Levy, 2012; Rosenthal et al., under review). Moreover, past international research from cultural psychology has been discussed as supporting the utility and value of polyculturalism (Morris, Chiu, & Liu, 2015). Future studies are needed that explore whether findings replicate in other universities across the United States as well as around the world, and that consider whether the amount of diversity at a university affects the association of polyculturalism with intergroup contact and friendship. It would also be interesting to explore whether polyculturalism has the same associations in other settings, including in elementary, middle, and high schools, or in workplaces.

Although the longitudinal design of the current investigation gives greater confidence in the direction of effects than past cross-sectional findings, experimental research is needed to understand how polyculturalism might be taught, primed, or promoted, and what the resulting effects would be. Indeed, it is not yet known how stable versus changeable endorsement of polyculturalism is, or what factors may increase or decrease endorsement of polyculturalism. Research exploring the antecedents of polyculturalism may help in this realm to identify what factors predict individuals' endorsement of polyculturalism that could potentially then be tested in experimental studies for causal effects, ultimately informing the development of interventions. What everyday and/or more major experiences (e.g., at home, at work, at school, while traveling) lead people to endorse polyculturalism more strongly, and how can those experiences with polyculturalism inform interventions, programs, and policies aimed at improving intergroup attitudes and relations? Despite the remaining unanswered questions, the growing body of promising evidence of the role of polyculturalism in intergroup relations suggests that polyculturalism deserves consideration in efforts to foster more positive intergroup relations. As discussed next, educational settings may be places where polyculturalism messages are learned and might be particularly well-suited as places that polyculturalism can be promoted (Rosenthal & Levy, 2010).

*Implications for Educational Policy and Programming*

How might polyculturalism fit into interventions, programs, and policies aimed at fostering positive intergroup contact in academic and other settings (e.g., workplace)? Diversity training programs are popular in university and workplace settings, but tend to focus on differences between groups and less so on connections among groups (e.g., Paluck, 2006), suggesting the need and potential benefit of incorporating polyculturalism into diversity training. There is increasing diversity on U.S. college campuses, and there have been many recent controversies over the handling of diversity- or prejudice-related issues on college campuses across the United States (e.g., Hartocollis & Bidgood, 2015, November 11), highlighting the significance of better understanding intergroup dynamics in these settings to inform institutional handling of these issues. Research finds that the campus climate around diversity predicts students' own acceptance of diversity (e.g., Simmons, Wittig, & Grant, 2010). Perceptions of institution-level support for diversity are therefore connected to support among and across students. Research also finds that students are more interested in intergroup contact when they perceive other students value diversity (e.g., Tropp & Bianchi, 2006).

In light of these findings and our program of research, we suggest future studies explore ways that polyculturalism could be incorporated and integrated with current institutional policies and programs tailored to students in college settings to foster valuing diversity and positive intergroup relations, including those based on multiculturalism (Rosenthal & Levy, 2010). As noted earlier, polyculturalism and multiculturalism are conceptually and empirically compatible because they both focus on recognizing and appreciating group identities, with multiculturalism focusing more on group distinctions and polyculturalism focusing more on interconnections among groups. Indeed, polyculturalism and multiculturalism are positively correlated in the current as well as in past investigations (e.g., Rosenthal & Levy, 2012), further suggesting the potential utility of pairing these beliefs together to promote positive intergroup relations.

Multiculturalism, for example, is often highlighted visually on campuses and schools' Web sites as well as through events on campus celebrating particular cultures, and multiculturalism is sometimes emphasized in coursework, such as in the humanities (e.g., Banks, 2013; Schultz, Barr, & Selman, 2001; Zirkel, 2008). Likewise, institutions' endorsement of polyculturalism could be communicated visually vis-a-vis events on campus, such as film screenings, music performances, or art exhibitions, as well as with food vendor options (e.g., fusion food) that implicitly or explicitly highlight cross-cultural, polycultural connections and influences. Because historical and contemporary examples of polyculturalism cut across many disciplines (e.g., art, dance, history, medicine, music, science), institutions could encourage examples of polyculturalism to be highlighted in courses already part of students' degree requirements.

Universities might also consider implementing more individual-level interventions that incorporate polyculturalism themes to promote positive views on diversity and intergroup contact. With a particular focus on the transition to college, polyculturalism messages could be incorporated into incoming undergraduates' orientations and/or courses that first year students are required to take. Those messages could even be tailored to individual students through text messages or emails, encouraging them to recognize and explore ways that their own cultures have influenced and been influenced by other cultures. Research could explore whether such an intervention promotes positive adjustment to a diverse university and results in increased intergroup contact and friendship.

Incorporating polyculturalism into intervention efforts at universities seems to be a promising application of the research findings to date. Such incorporation can also be done in conjunction with insights from research on other factors that have been found to increase positive intergroup contact and improve intergroup attitudes, including factors discussed in the current issue, such as self-expansion, allophilia, and opportunities for intimate and positive intergroup contact (Davies & Aron, 2016; Livert, 2016; Paolini, Wright, Dys-Steenbergen, & Favara, 2016; Pittinsky & Montoya, 2016).

## Conclusion

With increasing racial/ethnic diversity at U.S. colleges and universities, it is timely and important that researchers, educators, and policy makers consider factors that can foster positive intergroup contact and friendship, which are known to have many positive consequences, as opposed to self-segregation and/or intergroup conflict. Results from this longitudinal study suggest that greater belief in polyculturalism may help to promote increases in positive intergroup contact and friendship across the beginning of college. These findings, along with the growing body of research on polyculturalism, suggest that polyculturalism deserves future attention in research to continue to explore the role it plays in intergroup attitudes and interactions, and that it may be fruitful to explore ways that polyculturalism could be implemented into interventions, programs, and policies at universities and colleges, as well as in other diverse settings.

## References

Banks, J. A. (2013). *An introduction to multicultural education: Fifth edition*. United States: Pearson.

Barbarino, M.-L., & Stürmer, S. (2016). Different origins of xenophile and xenophobic orientations in human personality structure: A theoretical perspective and some preliminary findings. *Journal of Social Issues, 72*, 432–449.

Bernardo, A. B. I., Rosenthal, L., & Levy, S. R. (2013). Polyculturalism and attitudes toward people from other countries. *International Journal of Intercultural Relations, 37*, 335–344. doi: 10.1016/j.ijintrel.2012.12.005

Berryman-Fink, C. (2006). Reducing prejudice on campus: The role of intergroup contact in diversity education. *College Student Journal, 40*, 511–515.

Bonilla-Silva, E. (2003). *Racism without racists: Color-blind racism and the persistence of racial inequality in the United States*. Lanham, MD: Rowman & Littlefield.

Bowman, N. A., & Brandenberger, J. W. (2012). Experiencing the unexpected: Toward a model of college diversity experiences and attitude change. *The Review of Higher Education, 35*, 179–205. doi:10.1353/rhe.2012.0016

Bowman, N. A., & Denson, N. (2012). What's past is prologue: How precollege exposure to diversity shapes the impact of college diversity experiences. *Research in Higher Education, 53*, 406–425. doi:10.1007/s11162-011-9235-2

Chang, M. J. (1999). Does racial diversity matter? The educational impact of a racially diverse undergraduate population. *Journal of College Student Development, 40*, 377–395.

Chiu, C.-Y., Gries, P., Torelli, C. J., & Cheng, S. Y. Y. (2011). Toward a social psychology of globalization. *Journal of Social Issues, 67*, 663–676. doi:10.1111/j.1540-4560.2011.01721.x

Davies, K., & Aron, A. (2016). Friendship development and intergroup attitudes: The role of interpersonal and intergroup friendship processes. *Journal of Social Issues, 72*, 489–510.

Flint, K. (2006). Indian-African encounters: Polyculturalism and African therapeutics in Natal, South Africa, 1886-1950s. *Journal of Southern African Studies, 32*, 367–385.

Grasmuck, S., & Kim, J. (2010). Embracing and resisting ethnoracial boundaries: Second-generation immigrant and African-American students in a multicultural university. *Sociological Forum, 25*, 221–247. doi.10.1111/j.1573-7861.2010.01174.x

Gurin, P., Dey, E. L., Hurtado, S., & Gurin, G. (2002). Diversity and higher education: Theory and impact on educational outcomes. *Harvard Educational Review, 72*, 330–366. doi: 10.17763/haer.72.3.01151786u134n051

Hartocollis, A., & Bidgood, J. (2015, November 11). Racial discrimination protests ignite at colleges across the U.S. *The New York Times*. Retrieved from http://www.nytimes.com/2015/11/12/us/racial-discrimination-protests-ignite-at-colleges-across-the-us.html. Accessed at Dec 1, 2015.

Hurtado, S. (2005). The next generation of diversity and intergroup relations research. *Journal of Social Issues, 61*, 595–610. doi: 10.1111/j.1540-4560.2005.00422.x

Katz, I., & Hass, R. G. (1988). Racial ambivalence and American value conflict: Correlational and priming studies of dual cognitive structures. *Journal of Personality and Social Psychology, 55*, 893–905. doi: 10.1037/0022-3514.55.6.893

Kelley, R. D. G. (1999). The people in me. *Utne Reader, 95*, 79–81.

Levy, S. R., West, T., Ramirez, L., & Karafantis, D. M. (2006). The Protestant work ethic: A lay theory with dual intergroup implications. *Group Processes and Intergroup Relations, 9*, 95–115. doi: 10.1177/1368430206059874

Livert, D. (2016). A cook's tour abroad: Long term effects of intergroup contact on positive outgroup attitudes. *Journal of Social Issues, 72*, 524–547.

Locks, A. M., Hurtado, S., Bowman, N. A., & Oseguera, L. (2008). Extending notions of campus climate and diversity to students' transition to college. *The Review of Higher Education, 31*, 257–285. doi: 10.1353/rhe.2008.0011

London, B., Rosenthal, L., Levy, S. R., & Lobel, M. (2011). The influences of perceived identity compatibility and social support on women in nontraditional fields during the college transition. *Basic and Applied Social Psychology, 33*, 304–321. doi: 10.1080/01973533.2011. 614166

Lopez, G. (2004). Interethnic contact, curriculum, and attitudes in the first year of college. *Journal of Social Issues, 60*, 75–94. doi: 10.1111/j.0022-4537.2004.00100.x

Mendoza-Denton, R., Downey, G., Purdie, V., Davis, A., & Pietrzak, J. (2002). Sensitivity to status-based rejection: Implications for African American students college experiences. *Journal of Personality and Social Psychology, 83*, 896–918. doi: 10.1037/0022-3514.83. 4.896

Morris, M., Chiu, C.-Y., & Liu, Z. (2015). Polycultural psychology. *Annual Review of Psychology, 66*, 631–659. doi: 10.1146/annurev-psych-010814-015001

Nagda, B. A., Tropp, L. R., & Paluck, E. L. (2006). Looking back as we look forward: Integrating research, theory, and practice on intergroup relations. *Journal of Social Issues, 62*, 439–451. doi: 10.1111/j.1540-4560.2006.00467.x

Paluck, E. L. (2006). Diversity training and intergroup contact: A call to action research. *Journal of Social Issues, 62*, 577–595. doi: 10.1111/j.1540-4560.2006.00474.x

Paolini, S., Wright, S., Dys-Steenbergen, O., & Favara, I. (2016). Self-expansion and intergroup contact: Expectancies and motives to self-expand lead to greater interest in outgroup contact and more intergroup relations. *Journal of Social Issues, 72*, 450–471.

Pascarella, E. T., Martin, G., Hanson, J., Trolian, T., Gillig, B., & Blaich, C. (2014). Effects of diversity experiences on critical thinking skills over four years of college. *Journal of College Student Development, 55*, 86–92. doi: 10.1353/csd.2014.0009

Pettigrew, T. F., & Tropp, L. R. (2006). A meta-analytic test of intergroup contact theory. *Journal of Personality and Social Psychology, 90*, 751–783. doi: 10.1037/0022-3514.90.5.751

Pittinsky, T. L., & Montoya, R. M. (2016). Empathic joy in positive intergroup relations. *Journal of Social Issues, 72*, 511–523.

Pittinsky, T. L., Rosenthal, S. A., & Montoya, R. M. (2011). Measuring positive attitudes toward outgroups: Development and validation of the Allophilia Scale. In L. R. Tropp & R. K. Mallett (Eds.), *Beyond prejudice reduction: Pathways to positive intergroup relations (pp. 41–60)*. Washington, DC: American Psychological Association.

Prashad, V. (2001). *Everybody was Kung Fu fighting: Afro-Asian connections and the myth of cultural purity*. Boston: Beacon Press.

Prashad, V. (2003). Bruce Lee and the anti-imperialism of Kung Fu: A polycultural adventure. *Positions: East Asia Cultures Critique, 11*, 51–90.

Pratto, F., Sidanius, J., Stallworth, L. M., & Malle, B. F. (1994). Social dominance orientation: A personality variable predicting social and political attitudes. *Journal of Personality and Social Psychology, 67*, 741–763. doi: 10.1037/0022-3514.67.4.741

Rosenthal, L., & Levy, S. R. (2010). The colorblind, multicultural, and polycultural ideological approaches to improving intergroup attitudes and relations. *Social Issues and Policy Review, 4*, 215–246. doi: 10.1111/j.1751-2409.2010.01022.x

Rosenthal, L., & Levy, S. R. (2012). The relation between polyculturalism and intergroup attitudes among racially and ethnically diverse adults. *Cultural Diversity and Ethnic Minority Psychology, 18*, 1–16. doi: 10.1037/a0026490

Rosenthal, L., & Levy, S. R. (2013). Thinking about mutual influences and connections across cultures relates to more positive intergroup attitudes: An examination of polyculturalism. *Social and Personality Psychology Compass, 7*, 547–558. doi: 10.1111/spc3.12043

Rosenthal, L., Levy, S. R., Katser, M., & Bazile, C. (2015). Polyculturalism and attitudes toward Muslim Americans. *Peace and Conflict: Journal of Peace Psychology, 21*, 535–545. doi: 10.1037/pac0000133

Rosenthal, L., Levy, S. R., London, B., & Lewis, M. A. (2016). Polyculturalism among undergraduates at diverse universities: Associations through intergroup anxiety with academic and alcohol outcomes. *Analyses of Social Issues and Public Policy.* doi: 10.1111/asap.12121

Rosenthal, L., Levy, S. R., & Militano, M. (2014). Polyculturalism and sexist attitudes. *Psychology of Women Quarterly, 38,* 519–534. doi: 10.1177/0361684313510152

Rosenthal, L., Levy, S. R., & Moss, I. (2012). Polyculturalism and openness about criticizing one's culture: Implications for sexual prejudice. *Group Processes and Intergroup Relations, 15,* 149–166. doi: 10.1177/1368430211412801

Rosenthal, L., London, B., Levy, S. R., Lobel, M., & Herrera-Alcazar, A. (2011). The relation between the Protestant work ethic and undergraduate women's perceived identity compatibility in nontraditional majors. *Analyses of Social Issues and Public Policy, 11,* 241–262. doi: 10.1111/j.1530-2415.2011.01264.x

Rosenthal, L., Ramírez, L., Bernardo, A. B. I., & Levy, S. R. (under review). Polyculturalism: Viewing cultures as dynamically connected and its implications for intercultural attitudes in Colombia.

Ryan, C. S., Hunt, J. S., Weible, J. A., Peterson, C. R., & Casas, J. F. (2007). Multicultural and colorblind ideology, stereotypes, and ethnocentrism among Black and White Americans. *Group Processes and Intergroup Relations, 10,* 617–637. doi: 10.1177/1368430207084105

Schmid, K., Hewstone, M., Tausch, N., Cairns, E., & Hughes, J. (2009). Antecedents and consequences of social identity complexity: Intergroup contact, distinctiveness threat. *Personality and Social Psychology Bulletin, 35,* 1085–1098. doi: 10.1177/0146167209337037

Schultz, L., Barr, D. J., & Selman, R. L. (2001). The value of a developmental approach to evaluating character development programmes: An outcome study of Facing History and Ourselves. *Journal of Moral Education, 30,* 3–27. doi: 10.1080/03057240120033785

Sidanius, J., Levin, S., Van Laar, C., & Sears, D. O. (2010). *The diversity challenge: Social identity and intergroup relations on the college campus.* New York: Russell Sage Foundation.

Sidanius, J., Van Laar, C., Levin, S., & Sinclair, S. (2004). Ethnic enclaves and the dynamics of social identity on the college campus: The good, the bad, and the ugly. *Journal of Personality and Social Psychology, 87,* 96–110. doi: 10.1037/0022-3514.87.1.96

Siem, B., Stürmer, S., & Pittinsky, T. L. (2016). The psychological study of positive behavior across group boundaries: An overview. *Journal of Social Issues, 72,* 419–431.

Simmons, S. J., Wittig, M., & Grant, S. (2010). A mutual acculturation model of multicultural campus climate and acceptance of diversity. *Cultural Diversity and Ethnic Minority Psychology, 14,* 468–475. doi: 10.1037/a0020237

Stürmer, S., Benbow, A. E. F., Siem, B., Barth, M., Bodansky, A. N., & Lotz-Schmitt, K. (2013). Psychological foundations of xenophilia: The role of major personality traits in predicting favorable attitudes toward cross-cultural contact and exploration. *Journal of Personality and Social Psychology, 105,* 832–851. doi: 10.1037/a0033488

Tropp, L. R., & Bianchi, R. A. (2006). Valuing diversity and interest in intergroup contact. *Journal of Social Issues, 62,* 533–551. doi: 10.1111/j 1540-4560.2006.00472.x

Verkuyten, M. (2005). Ethnic group identification and group evaluation among minority and majority groups: Testing the multiculturalism hypothesis. *Journal of Personality and Social Psychology, 88,* 121–138. doi: 10.1037/0022-3514.88.1.121

Wolsko, C., Park, B., Judd, C. M., & Wittenbrink, B. (2000). Framing interethnic ideology: Effects of multicultural and color-blind perspectives on judgments of groups and individuals. *Journal Of Personality and Social Psychology, 78,* 635–654. doi: 10.1037/0022-3514.78.4.635

Zirkel, S. (2008). Creating more effective multiethnic schools. *Social Issues and Policy Review, 2,* 187–241. doi: 10.1111/j.1751-2409.2008.00015.x

LISA ROSENTHAL is an Assistant Professor of Psychology at Pace University in New York City. She earned her PhD in Social and Health Psychology from Stony Brook University in 2011. Her research focuses on stigma and social justice, including seeking to understand how experiences with prejudice, discrimination, stereotyping, marginalization, and inequality contribute to gender, racial/ethnic, and other academic and health disparities.

SHERI R. LEVY is an Associate Professor of Psychology at Stony Brook University in New York. She earned her PhD in Psychology from Columbia University. She studies factors that cause and maintain prejudice, stigmatization, and negative intergroup relations and that can be harnessed to reduce bias, marginalization, and discrimination. Her research focuses on bias based on age, ethnicity, gender, nationality, race, sexual orientation, social class, and weight. Levy was Editor of *Journal of Social Issues* from 2010 to 2013.

*Journal of Social Issues, Vol. 72, No. 3, 2016, pp. 489–510*
*doi: 10.1111/josi.12178*

# Friendship Development and Intergroup Attitudes: The Role of Interpersonal and Intergroup Friendship Processes

**Kristin Davies**[*]
*York College, City University of New York*

**Arthur Aron**
*Stony Brook University*

*Although there is a growing body of work concerning cross-group friendship and intergroup attitudes, this work typically focuses on a limited number of interpersonal processes among established friendships. In addition, little is known about the role of group-related processes within such friendships. Two studies were conducted to address this gap. Results from a retrospective online survey and a longitudinal study reveal that both interpersonal friendship processes (e.g., intimacy, affection, trust, self-disclosure) and intergroup friendship processes (e.g., belief that outgroup friend respects one's own group, spending time with outgroup friend's family members and friends) are associated with positive intergroup attitudes. Specifically, the current findings suggest that interpersonal friendship processes are vital to fostering positive attitudes for the outgroup early in the relationship, but that intergroup friendship processes become more strongly linked to attitudes once the relationship progresses. Results may inform interventions designed to promote positive interactions across "real-world" group boundaries.*

In his seminal work on intergroup relations, Pettigrew (1998) has advocated for cross-group friendships, as compared to general intergroup contact, in improving feelings about the outgroup (OG) as a whole, as these relationships typically involve longer-term contact, include both affective and cognitive underpinnings, and are likely to contain Allport's (1954) necessary conditions for success in prejudice reduction. Pettigrew (1997a) found strong support for the above notion

---

[*]Correspondence concerning this article should be addressed to Kristin Davies, Department of Behavioral Sciences, York College, City University of New York, 94 20 Guy R. Brewer Boulevard, Jamaica, New York, NY 11451. Tel: 718-262-5392 [e-mail: KDavies@york.cuny.edu].

This research was supported in part by a grant from the Society for the Psychological Study of Social Issues.

in his large study that surveyed four European nations, where cross-group friend-ships were associated with more positive OG attitudes to a greater degree than were general acquaintances. A meta-analysis (Davies, Tropp, Aron, Pettigrew, & Wright, 2011) investigating friendship contact and intergroup attitudes provides additional support for this view.

As we've previously discussed (See Davies, Wright, Aron, & Comeau, 2013), the experience of friendship tends to be highly valued; a study assessing beliefs about "what makes life meaningful" found that nearly all respondents included friendship in their answer (Klinger, 1977). Tesch and Martin (1983) found that def-initions of friendship most frequently include references to dependability, caring, commitment, and trust, followed by compatibility and similarity, and time spent together. In her extensive review of the friendship literature, Fehr (1996, 2008) describes "dyadic factors" that facilitate one's decision to pursue a friendship. These largely involve one's perception of how the other feels about the self, and include reciprocity of liking (e.g., Backman & Secord, 1959), and perception of the other's willingness to self-disclose (Altman & Taylor, 1973). As friendships deepen, partners enjoy easier and more meaningful communication (Knapp, Ellis, & Williams, 1980), have more frequent interactions, and are more likely to rely upon each other for emotional support (Hays, 1985).

Literature discussing cross-group friendship has identified interpersonal pro-cesses likely to underlie their positive impact on intergroup attitudes, including affection (e.g., Pettigrew, 1997b), self-disclosure (e.g., Turner, Tam, Hewstone, Kenworthy, & Cairns, 2013), and perceived partner responsiveness (Shelton, Trail, West, & Bergsieker, 2010). Cross-group friendships may also improve intergroup attitudes by realigning one's self-identity to be more inclusive of the OG (e.g., Wright, Aron, & Tropp, 2002), and the desire to expand one's sense of self may encourage individuals to seek out cross-group interactions (Paolini, Wright, Dys-Steenbergen, & Favara, 2016). Although these research endeavors make for an important first step, only a select few of the many interpersonal processes under-lying friendship have been examined in the context of cross-group relationships (Davies et al., 2011).

The intergroup literature has also highlighted group-related variables involved in the contact–prejudice relationship, including ingroup identification (Voci, Hewstone, Swart, & Veneziani, 2015), and perception of group norms (e.g., Jugert, Noack, & Rutland, 2011). Less is known, however, about more intimate group-relevant processes that are particularly likely to take place within the context of a cross-group friendship; what we will call "intergroup friendship processes." For example: discussions about friends' respective groups, interactions with OG friend's social network, and perceptions of OG friend's sensitivity for one's own group (i.e., the ingroup). These variables may be of particular importance to im-provements in intergroup attitudes because, due to their occurring within a close relationship, they are likely both interpersonal and intergroup in nature.

Finally, prior intergroup friendship research has primarily examined established relationships; less is known concerning the development of cross-group friendships, and the point at which the relationship begins to affect attitudes is unclear.

Therefore, this exploratory work sought to shed light on these issues. Our primary goals were: (1) to explore a wide variety of both interpersonal and intergroup friendship processes in relation to positive feelings toward the OG and (2) to gain a clearer picture of when feelings for OG improve. A retrospective survey was designed to recruit participants from the general adult population, while a longitudinal study of undergraduates observed changes over time. Although we had no specific hypotheses per se in this exploratory work, prior research on cross-group friendships (e.g., Davies et al., 2011; Pettigrew, 1997b) would suggest that higher levels of intimate processes such as self-disclosure, trust and spending time with friends (i.e., "interpersonal" friendship processes) would be associated with more positive feelings for the OG. Cross-group friendships provide a unique context in which intergroup processes can unfold at the interpersonal level, allowing for heightened levels of comfort, trust, and interest concerning the exchange of group-related information. Therefore, we expected that "intergroup" friendship processes would also have a positive connection to favorable perceptions of the OG.

## Study 1: A Retrospective Survey

*Methods*

*Participants.*      Participants were recruited during the summer of 2009 through a variety of means (e.g., emails, fliers, psychology listservs). Advertisements contained a direct link to the online survey (Surveymonkey.com), and informed potential participants that they would be entered in a random drawing for one of ten $50 Amazon gift cards upon survey completion. Anyone having a current friendship could participate, however, respondents were asked to complete the survey about a friend of a different racial or ethnic background if they currently had one (or the closest relationship, if having multiple). Given our research topic, analyses focused on those responding about OG members. The final sample[1] comprised 100 women, 22 men, aged 18 to 81 years ($M = 29.20$, $SD = 10.02$), 63% reported European ancestry (2% African, 17% Asian, 6% Hispanic or Latino, and 12% mixed or other category), and 78% were from the Northeastern United States.

---

[1] Of the original sample of 143 participants, 3 were removed due to missing data, 3 were removed due to having scores that were more than 3 *SD*s from the mean on predictor or outcome scales, and 15 were removed for responding to items using a "don't know" option that was provided, rather than the 7-point scale.

*Procedure.* Upon visiting the survey website potential participants were given a general overview of the study, and after giving consent they were presented with the survey items. When recruitment was complete, all participants were sent an email containing debriefing information.

*Measures.* The survey asked respondents to answer items concerning the beginning and current state of the relationship. All multiple-item measures were created by taking the average of the items. To inquire about a wide array of relevant friendship dimensions, we consulted the friendship literature (e.g., Fehr, 1996; Hays, 1984; Tesch & Martin, 1983) to guide the creation of items.

*Early interpersonal friendship processes.* The "Positive Qualities" scale ($\alpha = .86$) asked respondents to recall whether the person's specific attributes (e.g., warm, outgoing) made them think the person "might make a good friend," while the "Early Bonding" scale ($\alpha = .88$) assessed processes (e.g., helping, comfort) contributing to "thinking of (the person) as a friend."

*Current interpersonal friendship processes.* Measures assessing "as of to-day" friendship processes included "Reciprocal Caring" (You care about him/her, He/she cares about you; $\alpha = .91$); "Reciprocal Trust" (You trust him/her, He/she trusts you; $\alpha = .74$); "Intimacy" (You feel close, You feel important, He/she is important; $\alpha = .93$); a single-item measure of "Affection" (feeling "warmth, liking or love"); Due to conceptual similarities and strong relationships ($r$s ranging from .565 to .925) among the intimacy, caring, trust, and affection measures, these were combined to create a broader assessment of "Friendship Quality" ($\alpha = .93$). A single item assessed "Self-Disclosure" (You tell him/her things "you wouldn't share with everyone"), and the "Inclusion of Other in Self" scale (Aron, Aron, & Smollan, 1992) was utilized, which depicts seven increasingly overlapping circle pairs (i.e., Venn diagrams) in which each circle represents "self" or "other." Finally, "General Activity" level (spending time together, having conversations; $\alpha = .63$); and friend's "Supportive Behaviors" (e.g., asks about problems, offers help; $\alpha = .83$) were combined to form a composite measure of "Total Friendship Behaviors" ($\alpha = .81$).

*Current intergroup friendship processes.* These included: a single item of spending time with "OG Member's Family and Friends," "OG Member's Sensitivity for Ingroup" (perception of OG friend's understanding and respect for one's own ingroup; $\alpha = .66$), "Group-Related Activities" (how often one joins in OG activities, and how often the friend joins in activities relating to one's own ingroup; $\alpha = .78$), and frequency of "Group-Related Conversations" (how often group-related issues are discussed and explained; $\alpha = .82$).

*Intergroup attitudes.* Assessments of intergroup attitudes included "Empathy for OG" (understanding and feeling for friend's group; $\alpha = .71$), "Positive Regard for OG" (sympathy and admiration for OG of one's friend; Pettigrew & Meertens, 1995; $\alpha = .76$), and "Warmth for OG" (single feeling thermometer rating for friend's group). All items were answered on 7-point scales, except for warmth for OG (a "temperature" assigned from 0 to 100).

## Results

Based on prior literature, we anticipated that both types of friendship processes, interpersonal and intergroup, would relate to positive attitudes for the OG. Data were examined prior to analysis to confirm that assumptions for multiple regression (e.g., linearity, homoscedasticity) were met.

Bivariate correlations can be seen in Table 1. Our primary analyses were a series of hierarchical multiple regressions comparing the contributions of three sets of variables: early interpersonal friendship processes occurring during the initial stages of the relationship, current interpersonal friendship processes occurring at the time of the survey, and current intergroup friendship processes occurring at the time of the survey. We examined: (1) what each set contributed by itself with no others in the model, (2) what each set added over just one of the other sets, and (3) what each set added over both of the others. It should be noted that, in all cases, additional variance explained was due to variables in the set yielding positive changes in the outcome variable; greater amounts of positive intergroup attitudes were predicted.

*Predicting empathy for OG.* When investigating predictors of empathy for OG, we first observed that each of the three sets of predictors (early interpersonal processes, current interpersonal processes, and current intergroup processes) explained a significant portion of the variance when each was entered separately in a first step ($R^2$s were 15%, $p < .001$, 10%, $p = .015$, and 34%, $p < .001$, respectively). When entered separately in a second step, early interpersonal processes explained a significant additional proportion of the variance above and beyond both current interpersonal processes, (8%, $p = .006$), and current intergroup processes (4%, $p = .046$). Similarly, when entered in a second step, current intergroup processes explained another 26% of the variance above current interpersonal processes ($p < .001$), and 22% beyond early interpersonal processes ($p < .001$). Finally, when entered in a third and final step, only the set of predictors

---

[2] We wish to note that we repeated all of the Study 1 analyses checking the potential role of gender, given the greater proportion of females than males in the study. In no case did gender have a significant main or interaction effect, nor did controlling for it modify the pattern of significance of any of the reported results.

**Table 1.** Correlations between Interpersonal Friendship Variables (Early and Current), Intergroup Friendship Variables, and Positive Attitudes for the Outgroup in the Retrospective Study (Study 1)

| | $M$ | $SD$ | 1. | 2. | 3. | 4. | 5. | 6. | 7. | 8. | 9. | 10. | 11. | 12. | 13. |
|---|---|---|---|---|---|---|---|---|---|---|---|---|---|---|---|
| 1. Positive qualities of friend (early) | 5.52 | 1.22 | 1 | .42** | .36** | .26** | .19* | .07 | .14 | .37** | .05 | −.02 | .23* | .08 | .12 |
| 2. Early bonding processes | 5.43 | 1.09 | | 1 | .43** | .45** | .26** | .32** | .19* | .31** | .12 | .13 | .38** | .24** | .12 |
| 3. Friendship quality (current) | 5.92 | 1.49 | | | 1 | .81** | .55** | .48** | .34** | .25** | .23* | .09 | .30** | .24** | .11 |
| 4. Self-disclosure (current) | 5.61 | 1.58 | | | | 1 | .56** | .52** | .32** | .13 | .23* | .19* | .28** | .14 | .13 |
| 5. Inclusion of other in self (current) | 4.27 | 1.37 | | | | | 1 | .51** | .27** | .03 | .31** | .17 | .11 | .06 | .09 |
| 6. Total behaviors (current) | 4.74 | 1.00 | | | | | | 1 | .30** | −.01 | .33** | .29** | .14 | .04 | .01 |
| 7. OG family and friends | 3.67 | 2.10 | | | | | | | 1 | .04 | .49** | −.04 | .23* | .11 | .08 |
| 8. OG friend's sensitivity for IG | 5.61 | 1.05 | | | | | | | | 1 | .00 | .01 | .52** | .37** | .15 |
| 9. Group activities | 2.54 | 1.28 | | | | | | | | | 1 | .16 | .15 | .09 | −.08 |
| 10. Group conversations | 3.29 | 1.44 | | | | | | | | | | 1 | .15 | .16 | −.17 |
| 11. Empathy for OG | 4.97 | 1.52 | | | | | | | | | | | 1 | .57** | .29** |
| 12. Positive regard for OG | 4.27 | 1.52 | | | | | | | | | | | | 1 | .39** |
| 13. Warmth for OG | 76.34 | 16.91 | | | | | | | | | | | | | 1 |

*Note.* In the above table, "OG" denotes "outgroup" and "IG" denotes "ingroup." $N = 122$.
**Correlation is significant at the .01 level (two-tailed).
*Correlation is significant at the .05 level (two-tailed).

concerning current intergroup processes provided a significant gain in variance explained beyond both of the other sets (21%, $p = .000$). As individual predictors in the final model, both early bonding and OG member's sensitivity for one's own ingroup made significant unique contributions to the variance explained ($\beta = .19$, $p = .041$, and $\beta = .46$, $p < .001$, respectively).

*Predicting positive regard for OG.* We next explored models predicting positive regard for OG, and initially observed that both early interpersonal processes and current intergroup variables explained significant portions of the variance when each was entered individually in a first step ($R^2$s were 6%, $p = .025$, and 17%, $p < .001$, respectively). When each of the three sets was entered individually in a second step, however, only current intergroup processes explained a significant amount of additional variance above either of the other sets ($R^2$ was 12%, $p = .003$, above current interpersonal processes, and 13%, $p = .002$, above early interpersonal processes). Similarly, only current intergroup processes provided a significant gain in variance explained (11%, $p = .004$) beyond each of the other sets when entered in a third and final step. Both current relationship quality and OG member's sensitivity for one's own ingroup made significant unique contributions to the variance explained in the final model ($\beta = .31$, $p = .050$, and $\beta = .32$, $p = .001$, respectively).

*Predicting warmth for OG.* Somewhat surprisingly, we found that no set of variables (early interpersonal processes, current interpersonal processes, or current intergroup processes) acted as significant predictors of Warmth for OG at any stage of any model in this study.[2]

## Discussion: Retrospective Study

The retrospective study found support for our general expectation that positive interpersonal friendship and intergroup friendship processes would relate to positive intergroup attitudes. Several interpersonal friendship and intergroup friendship variables had significant bivariate relationships with intergroup attitudes (Table 1), and in investigating larger models using hierarchical regression, early "bonding" processes, current friendship quality, and feeling that the OG member respects and understands one's own group (i.e., ingroup), were each significant unique predictors of positive intergroup attitudes in at least one final model.

Surprising was our finding that, as a set, the current interpersonal friendship processes mainly failed to make significant contributions to the models explored, except for the first step in the model for empathy for OG. Early interpersonal friendship processes made a significant contribution in a first step when predicting positive regard for OG, and in first and second steps in models predicting empathy for OG, but they failed to explain a significant increase in variance when added in the third stage for all models. It was the set of variables concerning current intergroup processes that most often explained a significant portion of the variance beyond that of the other sets (i.e., the interpersonal friendship variables). This may suggest that although interpersonal friendship processes transpiring between members of differing groups do generally tend to encourage more positive perceptions of the OG, the group-related one-on-one interactions that occur within this context may ultimately have a greater influence on one's intergroup attitudes. Also surprising, and counter to prior work in this area (e.g., Davies et al., 2011; Wright et al., 2002), was the observation that inclusion of other in self, and current activity/behaviors had little connection to intergroup attitudes in this study.

## Study 2: A Longitudinal Survey

In the longitudinal study, we examined newly formed friendships. This allowed for the collection of (potentially) more accurate information about friendship processes due to their having recently occurred. In addition, a longitudinal design allows for a clearer picture of how associations between variables may change over time, as the friendship progresses. As in the retrospective survey, we expected that both interpersonal and intergroup friendship processes would predict positive changes in intergroup attitudes. It should be noted that because the retrospective and longitudinal studies were conducted around the same period of time they were not able to inform each other; some variables assessed in one study were not assessed in the other. Most variables are the same or comparable across studies, however.[3]

### *Methods*

*Design.*    We assessed interpersonal and intergroup friendship processes using surveys at three time points across a university semester during the fall of 2008 and spring of 2009. The first survey inquired about someone met within the past month with whom the respondent may "become friends," and instructed respondents to think of a potential friend of another ethnicity. If an OG potential friend did not exist, the respondent selected a potential ingroup friend. Those without a potential friend answered about a current or past ingroup friend. The

---

[3]Generally, measures were briefer in the longitudinal study due to limitations on survey length. Major differences in survey content are that the retrospective study, unlike the longitudinal survey, included the Inclusion of Other in Self scale, a more detailed assessment of friendship behaviors, and assessments of group-related activities and conversations. Also, the retrospective study asked participants to recall earliest aspects of the relationship (i.e., initial "bonding" events, and recognized "positive qualities" of the then potential friend) whereas the longitudinal study did not, given it concerned relationships that were only 1 month old at T1. The longitudinal study also differs in that it included an assessment of perceived similarity to outgroup member, and "learning" about the outgroup.

first (paper) survey was administered during a "mass testing" session in which introductory psychology students are required to take a number of questionnaires at the beginning of the semester (T1). The second (T2) and third (T3) surveys, which inquired about the relationship identified at T1, were administered via the internet about 6 and 10 weeks later, respectively.

*Participants.*     Of the 328 students completing the first survey, 183 (56%) reported having recently met a potential friend (ingroup or OG), and were invited to take part in the later surveys, for which they received either $10 or one additional research credit for their psychology course.

Of all eligible respondents, 70 (38%) accepted, and the final sample consisted of 52 cross-group participants and 18 same-group participants (70% female, mean age of 18.50 years). The sample was 9% African American or Black, 37% Asian American, 7% Hispanic or Latino, 44% European American or White, and 3% mixed or other category. It is worth noting that this final sample, as compared to those not volunteering for the later surveys ($n = 114$), contains a higher percentage of female participants (70% vs. 49%, respectively). Although "volunteer bias" of this sort is not unusual in studies of friendship (Lewis, Winstead, & Derlega, 1989), it should be considered during the interpretation of findings. Those taking all three surveys were generally similar to those completing just the first survey in terms of age ($M = 18.50$ and 18.47 years, respectively) and racial composition (44% White and 54% White, respectively).

*Final sample.*     Given the small number of participants reporting a same-group friendship, primary analyses focused on just those in cross-group relationships. In addition, because contact theory (e.g., Pettigrew, 1998) emphasizes the need for "friendship potential" to encourage positive intergroup attitudes, our analyses excluded participants describing a relationship in which friendship was considered "unlikely" at T3 (seven people), or who demoted their T2 "friendship" to a T3 "potential" friendship (two people). Two participants reporting romantic developments were also excluded, resulting in a final sample of 41 cross-group participants.

*Procedure.*     After agreeing to participate, volunteers were reminded who they had answered the initial survey about, and were given a code granting access to the additional online surveys. When recruitment was complete, participants were debriefed via email.

*Measures*

*Interpersonal friendship processes.*     As in the retrospective study, scales for the longitudinal data were created based on relevant theory. The "Intimacy" scale (T1 $\alpha$ = .92; T2 $\alpha$ = .91; T3 $\alpha$ = .96) assessed meaningful connection to potential friend (e.g., feeling close, feeling that one is important to their potential friend), while "Affection" (T1 $\alpha$ = .84; T2 $\alpha$ = .85; T3 $\alpha$ = .89) assessed positive feelings for potential friend (e.g., liking the individual, enjoying the time spent together). Concerning perceived characteristics of the potential friend, we assessed "Reliability" (potential friend is "trustworthy" and can be depended upon; T1 $\alpha$ = .75; T2 $\alpha$ = .76; T3 $\alpha$ = .86) and degree of "Caring" (e.g., is concerned for one's well-being, makes one feel comfortable; T1 $\alpha$ = .91; T2 $\alpha$ = .93; T3 $\alpha$ = .95). A single-item measure of "Self-Disclosure" inquired about the "most personal or sensitive thing ever discussed" at T1, T2, and T3. The "General Activity" scale assessed the broad activity level of the relationship by inquiring about frequency of time spent together and communication (T1 $\alpha$ = .86; T2 $\alpha$ = .87; T3 $\alpha$ = .91). Scales assessing "Personal Similarity" (e.g., similar personality, values, artistic interests; T1 $\alpha$ = .75; T2 $\alpha$ = .78; T3 $\alpha$ = .86) and "Societal Similarity" (e.g., similar financial background, political views, academic goals; T1 $\alpha$ = .76; T2 $\alpha$ = .72; T3 $\alpha$ = .78) were also employed. In an effort to simplify our analyses, all of the above interpersonal friendship measures were averaged to create one global score for total interpersonal friendship processes (T1 $\alpha$ = .81; T2 $\alpha$ = .86; T3 $\alpha$ = .89).

*Intergroup friendship processes.*     Regarding intergroup variables, single-item measures assessed belief that one's potential friend respects their ethnic group ("OG Member's Sensitivity for Ingroup"), belief that one learned "new things" about the OG through their relationship ("Learning about OG"), and degree of interaction with the potential friend's (OG) friends and family members ("OG Member's Family and Friends"). As with the interpersonal measures, all intergroup friendship measures were averaged to create one global score for total intergroup friendship processes (T1 $\alpha$ = .49; T2 $\alpha$ = .61; T3 $\alpha$ = .65).

*Intergroup attitudes.*     As in the retrospective study, a feeling thermometer measured "Warmth" felt for the racial group of one's potential friend, and two items from Pettigrew and Meertens (1995) assessed "Positive Regard" (T1 $\alpha$ = .74; T2 $\alpha$ = .82; T3 $\alpha$ = .85).

All items were answered on 7-point scales, except for "General Activity" (5-point scale) and "Warmth" for OG (assigned feeling thermometer "temperature" from 0 to 100).[4]

---

[4]On the few occasions where data were missing, the series mean was replaced in an effort to maintain the original sample. Four replacements were made for "Learning about the OG" and "OG Member's Sensitivity for IG" and "Positive Regard for OG" at time one, three were made for "OG Member's Friends and Family" at time one, and one was made for "Positive Regard for OG" at time two and time three.

*Results*

Analyses were conducted on those in cross-group potential friendships.[5] Means, *SD*s, and correlations among main variables can be seen in Table 2. As in Study 1, we examined potential models using hierarchical multiple regression. To assess improvements in intergroup attitude over time, we used residual scores as our dependent variables; this is what remains of the attitude at T2 or T3 after being predicted by the earlier measurement of the attitude (i.e., T1 or T2) in a regression. In addition, in each analysis, the interpersonal friendship processes predictor and intergroup friendship processes predictor for a given time point were added in a second step after their values at an earlier time point, which acted as controls. For example, when looking at change in attitude between time one (T1) and time two (T2), T1 interpersonal and intergroup friendship processes would be entered in the first step as controls, and T2 interpersonal and intergroup friendship processes would be entered in the second, to see what additional variance they explained beyond the T1 processes. Statistical details of the regression analyses can be seen in Table 3.

*Intergroup attitude improvements between T1 and T2.*    We first explored a model predicting improvements in positive regard for OG (i.e., sympathy and admiration) between T1 and T2. In the first step, the T1 predictors did not explain a significant portion of the variance (0%). In the second step, the overall model was non-significant, but the T2 predictors explained a marginally significant amount of additional variance (13%), suggesting that greater levels of interpersonal and intergroup friendship processes at T2 may predict greater improvements in positive regard for OG between T1 and T2. Turning to improvements in warmth for OG between T1 and T2, we observed that the T1 predictors explained 16% of the variance in the first step, with T1 interpersonal friendship processes making a significant unique contribution to the model. T2 predictors failed to explain a significant amount of additional variance (1%) when added in the second step. The overall model was nonsignificant ($p = .134$), but T1 interpersonal friendship processes made a significant unique contribution in each step, with higher levels predicting greater improvements in warmth for OG from T1 to T2.

---

[5]Analyses were also conducted comparing same-group friendships ($N = 18$) to cross-group friendships ($N = 41$). However, given that the sample size for the former was particularly small, these analyses should be considered preliminary. Using a series of independent samples *t*-tests, we found that T1–T2 improvements in positive regard for OG and warmth for OG were significantly different, with positive shifts in attitude occurring for those in cross-group rather than same-group relationships. Surprisingly, differences between the groups in T3 (predicted from T2) residual attitudes were not significant.

**Table 2.** Correlations between Interpersonal Friendship Variables, Intergroup Friendship Variables, and Improvements in Positive Attitudes for the Outgroup in the Longitudinal Study (Study 2)

| | M | SD | 1. | 2. | 3. | 4. | 5. | 6. | 7. | 8. | 9. | 10. |
|---|---|---|---|---|---|---|---|---|---|---|---|---|
| 1. T1 Interpersonal processes | 4.31 | 0.93 | 1 | .52** | .39* | .38* | .13 | .16 | −.04 | .40* | −.13 | .00 |
| 2. T2 Interpersonal processes | 4.01 | 1.03 | | 1 | .87** | .16 | .30 | .36* | .21 | .12 | .19 | .17 |
| 3. T3 Interpersonal processes | 4.22 | 1.15 | | | 1 | .09 | .32* | .48** | .24 | −.00 | .19 | .28 |
| 4. T1 Intergroup processes | 4.74 | 1.30 | | | | 1 | .38* | .33* | .03 | .07 | −.05 | .20 |
| 5. T2 Intergroup processes | 4.77 | 1.50 | | | | | 1 | .51** | .29 | −.01 | −.22 | .49** |
| 6. T3 Intergroup processes | 4.98 | 1.37 | | | | | | 1 | .09 | .02 | .01 | .45** |
| 7. T2 Residual positive regard for OG | 0 | 1.22 | | | | | | | 1 | −.18 | −.09 | .20 |
| 8. T2 Residual warmth for OG | 0 | 14.09 | | | | | | | | 1 | −.06 | −.10 |
| 9. T3 Residual positive regard for OG | 0 | 0.79 | | | | | | | | | 1 | .11 |
| 10. T3 Residual warmth for OG | 0 | 13.31 | | | | | | | | | | 1 |

*Note.* In the above table, "OG" denotes "outgroup." $N = 41$.
**Correlation is significant at the .01 level (two-tailed).
*Correlation is significant at the .05 level (two-tailed).

**Table 3.** Hierarchical Regressions Predicting Intergroup Attitude Improvements in the Longitudinal Study (Study 2)

| Model | | $R$ | $R^2$ | $R^2$ Change | | $B$ | Standard Error | $\beta$ | $t$ |
|---|---|---|---|---|---|---|---|---|---|
| T2 Residual | Step 1: | .06 | .00 | — | T1 Interpersonal Processes | −0.08 | 0.23 | −.06 | −0.35 |
| Positive Regard for OG | | | | | T1 Intergroup Processes | −0.05 | 0.17 | .05 | 0.29 |
| $F (2,38) = 0.01$ | | | | | | | | | |
| T2 Residual | Step 2: | .36 | .13 | .13 | T1 Interpersonal Processes | −0.24 | 0.26 | −.18 | −0.91 |
| Positive Regard for OG | | | | | T1 Intergroup Processes | −0.04 | 0.17 | −.04 | −0.23 |
| $F (4,36) = 1.36$ | | | | | T2 Interpersonal Processes | 0.28 | 0.23 | .23 | 1.21 |
| | | | | | T2 Intergroup Processes | 0.21 | 0.15 | .26 | 1.47 |
| T2 Residual | Step 1: | .40 | .16* | — | T1 Interpersonal Processes | 6.50 | 2.43 | .43 | 2.68* |
| Warmth for OG | | | | | T1 Intergroup Processes | −0.98 | 1.74 | −.09 | −0.56 |
| $F (2,38) = 3.71^{*}$ | Step 2: | .42 | .17 | .01 | T1 Interpersonal Processes | 7.45 | 2.92 | .49 | 2.55* |
| T2 Residual | | | | | T1 Intergroup Processes | −1.04 | 1.94 | −.10 | −0.53 |
| Warmth for OG | | | | | T2 Interpersonal Processes | −1.62 | 2.57 | −.12 | −0.63 |
| $F (4,36) = 1.89$ | | | | | T2 Intergroup Processes | −0.08 | 1.63 | −.00 | −0.01 |
| T3 Residual | Step 1: | .49 | .24** | — | T2 Interpersonal Processes | 0.37 | 1.92 | .03 | 0.19 |
| Warmth for OG | | | | | T2 Intergroup Processes | 4.27 | 1.32 | .48 | 3.23** |
| $F (2,38) = 5.96^{**}$ | | | | | | | | | |
| T3 Residual | Step 2: | .56 | .31** | .07 | T2 Interpersonal Processes | −3.47 | 3.75 | −.27 | 0.93 |
| Warmth for OG | | | | | T2 Intergroup Processes | 3.23 | 1.45 | .36 | 2.23* |
| $F (4,36) = 4.05^{**}$ | | | | | T3 Interpersonal Processes | 3.30 | 3.52 | .29 | 0.94 |
| | | | | | T3 Intergroup Processes | 2.17 | 1.72 | .22 | 1.26 |

*Note.* In the above table, "OG" denotes "Outgroup." $N = 41$.
*$p < .05$, **$p < .01$

*Intergroup attitude improvements between T2 and T3.*     Regarding improvements in positive regard for the OG, surprisingly, neither interpersonal nor intergroup variables were significant predictors at either step of the model. Regarding improved warmth for OG, we found that the T2 predictors accounted for a significant portion of the variance (24%) when entered in the first step. The T3 predictors did not explain a significant amount of additional variance in the second step, however, the overall model was significant, and T2 intergroup friendship processes made significant unique contributions in each step, suggesting that earlier group-related interactions predicted increased warmth for OG between T2 and T3.[6]

## Discussion: Longitudinal Study

As in the retrospective study, the longitudinal study found evidence that, as expected, interpersonal and intergroup processes transpiring within a cross-group friendship correspond to better attitudes for the OG. Importantly, the longitudinal nature of this study allowed us to take into account prior attitudes, so that associations with positive changes in attitudes could be assessed. Somewhat surprisingly, in both of the models yielding significant predictors, friendship processes occurring at an earlier time point, rather than the current time point, were the strongest predictors of attitudes at the current time point. In addition, in the final model for residual T2 warmth for OG, T1 interpersonal friendship processes were a much stronger predictor ($\beta = .49$) than T1 intergroup processes ($\beta = -.10$, n.s.). Conversely, in the final model for residual T3 warmth for OG, T2 intergroup friendship processes were a much stronger predictor ($\beta = .36$) than T2 interpersonal processes ($\beta = -.27$, n.s.). As in the retrospective study, these findings may suggest that positive interpersonal interactions are particularly important for establishing initial improvements in intergroup attitudes but that group-related interactions play a key role in maintaining those positive views about the OG. Somewhat surprising was the finding that neither interpersonal nor intergroup friendship processes predicted improvements in positive regard for the OG between T2 and T3.

Of course, it is very important to note that the longitudinal study had a small sample size, and so some of the relationships between the variables may have failed to reach significance due to low power. Despite this, several interesting results were identified.

---

[6]As in the retrospective study, no significant main effects or interactions involving gender were observed in the current models.

## General Discussion

Intergroup contact research has traditionally utilized very general assessments of cross-group interaction when examining links to intergroup attitudes, and in addition, has typically focused on the negative outcomes (e.g., prejudice). In keeping with the current issue's special focus on positive behavior across group boundaries, our work explores connections between meaningful one-on-one processes and positive intergroup attitudes within the context of a developing cross-group friendship. Using bivariate and regression analyses, across both studies, we found that positive interpersonal friendship processes are generally linked to more favorable attitudes for the OG as a whole. These results converge with earlier work highlighting the importance of interpersonal factors such as affection (e.g., Pettigrew, 1997b). In addition, our retrospective and longitudinal studies extend prior work concerning intergroup friendship in several important ways. First, we simultaneously employed several measures of interpersonal factors, including many (e.g., caring, reliability, similarity) not utilized in prior research. In addition, we examined the earlier stages of cross-group friendships, to gain a more accurate picture of when positive attitudes for the OG emerge. Results from both the retrospective and longitudinal study suggest that intergroup attitudes and interpersonal processes are already linked at even the earliest stages of friendship development. Furthermore, across both studies, we assessed intergroup friendship processes, including perception of OG friend's respect for one's own group ("Ingroup Sensitivity"), and spending time with OG member's family and friends. We sought to explore the connections that group-related cognitions and experiences may have to intergroup attitudes within the unique context of a cross-group friendship, and found that these processes were largely associated with more positive evaluations of the OG.

Somewhat surprising, however, was the observation that the intergroup friendship processes often had a stronger relationship to attitudes than interpersonal processes; this was especially true in the retrospective study. Taken as a whole, results of these studies may reveal that interpersonal processes may be particularly relevant to positive intergroup attitudes at the beginning of a cross-group friendship, before more serious exchanges concerning group-related issues are likely to have transpired. In the retrospective study of well-established cross-group friendships, although having significant bivariate relationships with positive intergroup attitudes and acting as significant contributors in some earlier stages of models, both early and current interpersonal processes failed to provide significant gains in variance explained when added as final steps in the models predicting positive intergroup attitudes. Only the set of predictors concerning intergroup friendship processes made a significant contribution in the final stages of models predicting empathy for the OG and positive regard (i.e., sympathy and admiration) for the OG, above the contributions made by interpersonal processes.

Similarly, in the longitudinal study, although we observed that improvements in warmth felt for the OG between T1 and T2 were significantly predicted by T1 interpersonal processes, it was T2 intergroup processes that significantly predicted positive shifts between T2 and T3 warmth for the OG. Therefore, positive interpersonal encounters may be given more weight in the determination of one's intergroup attitudes during the earlier stages of the relationship, but as the friendship progresses and more meaningful group-related exchanges occur, these intergroup processes may come to have a stronger connection to one's intergroup attitudes. These results are in agreement with other work suggesting that group-related factors are linked to positive intergroup behaviors and attitudes. For example, Rosenthal and Levy (2016) find that polyculturalism (i.e., the belief that different racial and ethnic groups have interacted and influenced each other's cultures throughout history) predicts cross-group friendship development, and Montoya and Pinter (2016) argue that ingroup-favoring norms can be used to facilitate harmonious intergroup relations. Our findings add to this work by revealing that intergroup experiences vital to positive attitudes may actually arise from meaningful interpersonal connections between group members. The greater degree of intimacy in these relationships likely provides the comfort necessary to have more serious and nuanced discussions about group issues (e.g., "Why is the 'Black Lives Matter' movement important to you?"), and encourages a greater interest and personal investment in the OG (e.g., "respect" or "sensitivity"). Consequently, these more meaningful cross-group processes are more likely than superficial discussions/experiences to yield the deepest levels of understanding and appreciation for the OG. It's worth noting that one's belief that the OG member respects and understands one's own group (i.e., the ingroup) was a particularly strong predictor of positive feelings for the OG. This finding underscores the role of perceived partner reciprocation in this context. The importance of perceived reciprocity in relationship development and maintenance is well-noted within the close relationships and friendship literatures (e.g., Altman & Taylor, 1973), and is starting to gain attention in intergroup relations research (e.g., Shelton et al, 2010).

Somewhat surprisingly, given the relevant interpersonal and intergroup literatures, was the observation that little support emerged for the roles of inclusion of other in self, time spent with the OG member, and feeling similar to the OG member. Including an OG member (and thus, the OG) in the self has been identified as an avenue by which positive attitudes for the OG may form (e.g., Wright et al., 2002), however, we failed to observe this in the retrospective study, perhaps due to the subjective nature of this measure. Similarly, spending time and engaging in activities with OG members has been linked to positive intergroup attitudes (e.g., Davies et al., 2011), but this was not observed in these studies, perhaps due to the use of a rather simplistic assessment of activity (i.e., frequency of spending time together and communicating) rather than one assessing more intimate encounters (e.g., attending social events together). Finally, the relationships observed between similarity and intergroup attitudes in the longitudinal study were inconsistent; the concept of perceived similarity is likely complex, with different domains (e.g., personality, culture) likely having different connections to intergroup attitudes. Future work will be needed to clarify the apparent discrepancies described above.

*Limitations and Future Directions*

Although an interesting exploration of the processes underlying cross-group friendship development, these studies are certainly not without limitations. Perhaps the largest weakness in this work, the longitudinal study had a very small sample size, which may have left some effects undetected. The restriction that one must have met a "potential friend" in the prior month substantially reduced the final sample (by 44%), and for unknown reasons, recruitment for the follow-up surveys was slow. Future research will undoubtedly need to recruit a larger sample to lend credibility to these initial findings. Despite this, we discovered a number of significant results with the current longitudinal data, and importantly, many converged with results from the larger retrospective study. Nonetheless, confirmation of the current longitudinal results with a larger sample is imperative; it must be emphasized that the current longitudinal study was exploratory in nature, and as such, the findings should be considered preliminary.

In both the retrospective and longitudinal studies, samples describing a same-group friendship or a cross-group friendship had similar demographic characteristics (i.e., statistics for gender, age, and ethnic background).[7] However, within both studies, each sample contained more women than men and, as stated earlier, research on friendship tends to attract more female than male participants (Lewis et al., 1989). This may impact the ability of the current study findings to generalize to the cross-group relationships of men. The lack of significant main or interaction effects involving gender gives us greater confidence that our results should apply to male relationships, however. Finally, participants in both studies were primarily from North America, younger (i.e., 20s), and White or European American. Age has been found to play a role in the desire and ability to recruit and maintain friends, (Wrzus, Hänel, Wagner, & Neyer, 2013), and cross-group

---

[7]Although the circumstances surrounding cross-group (as compared to same-group) friendship formation were not presented in the current paper, which focused instead on intergroup attitudes, a separate set of hypotheses concerning this issue and utilizing the current data sets are reported in the first author's doctoral dissertation (Davies, 2009). Key results indicate that developing cross-group and same-group friendships are much more similar than different, however, cross-group friendships are more likely to begin due to involuntary interactions (e.g., via work, school) rather than through existing social networks, and that intimate processes (e.g., trust, closeness) are more interconnected in cross-group friendships, making them vital to the progression of the relationship. This underscores the importance of making cross-group interactions both comfortable and meaningful for individuals who have little experience interacting with members of an outgroup.

contact experiences of minority group members may differ from those of majority group members (e.g., Mendoza-Denton, Downey, Purdie, Davis, & Pietrzak, 2002). Therefore, in addition to larger samples, future studies may wish to recruit from other geographic locations, and include a more diverse group of participants with regard to gender, age, and ethnic background.

There are a number of important ways in which this work could be extended for future studies. In the longitudinal study, we recruited participants who met someone "within the past month" who "may become a friend," however, when participants were surveyed again 6 weeks later, most relationships had already become friendships. It may be advantageous to observe a cross-group relationship closer to the time that the OG member is promoted from acquaintance to friend, or perhaps better yet, around the time of the initial meeting. The current findings suggest that friendship processes and shifts in intergroup attitudes may progress quite rapidly, so capturing these variables at the time that they first emerge will aid in clarifying their interconnections. In addition, given the growing role of social media in maintaining relationships, future work could investigate the utility of online interactions in fostering meaningful relationships between members of differing groups; do interpersonal and intergroup friendship processes unfold successfully via the internet, and if so, do attitudes for OG improve?

*Implications for Social Issues*

Knowing how to promote conditions vital to successful cross-group relationships is necessary in today's increasingly diverse and globalized world, particularly for those working to foster positive intergroup relations. Our results imply that positive interpersonal processes (e.g., activities designed to encourage trust, caring, affection) are crucial to building positive intergroup attitudes during initial contact sessions, but that as cross-group relationships progress, encouragement must be given to positive intergroup friendship processes (e.g., messages of understanding and respect, learning about the OG and about other OG members). At both the interpersonal and intergroup levels, reciprocation between interaction partners will be instrumental in fostering these crucial cross-group friendship processes. The findings from this study may be used to inform individuals who are in a position to encourage meaningful one-on-one interactions between group members, such as a community group leaders, public administrators, and educators. Our work suggests that program developers should provide sufficient opportunity for individuals to explain, within the context of a meaningful interpersonal exchange, how their group membership impacts them personally. Rather than, for example, having individuals provide a general description of their culture to a larger group, they should first get to know specific OG members on a personal level, giving each interaction partner the chance to discuss how their group membership plays a role in their own life.

In addition, existing interpersonal interventions aimed at creating more harmonious relationships between groups could be easily adapted for greater effectiveness using the current results. For example, the "Fast-Friends" activity (Aron, Melinat, Aron, Vallone, & Bator, 1997) is an experimental procedure in which participants each take turns revealing increasingly personal information (e.g., self-disclosure) to encourage feelings of closeness and trust between partners. When used with cross-group participants, this paradigm has been shown to improve intergroup attitudes in a number of contexts including general race relations (e.g., Page-Gould, Mendoza-Denton, & Tropp, 2008; Wright et al., 2002), police-community relations (Aron, Eberhardt, Davies, Bergsieker, & Wright, 2015), and cross-sexual orientation contact (Lytle & Levy, 2015). To make this intervention strategy even stronger, results from these studies would suggest that after undergoing sessions establishing general interpersonal connections, that special opportunities for positive group-related interpersonal exchanges be provided. For instance, interaction partners could each identify aspects of their partner's culture or group that they find to be interesting, and would like to hear more about from their partner. Such conversations could help to promote the development of respect, understanding, and concern for the group of one's partner.

Given the increasing diversity of many countries, policies and programs aimed at promoting positive interactions across group boundaries will be critical to ensuring harmonious intergroup relations. Augmenting interpersonal interventions with meaningful group-related exchanges could be a practical way to promote positive intergroup relations, and could be adopted in wide variety of real-world contexts, including (but not limited to) conflicts concerning immigration, police–community relations, cross-religious interactions, and attitudes about sexual orientation.

*Conclusion*

In conclusion, results of these studies highlight the importance of *both* interpersonal and intergroup friendship processes in encouraging positive views for the OG within a developing cross-group friendship. Specifically, interpersonal friendship processes (e.g., affection, caring, trust) are crucial to establishing meaningful connections to an OG member and initial improvements in intergroup attitudes. As the friendship deepens over time, intergroup attitudes may become more strongly linked to group-related behaviors and cognitions that have likely become more sophisticated and meaningful given the intimate nature of the relationship. Future research should continue to investigate how both interpersonal and intergroup processes develop and relate to intergroup attitudes within cross-group friendships, perhaps over a longer period of time and starting at the very beginning of the relationship. Interpersonal interventions striving to improve intergroup relations should incorporate group-relevant activities for interaction partners after interpersonal connections are established; this could serve to generate even greater improvements in intergroup attitudes.

# References


Allport, G. W. (1954). *The nature of prejudice*. Reading, MA: Addison-Wesley.

Altman, I., & Taylor, D. A. (1973). *Social penetration: The development of interpersonal relationships*. New York: Holt, Rinehart & Winston.

Aron, A., Aron, E., & Smollan, D. (1992). Inclusion of other in the self scale and the structure of interpersonal closeness. *Journal of Personality and Social Psychology, 63*, 596–612. doi: 10.1037/0022-3514.63.4.596

Aron, A., Eberhardt, J. L., Davies, K., Bergsieker, H. B., & Wright, S. C. (2015). *Initial test of asocial-psychological intervention to improve community relations with police*. Manuscript in preparation.

Aron, A., Melinat, E., Aron, E. N., Vallone, R. D., & Bator, R. J. (1997). The experimental generation of interpersonal closeness: A procedure and some preliminary findings. *Personality and Social Psychology Bulletin, 23*, 363–377.

Backman, C. W., & Secord, P. F (1959). The effect of perceived liking on interpersonal attraction. *Human Relations, 12*, 379–383. doi: 10.1177/001872675901200407

Davies, K. (2009). *Identifying key themes in cross-group friendship formation*. Doctoral Thesis. Retrieved from ProQuest Dissertations and Theses. (Accession Order No. AAI 3399740).

Davies, K., Tropp, L. R., Aron, A., Pettigrew, T. F., & Wright, S. C. (2011). Cross-group friendships and intergroup attitudes: A meta-analytic review. *Personality and Social Psychology Review, 15*, 332–351. doi: 10.1177/1088868311411103

Davies, K., Wright, S. C., Aron, A., & Comeau, J. (2013). Intergroup contact through friendship: Intimacy and norms. In G. Hodson, M. Hewstone, G. Hodson, M. Hewstone (Eds.), *Advances in intergroup contact* (pp. 200–229). New York, NY, US: Psychology Press.

Fehr, B. (1996). *Friendship processes*. Thousand Oaks, CA: Sage.

Fehr, B. (2008). Friendship formation. In S. Sprecher, A. Wenzel, J. Harvey, S. Sprecher, A. Wenzel, & J. Harvey (Eds.), *Handbook of relationship initiation* (pp. 29–54). New York: Psychology Press.

Hays, R. B. (1984). The development and maintenance of friendship. *Journal of Social and Personal Relationships, 1*, 75–98. doi: 10.1177/0265407584011005

Hays, R. B. (1985). A longitudinal study of friendship development. *Journal of Personality and Social Psychology, 48*, 909–924. doi: 10.1037/0022-3514.48.4.909

Jugert, P., Noack, P., & Rutland, A. (2011). Friendship preferences among German and Turkish preadolescents. *Child Development, 82*, 812–829. doi: 10.1111/j.1467-8624.2010.01528.x

Klinger, E. (1977). *Meaning and void: Inner experience and the incentives in people's lives*. Minneapolis, MN: U Minnesota Press.

Knapp, M. L., Ellis, D. G., & Williams, B. A. (1980). Perceptions of communication behavior associated with relationships terms. *Communication Monographs, 47*, 262–278. doi: 10.1080/03637758009376036

Lewis, R. J., Winstead, B. A., & Derlega, V. J. (1989). Gender differences in volunteering for friendship research. *Journal of Social Behavior and Personality, 4*, 623–632.

Lytle, A., & Levy, S. R. (2015). Reducing heterosexuals' prejudice toward gay men and lesbian women via an induced cross-orientation friendship. *Psychology of Sexual Orientation and Gender Diversity, 2*, 447–455. doi: 10.1037/sgd0000135

Mendoza-Denton, R., Downey, G., Purdie, V. J., Davis, A., & Pietrzak, J. (2002). Sensitivity to status-based rejection: Implications for African American students' college experience. *Journal of Personality and Social Psychology, 83*, 896–918. doi: 10.1037/0022-3514.83.4.896

Montoya, R. M., & Pinter, B. (2016). A model for understanding positive intergroup relations using the ingroup-favoring norm. *Journal of Social Issues, 72*, 584–600.

Page-Gould, E., Mendoza-Denton, R., & Tropp, L. R. (2008). With a little help from my cross-group friend: Reducing anxiety in intergroup contexts through cross-group friendship.

*Journal of Personality and Social Psychology, 95,* 1080–1094. doi: 10.1037/0022-3514.95.5. 1080

Paolini, S., Wright, S. C., Dys-Steenbergen, O. & Favara, I. (2016). Self-expansion and intergroup contact: Expectancies and motives to self-expand lead to greater interest in outgroup contact and more positive intergroup relations. *Journal of Social Issues, 72,* 450–471.

Pettigrew, T. F. (1997a). Generalized intergroup contact effects on prejudice. *Personality and Social Psychology Bulletin, 23,* 173–185. doi: 10.1177/0146167297232006

Pettigrew, T. F. (1997b). The affective component of prejudice: Empirical support of the new view. In S. Tuch & J. K. Martin (Eds.), *Racial attitudes in the 1990s: Continuity and change* (pp. 76–90). Westport: Praeger.

Pettigrew, T. F. (1998). Intergroup contact theory. *Annual Review of Psychology, 49,* 65–85. doi: 10.1146/annurev.psych.49.1.65

Pettigrew, T. F., & Meertens, R. W. (1995). Subtle and blatant prejudice in Western Europe. *European Journal of Social Psychology, 25,* 57–75. doi: 10.1002/ejsp.2420250106

Rosenthal, L., & Levy, S. R. (2016). Endorsement of polyculturalism predicts increased positive intergroup contact and friendship across the beginning of college. *Journal of Social Issues, 72,* 472–488.

Shelton, J. N., Trail, T. E., West, T. V., & Bergsieker, H. B. (2010). From strangers to friends: The interpersonal process model of intimacy in developing interracial friendships. *Journal of Social and Personal Relationships, 27,* 71–90. doi: 10.1177/0265407509346422

Tesch, S. A., & Martin, R. R. (1983). Friendship concepts of young adults in two age groups. *Journal of Psychology: Interdisciplinary and Applied, 115,* 7–12. doi: 10.1080/00223980.1983.9923591

Turner, R. N., Tam, T., Hewstone, M., Kenworthy, J., & Cairns, E. (2013). Contact between Catholic and Protestant schoolchildren in Northern Ireland. *Journal of Applied Social Psychology, 43*(Suppl 2), E216–E228. doi: 10.1111/jasp.12018

Voci, A., Hewstone, M., Swart, H., & Veneziani, C. A. (2015). Refining the association between intergroup contact and intergroup forgiveness in Northern Ireland: Type of contact, prior conflict experience, and group identification. *Group Processes and Intergroup Relations, 18,* 589–608. doi: 10.1177/1368430215577001

Wright, S. C., Aron, A., Tropp, L. R. (2002). Including others (and groups) in the self: Self-expansion and intergroup relations. In J. P. Forgas & K. D. Williams (Eds.), *The social self: Cognitive, interpersonal, and intergroup perspectives* (pp. 343–363). New York: Psychology Press.

Wrzus, C., Hänel, M., Wagner, J., & Neyer, F. J. (2013). Social network changes and life events across the life span: A meta-analysis. *Psychological Bulletin, 139,* 53–80. doi: 10.1037/a0028601

KRISTIN DAVIES received her BA from The Pennsylvania State University and earned her MA and PhD from Stony Brook University in the area of Social Psychology. She is currently an Assistant Professor of Psychology at York College of the City University of New York. Throughout her various research projects, she seeks to identify relationships between interpersonal and intergroup processes; how do our meaningful interactions with outgroup members inform our views of the outgroup as a whole? Recently, her work has focused on understanding cross-group friendship development via the Internet, as well as the role of reciprocal processes (e.g., trust, respect, etc.) and culture in the improvement of intergroup attitudes.

ARTHUR ARON (BA, MA, University of California, Berkeley; PhD, University of Toronto, Social Psychology) is a Research Professor of Psychology at Stony Brook University and Visiting Scholar at University of California, Berkeley. His research centers on the self-expansion model of motivation cognition in personal relationships, including neural underpinnings and real-world applications. He is on the editorial boards of the Journal of Personality and Social Psychology, Personal Relationships, and Journal of Social and Personal Relationships. He is a Fellow of the American Psychological Association, the Association for Psychological Science, and the Society for the Psychological Study of Social Issues, and the Society of Personality and Social Psychology. He has received major grants from the National Science Foundation, the Fetzer Foundation, the Templeton Foundation, and the Social Science and Humanities Research Council of Canada. He is a recipient of the Distinguished Research Career Award for the International Association for Relationship Research.

*Journal of Social Issues, Vol. 72, No. 3, 2016, pp. 511–523*
doi: 10.1111/josi.12179

# Empathic Joy in Positive Intergroup Relations

**Todd L. Pittinsky**[*]
*Stony Brook University*


**R. Matthew Montoya**
*University of Dayton*

*Research on empathy focuses almost exclusively on its negative variety, empathic sorrow, either by defining empathy as a state involving negative emotions or by confining its empirical study to the negative. In contrast, we investigate empathy's positive variety, empathic joy. We do so in the context of intergroup relations. A total of 1,216 predominantly White teachers participated in a yearlong investigation of whether their attitudes toward, and empathy for, their predominantly ethnic minority students affected their teaching style and the students' learning. Consistent with expectations, we found that teachers' experience of empathic joy predicted better student outcomes and that it did so by leading to more allophilia toward students and, in turn, toward more proactive and positive interactions with students. Implications are considered for the role of empathic joy in positive intergroup relations more generally.*

> "Our sympathy with sorrow, though not more real, has been more taken notice of than our sympathy with joy."
>
> — Adam Smith, *Theory of Moral Sentiments*, p. 39.

The empathic joy that Adam Smith observed—a person's "interest in the fortunes of others . . . [that] render[s] their happiness necessary to him" (Smith, 1759/1976)—is echoed in the Buddhist concept of *Mudita*, the "divine state" or "virtue" of delighting in other people's well-being (Wallace & Shapiro, 2006). In social science research, however, it has received little attention.

Yet, what little research there is suggests a relation between more positive empathic emotion and more positive attitudinal responses. We seek to demonstrate the existence and practical importance of that relation in the intergroup context.

---

[*]Correspondence concerning this article should be addressed to Todd L. Pittinsky, Department of Technology and Society, Stony Brook University, 347 Harriman Hall, Stony Brook, NY 11794. [e-mail: Todd.Pittinsky@stonybrook.edu].

511

We test a model of empathic joy in intergroup relations in which empathic joy for the members of a different social group leads to more positive intergroup attitudes toward members of that group that, in turn, lead to more positive intergroup behaviors toward them.


## Defining Empathic Joy


Empathy research in the social and behavioral sciences has been fixated on empathic sorrow, understood as "a negative emotional state anchored in and tending toward the alleviation of another's *misfortune* [italics added]" (Royzman & Rozin, 2006) or as the ability to understand the *suffering* of other people. A typical experiment involves inducing empathy by asking participants to read about someone who is homeless, addicted to drugs, or ravaged by AIDS (e.g., Batson, Chang, Orr, & Rowland, 2002; Eisenberg et al., 1989; Finlay & Stephan, 2000; Hoffman, 2000; Weiner & Wright, 1973; Xu, Zuo, Wang, & Han, 2009). Empathic responses are then typically measured by assessing the degree to which one feels "sympathetic, compassionate, softhearted, warm, tender and moved" (Batson, 1991) or by assessing the "tendency to experience feelings of sympathy and compassion for unfortunate others" (Davis, 1994) or to have "tender, concerned feelings for people less fortunate than [oneself]" (Davis, 1980).

As may be noted from the previously mentioned definitions, researchers tend to explicitly ignore the possibility of empathic joy. However, even research that does consider empathy as either a positive or negative force in human relations exclusively studies negative emotions such as pity, sympathy, sadness, and sorrow. Tam et al. (2008), for example, set forth to explore the more positive and "hopeful" sides of intergroup relations, yet measured empathy with items such as "I often feel very sorry for people from the other community when they are having problems" and "When I see someone from the other community being treated unfairly, I sometimes don't feel very much pity for them." Even the promisingly named "empathic-joy hypothesis" (Smith, Keating, & Stotland, 1989), a well-studied phenomenon in the psychological sciences, takes as its starting point another person's suffering and seeks to understand the experience of finding out that the suffering has been alleviated.

In the empathy literature, there is a diversity of views regarding the definition and components of the experience of empathy. One perspective is that the word "empathy" refers strictly to the emotional experience of being affected by someone else's condition, often through the cognitive act of perspective-taking. A second perspective is that "empathy" refers strictly to the perspective-taking process itself, with "sympathy" being the resulting emotion (e.g., Mathiasen, 2006). A third perspective is that "empathy" refers to an experience that is both emotional and cognitive, either because the two elements are intertwined or because the emotion results immediately from the cognitive state of perspective-taking (Duan & Hill, 1996; Finlay & Stephan, 2000; Shechtman & Basheer, 2005).

We follow the third perspective: We defined empathic joy as the combined experience of perspective-taking and the resulting joy or happiness. Note that this definition neither presuppose either a direct or an indirect exposure to whatever stimulates the empathy, nor does it presuppose anything about the relation of the person feeling the empathy with the person whose situation provoked it.

## Importance of Positive Emotions versus Negative Emotions

There is evidence to indicate that there is a value in studying the positive versus negative variety of empathy. Specifically, a wealth of research indicates that positive and negative emotions operate differently (Dijker, Koomen, van den Heuvel, & Frijda, 1996; Stangor, Sullivan, & Ford, 1992) and that positive emotions play a unique role in intergroup relations (e.g., Dijker, 1987). Although positive empathy is not widely acknowledged as a construct distinct from empathic sorrow, increasing evidence indicates that it is independent of potentially related constructs, such as general positivity and empathy for others' distress (Morelli, Lieberman, & Zaki, 2015). Positive emotions are particularly important for building connections among groups (Fredrickson, 2001; Fredrickson & Branigan, 2001) and have been found to be better predictors of positive attitudes and behaviors toward an "other" (Pittinsky, Rosenthal, & Montoya, 2011b; Tam et al., 2008). Studies in places such as Israel and Northern Ireland indicate that positive emotions and associated attitudes are present even during long-standing intergroup conflicts and that these positive intergroup emotions operate distinctly from negative emotions (for a review, see Pittinsky, 2012; Stürmer et al., 2013). Such a distinction has also been observed in attitudes toward African Americans. Although one body of intergroup relations research defines "pro-Black attitudes" as feelings that blacks are disadvantaged and deserve sympathy (Katz, Wackenhut, & Haas, 1986), such sympathetic recognition of prejudice toward African Americans is not the same as positive feelings or beliefs about them (Czopp & Monteith, 2006).

## Empathic Joy in the Social Context

Several strands of research do suggest that there may be a distinct and important role for empathic joy in intergroup relations. First, empathic joy has been found for a range of social targets—not only close relationships such as family, friends, romantic partners, and roommates, but also strangers, coworkers, and acquaintances (e.g., Gable, Reis, Impett, & Asher, 2004). Specifically, the close relationship literature has identified a positive association of perceived positive empathy with relationship satisfaction, commitment, intimacy, and trust (Gable,

Gonzaga, & Strachman, 2006; Gable, Gosnell, Maisel, & Strachman, 2012; Gable et al., 2004). Gable et al. (2006), for example, used observational coding of positive discussions to reveal that verbal and nonverbal displays of positive empathy predicted better relationship well-being and lower likelihood of breakup two months later. Similarly, studies using self-reports of trait and daily positive empathy showed a strong association between positive empathy and feelings of social connection (Morelli et al., 2015). Specifically, across several samples, trait positive empathy showed a positive association with trait social connection, but also a negative association with trait loneliness. In two daily diary studies, similar associations emerged at the within-subject level: daily positive empathy showed a positive relation with daily social connection and a negative relation with daily loneliness. Taken together, these studies demonstrate that positive empathy is associated with better relationships.

In addition, Fredrickson's broaden-and-build theory holds that positive emotions can help one develop friendships and social-support networks (Fredrickson, 2001; Fredrickson & Branigan, 2001). Fredrickson's (2001) and Fredrickson and Branigan's (2001) work indicates that arousing empathic joy generates positive emotions, positive thoughts, enhanced memory (including better recall of pleasant events), more exploratory and more flexible thinking, and the psychological states that prepare a person to build friendships and social networks.

In perhaps the most direct examination of empathic joy in positive intergroup relations to date, Pittinsky and Montoya (2009b) explored the contribution of empathic joy to positive intergroup attitudes toward outgroup members. Specifically, the authors assessed the attitudes of American White high school students at predominantly White schools, measuring their levels of empathic sorrow (sympathy) and empathic joy for the members of ethnic minorities. Empathic joy, relative to empathic sorrow, was more strongly tied to higher levels of positive intergroup attitudes toward ethnic minorities. Although this study provided clear evidence for the importance of empathic joy to positive attitudes, it did not examine the impact of empathic joy on subsequent positive behaviors. As has been noted more recently, it remains important "to more formally establish a causal relationship between positive empathy and important outcomes" (Morelli et al., 2015, p. 59).

## The Current Study

We test a model of empathic joy in which empathic joy leads to more positive intergroup attitudes and behaviors toward outgroup members, which, in turn, lead to better outcomes for them. We test our model in the context of education, partnering with a national organization that places a predominantly White cadre of teachers in schools with predominantly ethnic minority students. Specifically, we investigated our hypotheses over the course of an academic school year, in which we tested whether empathic joy and allophilia assessed midway through the school year, would affect the positivity of their teaching style (assessed midway through the second semester), and produce better student outcomes (assessed during an end-of-term exam).

## Method

*Participants*

Of the teachers in this organization who were active during the 2010–2011 academic year, a randomly selected subsample of 1,216 (29.6 percent) participated in this study. Their average age was 23.50 years old. Eighty percent were Caucasian, 10% were African American, 8% were Hispanic/Latino, and 2% identified as another ethnicity or chose not to identify their ethnicity. The teachers were selected in roughly equal percentages from schools in 14 states: Alabama, Arizona, California, Colorado, Connecticut, Delaware, the District of Columbia, Georgia, Kansas, Louisiana, New York, North Carolina, South Carolina, and Washington.

*Materials*

*Positive intergroup attitudes.*　The degree to which teachers liked their students was assessed using the intergroup affection subscale of the Allophilia Scale (Pittinsky, Rosenthal, & Montoya, 2011a). Participants indicated their responses to four items on a seven-point scale, ranging from 1 (*strongly disagree*) to 7 (*strongly agree*). Sample items included "In general, I have positive attitudes about my students" and "I feel positively toward my students." The scale was reliable, $\alpha = .91$.

*Empathy.*　The degree to which teachers experienced empathic joy for their students was assessed using four items adapted from the Interpersonal Reactivity Index (Davis, 1980). Sample items for empathic joy included "When my students celebrate things, I am happy for them" and "When my students feel happy, I feel happy." Participants recorded their responses on a seven-point scale ranging from 1 (*strongly disagree*) to 7 (*strongly agree*). The empathic joy items were combined to form a reliable index, $\alpha = .92$.

*Positive achievement teacher behavior.*　To assess the degree to which a teacher was proactively and positively engaged with his or her students, we used data collected by the teacher organization to assess the global degree to which he or she was engaged in building a culture of achievement and fostering an environment of positive academic growth for all students in the classroom. The assessment was conducted by a trained expert in the professional development

**Table 1.** Means, Standard Deviations, Reliabilities, and Correlation between Teacher Assessments and Student Achievement

| | | | Correlation | | |
|---|---|---|---|---|---|
| Variable | *M* | *SD* | 1 | 2 | 3 |
| 1. Empathic joy | 6.36 | 0.67 | | | |
| 2. Allophilia | 6.31 | 0.76 | .46[*] | | |
| 3. Teaching culture | 2.35 | 0.73 | .15[*] | .21[*] | |
| 4. Student achievement | 77.73 | 40.40 | .06[*] | .16[*] | .26[*] |

*Note.* $N = 1{,}216$. *$p < .05$.

of teachers and used a standardized coding rubric. The assessment was scaled between 0 (*apathetic/unruly*) and 4 (*passionate/caring*).

*Student achievement.* Students' academic performance was assessed using a composite of nonproprietary, standardized academic achievement scores administered at the end of each academic year to all students taught by members of the teaching organization as a way to quantify teachers' impact. The test included questions relevant to the subject a given teacher teaches, such as English, mathematics, art, and science. A student achievement score was then assigned to each teacher.

## Procedure

As part of a midyear assessment, teachers completed a large set of online questionnaires in December 2010. They were instructed to complete it in private and were assured that their responses would remain anonymous. The questionnaires of interest for this study—the assessments of empathic joy and allophilia—were included among a larger set of questionnaires unrelated to the current project.

About halfway through the spring semester, each teacher was evaluated by a member of the teaching organization's staff. This included an evaluation of the teacher's curriculum, an in-depth interview, and an observation of the teacher's classroom teaching style, which included scoring the aforementioned "positive achievement teacher behavior." At the end of the school year, the student achievement test was administered and scored by national staff of the teacher organization.

## Results

The correlations between the variables are presented in Table 1. Prior to conducting our main analyses, all variables were standardized.

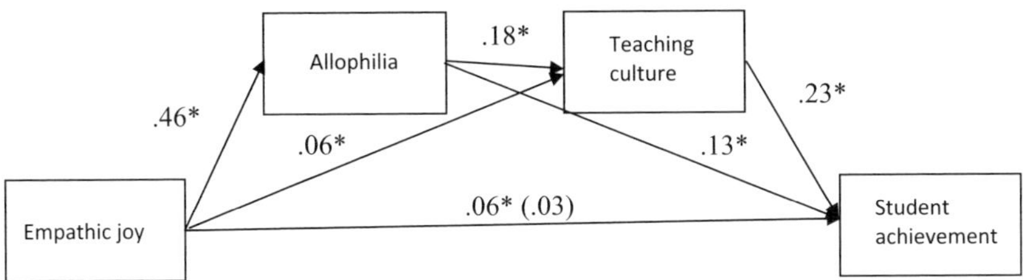


**Fig. 1.** Results of the serial mediation model assessing the relation between empathic joy and student achievement through allophilia and teaching culture. *$p$ < .05.

The methods used to collect the data allowed us to test a temporal sequence from empathic joy to student outcomes. Early in the school year, teachers reported their experience of empathic joy and their degree of positive intergroup attitudes for their students. Midway through the year, the teachers' degree of positive achievement behaviors was coded. At the end of the school year, student performance was measured.

To conduct the key analyses, we conducted serial mediational analyses to test whether the proposed mediators (allophilia and teaching culture) produced indirect effects on the relation between empathic joy and student achievement. We used the PROCESS macro (Model 6) developed by Hayes (2013) to estimate direct and indirect effects and confidence intervals using bootstrapping methods. The PROCESS macro produces point estimates for the size of the indirect effect and a 95% confidence interval (95% CI) based on the distribution of the 5,000 bootstrapped samples. The mediation pathway is considered significant if the confidence interval does not include zero.

In terms of our model, we first tested the pathway from empathic joy to allophilia to teaching culture to student achievement. The results of the sequential mediation are presented in Figure 1. Consistent with the model's predictions, there was a significant total effect of empathic joy on student achievement ($\beta$ = .06, $t$ = 2.26, $p$ < .05). Next, we tested whether the relation between empathic joy and student achievement was mediated by the sequential allophilia-to-teaching-culture processes. Consistent with expectations, there was an overall indirect effect through allophilia to teaching culture (*estimate* = .09, 95% CI = .06, .13). When the mediators were included in the model, the direct influence of empathic joy on student achievement was no longer significant ($\beta$ = .03, $p$ = .28).

## Discussion

We examined empathic joy in an intergroup context and empirically tested a model in which predominantly White teachers' experience of empathic joy for their predominantly ethnic minority students produces better learning outcomes for those students. Consistent with expectations, teachers' experience of empathic joy and positive intergroup attitudes (i.e., allophilia) was associated with positive achievement teacher behavior, which then produced better learning outcomes. Our study provides evidence for the importance of empathic joy in intergroup contexts and its importance in promoting positive intergroup attitudes and outcomes. Whereas the literature on empathic joy has tended to focus on close interpersonal relationships, our findings provide clear evidence of its importance in a larger social context. They also contribute to a body of studies finding that the presence of positive intergroup attitudes such as allophilia, rather than the absence of negative intergroup attitudes, is an important antecedent to positive intergroup relations that involve positive, proactive engagement and behaviors across groups divides (e.g., Pittinsky & Montoya, 2009a; Pittinsky et al., 2011a).

Whether positive empathy is a cause of prosocial behavior or an effect of it has been questioned repeatedly in the literature (e.g., Batson et al., 1991; Smith et al., 1989). For example, two studies found that participants were more likely to help if they anticipated seeing the positive reaction of the recipient than if they were told they would not see that reaction (Batson et al., 1991; Smith et al., 1989). It is possible that they were motivated by the anticipation of empathic joy (that is, that empathy caused the prosocial behavior). Furthermore, the research on empathic joy in the intergroup context (e.g., Pittinsky & Montoya, 2009b) has only revealed correlational evidence regarding the relation between (i) positive intergroup attitudes such as allophilia and empathic joy and (ii) student outcomes. However, our findings provide an example of empathic joy preceding student achievement and document the causality in the relation between the measurement of empathic joy and allophilia and the subsequent assessment of student outcomes.

Although the direct relation between empathic joy and student outcomes ($r = .06$) appears to be only a trivial effect, the Institute of Education Sciences recently issued a report (Lipsey et al., 2012) that focused on how to interpret effect sizes in education. Specifically, the report dismisses the traditional characterization of effect sizes—such as those established by Cohen (1977, 1988)—often used in the context of laboratory studies by noting that in randomized studies using "broad measures" (such as state test scores or standardized measures), effect sizes across elementary and middle school studies will be relatively small (for example, .08). Our study, though finding a "small" effect size, meets all of Lipsey et al.'s (2012) criteria for a meaningful and "high-quality study": We used a large sample, used independently collected and objective measures of student performance, and conducted the study over the course of a school year. Moreover, there is a research literature on the impact a particular teacher can have on student achievement, despite the many other possible factors at play (e.g., Darling-Hammond, 2000;

Sanders & Rivers, 1996; Wright, Horn, & Sanders, 1997). Learning gains achieved during a year with an effective teacher last beyond that year (Konstantopoulos & Chung, 2011a, 2011b).

We would also point out the possibility that empathic joy, although associated with a small effect size in our study, may have meaningful effects by virtue of acting as a catalyst. We often hear of vicious cycles, in which reciprocal causes and effects intensify and aggravate each other, there can also be *virtuous* cycles, in which reciprocal causes and effects produce increasingly favorable results. Empathic joy may, for example, help trigger moral elevation (e.g., Aquino, McFerran, & Laven, 2011). Moral elevation is a state that individuals may experience after witnessing— or even merely hearing about—a virtuous act. In the intergroup context, a show of unexpected compassion, forgiveness, or proactive engagement may produce more altruism and helpful behavior simply by being a witness. In this way, empathic joy may be a critical part of the virtuous cycle observed in moral elevation research and in intergroup relations more generally.

*Implications for Practice*

Anecdotal evidence for the power of empathic joy in education includes the popularity of films such as *Stand and Deliver* (1988), in which ethnic minority dropout students learn to excel in calculus, and *Knights of the South Bronx* (2007), in which a teacher creates a championship chess team out of fourth-grade students whose families confront social problems such as poverty, prison, and drug addiction. Audience members, many of them White and middle class, feel joyful as the characters—minority youth—persevere and triumph.

Indeed, there are many opportunities for the use of empathic joy to complement or replace the use of empathic sorrow in education. The American educational system is steeped in empathic sorrow and it sometimes goes to extremes (Davis, 2001). In the many educational domains in which empathic sorrow is put to use—such as history, civics, and English—it seems important to investigate how empathic joy might play a role that is not only complementary but possibly more constructive.

The implications of our findings extend well beyond our experimental context, because educational attainment (our measured outcome) can predict adult well-being (emotional, physical, and material) in industrialized countries. Any gain in educational attainment is therefore important, especially given the wealth of findings on self-fulfilling prophecies and on vicious and virtuous cycles.

Finally, we note that education is not the only sector in which empathic joy on the part of those who serve members of disadvantaged communities might be valuable. Youth guidance, criminal justice, and community relations more generally might benefit from greater attention to empathic joy alongside empathic sorrow.

*Social Policy Considerations*

There is debate about how student outcomes may be affected by the combination of the teacher's ethnicity and the student's ethnicity. Some education leaders submit that because role-modeling effects may trump other effects, ethnic minority students must have teachers of the same ethnic identity. Other researchers propose that the teacher's skills and attitudes are paramount. Caught in the middle are the teacher and tutor corps—organizations such as Alliance for Catholic Education, Americorps Builds Lives through Education (ABLE), Citizen Schools National Teaching Fellowship, Teach for America, and city-government sponsored teaching fellowship programs such as those run in New York and Boston—whose members, often largely White, seek to address the shortages of qualified teachers in struggling schools serving predominantly ethnic minority students. Our findings indicate that an ability to empathize with students' joy can increase teachers' effectiveness, even when they differ ethnically and socioeconomically from their students.

*Limitations and Directions for Future Work*

Although our findings raise several intriguing possibilities, future work remains to understand more deeply the role of empathic joy in intergroup relations, both in education and more generally. More specifically, other external variables and more general dispositional characteristics of the teachers that might underpin observed differences in teacher orientation, but for which our data do not allow us to test. Future work might directly consider possible external variables that could influence both empathic joy and allophilia, as well as more general characteristic such as optimism or sociability. We note this in light of Barbarino and Stürmer's (2016) findings, who noted that xenophilic orientations can be predicted by major personality traits. Similarly, Paolini, Wright, Dys-Steenbergen, and Favara (2016) found that individuals' expectations, desires, and motives are factors that can lead to more and better intergroup interactions. Understanding how expectations, desires, and motives affect the experience of empathic joy in intergroup contexts is therefore a rich area for consideration.

## Conclusion

Our goal was to investigate the impact of empathic joy on objective student outcomes. Consistent with expectations, we found that empathic joy can indeed create conditions that improve student outcomes. Education has always been seen as a key to what is best about American society: mobility and success through personal ability and effort. To the extent that American education is not serving that purpose today as well as it has in the past, we need teachers who empathize with their students fully—that is, who experience empathic joy but also empathic sorrow.

# References

Aquino, K., McFerran, B., & Laven, M. (2011). Moral identity and the experience of moral elevation in response to acts of uncommon goodness. *Journal of Personality and Social Psychology, 100*, 703–718. doi: 10.1037/a0022540.

Barbarino, M. L., & Stürmer, S. (2016). Different origins of xenophile and xenophobic orientations in human personality structure: A theoretical perspective and some preliminary findings. *Journal of Social Issues, 72*, 432–449.

Batson, C. D. (1991). *The altruism question: Toward a social-psychological answer.* Hillsdale, NJ: Erlbaum.

Batson, C. D., Batson, J. G., Slingsby, J. K., Harrell, K. L., Peekna, H. M., & Todd, R. M. (1991). Empathic joy and the empathy–altruism hypothesis. *Journal of Personality and Social Psychology, 61*, 413–426. doi: 10.1037/0022-3514.61.3.413

Batson, C. D., Chang, J., Orr, R., & Rowland, J. (2002). Empathy, attitudes, and action: Can feeling for a member of a stigmatized group motivate one to help the group? *Personality and Social Psychology Bulletin, 28*, 1656–1666.

Cohen, J. (1977). *Statistical power analysis for the behavioral sciences* (revised ed.). New York: Academic Press.

Cohen, J. (1988). *Statistical power analysis for the behavioral sciences* (2nd ed.). Hillsdale, NJ: Erlbaum.

Czopp, A. M., & Monteith, M. (2006). Thinking well of African Americans: Measuring complimentary stereotypes and negative prejudice. *Basic and Applied Social Psychology, 28*, 233–250. doi: 10.1207/s15324834basp2803_3

Darling-Hammond, L. (2000). Teacher quality and student achievement: A review of state policy evidence. *Education Policy Analysis Archives, 8*(1). Retrieved June 3, 2016 from http://epaa.asu.edu/ojs/article/view/392

Davis, M. H. (1980). A multidimensional approach to individual differences in empathy. *JSAS Catalog of Selected Domains in Psychology, 10*, 85.

Davis, M. H. (1994). *Empathy: A social psychological approach.* Boulder, CO: Westview.

Davis, O. L., Jr. (2001). In pursuit of historical empathy. In O. L. Davis, Jr., E. A. Yeager, & S. J. Foster (Eds.), *Historical empathy and perspective taking in the social studies* (pp. 1–11). Lanham, MD: Rowman & Littlefield.

Dijker, A. J. (1987). Emotional reactions to ethnic minorities. *European Journal of Social Psychology, 17*, 305–325. doi: 10.1002/ejsp.2420170306

Dijker, A. J., Koomen, W., van den Heuvel, H., & Frijda, N. H. (1996). Perceived antecedents of emotional reactions in inter-ethnic relations. *British Journal of Social Psychology, 35*, 313–329. doi: 10.1111/j.2044-8309.1996.tb01100.x

Duan, C. & Hill, C. (1996). The current state of empathy research. *Journal of Counseling Psychology, 43*, 261–274. doi: 10.1037/0022-0167.43.3.261

Eisenberg, N., Fabes, R. A., Miller, P. A., Fultz, J., Mathy, R. M., Shell, R., & Reno, R. (1989). Relation of sympathy and personal distress to prosocial behavior: A multimethod study. *Journal of Personality and Social Psychology, 57*, 55–66. doi: 10.1037/0022-3514.57.1.55

Finlay, K. A., & Stephan, W. G. (2000). Improving intergroup relations: The effects of empathy on racial attitudes. *Journal of Applied Social Psychology, 30*, 1720–1737. doi: 10.1111/j.1559-1816.2000.tb02464.x

Fredrickson, B. L. (2001). The role of positive emotions in positive psychology. *American Psychologist, 56*, 218–226. doi: 10.1037//0003-066X.56.3.218

Fredrickson, B. L., & Branigan, C. (2001). Positive emotions. In T. J. Mayne & G. A. Bonnano (Eds.), *Emotion: Current issues and future directions* (pp. 123–151). New York: Guilford.

Gable, S., Gonzaga, G., & Strachman, A. (2006). Will you be there for me when things go right? Supportive responses to positive event disclosures. *Journal of Personality and Social Psychology, 91*, 904–917. doi: 10.1037/0022-3514.91.5.904

Gable, S. L., Gosnell, C. L., Maisel, N. C., & Strachman, A. (2012). Safely testing the alarm: Close others' responses to personal positive events. *Journal of Personality and Social Psychology, 103*, 963–981. doi: 10.1037/a0029488

Gable, S. L., Reis, H. T., Impett, E., & Asher, E. R. (2004). What do you do when things go right? The intrapersonal and interpersonal benefits of sharing positive events. *Journal of Personality and Social Psychology, 87*, 228–245. doi: 10.1037/0022-3514.87.2.228

Hayes, A. F. (2013). *Introduction to mediation, moderation, and conditional process analysis: A regression-based approach.* New York: Guilford.

Hoffman, M. L. (2000). *Empathy and moral development: Implications for caring and justice.* Cambridge, UK: Cambridge University Press.

Katz, I., Wackenhut, J., & Hass, R. G. (1986). Racial ambivalence, value duality, and behavior. In J. F. Dovidio & S. L. Gaertner (Eds.), *Prejudice, discrimination, and racism* (pp. 35–59). New York: Academic Press.

Konstantopoulos, S., & Chung, V. (2011a). The persistence of teacher effects in elementary grades. *American Educational Research Journal, 48*, 361–386. doi: 10.3102/0002831210382888

Konstantopoulos, S., & Chung, V. (2011b). Teacher effects on minority and disadvantaged students' fourth grade achievement. *Journal of Educational Research, 104*, 73–86. doi: 10.1080/00220670903567349

Lipsey, M. W., Puzio, K., Yun, C., Hebert, M. A., Steinka-Fry, K., Cole, M., Roberts, M., Anthony, K. S., & Busick, M. D. (2012). *Translating the statistical representation of the effects of education interventions into more readily interpretable forms.* NCSER 2013-3000. Washington, DC: U.S. Government Printing Office.

Mathiasen, H. (2006). Empathy and sympathy: Voices from literature. *American Journal of Cardiology, 5*(97), 1789–1790.

Morelli, S. A., Lieberman, M. D., & Zaki, J. (2015). The emerging study of positive empathy. *Social and Personality Psychology Compass, 9*, 57–68. doi: 10.1111/spc3.12157.

Paolini, S., Wright, S., Dys-Steenbergen, O., & Favara, I. (2016). Self-expansion and intergroup contact: Expectancies, motives, and desires to self-expand lead to greater interest in outgroup contact and more positive cross-group contact. *Journal of Social Issues, 72*, 450–471.

Pittinsky, T. L. (2012). *Us plus them: Tapping the positive power of difference.* Boston: Harvard Business School Press.

Pittinsky, T. L., & Montoya, R. M. (2009a). Is valuing equality enough? Equality values, allophilia, and social policy support for multiracial individuals. *Journal of Social Issues, 65*, 151–163. doi: 10.1111/j.1540-4560.2008.01592.x

Pittinsky, T. L., & Montoya, R. M. (2009b). Symhedonia in intergroup relations: The relationship of empathic joy to prejudice and allophilia. *Psicologia Sociale, 3*, 347–364.

Pittinsky, T. L., Rosenthal, S. A., & Montoya, R. M. (2011a). Measuring positive attitudes toward outgroups: Development and validation of the Allophilia Scale. In L. Tropp & R. Mallett (Eds.), *Beyond prejudice reduction: Pathways to positive intergroup relations* (pp. 41–60). Washington, DC: American Psychological Association.

Pittinsky, T. L., Rosenthal, S. A., & Montoya, R. M. (2011b). Liking is not the opposite of disliking: The functional separability of positive and negative attitudes toward minority groups. *Cultural Diversity and Ethnic Minority Psychology, 17*, 134–143. doi: 10.1037/a0023806

Royzman, E. B., & Rozin, P. (2006). Limits of symhedonia: The differential role of prior emotional attachment in sympathy and sympathetic joy. *Emotion, 6*, 82–93. doi: 10.1037/1528-3542.6.1.82

Sanders, W. L., & Rivers, J. C. (1996). *Cumulative and residual effects of teachers on future student academic achievement.* Research Progress Report. Knoxville, TN: University of Tennessee Value-Added Research and Assessment Center.

Shechtman, Z., & Basheer, M. (2005). Normative beliefs supporting aggression of Arab children in an intergroup conflict. *Aggressive Behavior, 31*, 324–335. doi: 10.1002/ab.20069.

Smith, A. (1976). *The theory of moral sentiments.* Oxford, UK: Clarendon.

Smith, K. D., Keating, J. P., & Stotland, E. (1989). Altruism reconsidered: The effect of denying feedback on a victim's status to empathic witnesses. *Journal of Personality and Social Psychology, 57*(4), 641–650. doi: 10.1037/0022-3514.57.4.641

Stangor, C., Sullivan, L. A., & Ford, T. E. (1992). Affective and cognitive determinants of prejudice. *Social Cognition, 9*, 359–380. doi: 10.1521/soco.1991.9.4.359.

Stürmer, S., Benbow, A. E. F., Siem, B., Barth, M., Bodansky, A. N., & Lotz-Schmitt, K. (2013). Psychological foundations of xenophilia: The role of major personality traits in predicting favorable attitudes toward cross-cultural contact and exploration. *Journal of Personality and Social Psychology, 105*(5), 832–851. doi: 10.1037/a0033488

Tam, T., Hewstone, M., Kenworthy, J. B., Cairns, E., Marimetti, C., Geddes, L., & Parkinson, B. (2008). Post-conflict reconciliation: Intergroup forgiveness and implicit biases in Northern Ireland. *Journal of Social Issues, 64*, 303–320. doi: 10.1111/j.1540-4560.2008.00563.x.

Wallace, B. A., & Shapiro, S. L. (2006). Mental balance and well-being: Building bridges between Buddhism and western psychology. *American Psychologist, 61*, 690–701.

Weiner, M. J., & Wright, F. E. (1973). Effects of undergoing arbitrary discrimination upon subsequent attitudes toward a minority group. *Journal of Applied Social Psychology, 3*, 94–102. doi: 10.1111/j.1559-1816.1973.tb01298.x

Wright, S., Horn, S., & Sanders, W. (1997). Teacher and classroom context effects on student achievement: Implications for teacher evaluation. *Journal of Personnel Evaluation in Education, 11*(1), 57–67. doi: 10.1023/A:1007999204543.

Xu, X., Zuo, X., Wang, X., & Han, S. (2009). Do you feel my pain? Racial group membership modulates empathic neural responses. *Journal of Neuroscience, 29*(26), 8525–8529. doi: 10.1523/JNEUROSCI.2418-09.2009.

TODD L. PITTINSKY is Professor at Stony Brook University (SUNY). He was previously associate professor at the Harvard Kennedy School, where he served as research director for Harvard's Center for Public Leadership. His recent projects include Us Plus Them: Tapping the Positive Power of Difference (Harvard Business Publishing). He received his BA in psychology from Yale and his PhD jointly from Harvard's Graduate School of Arts and Science and Harvard Business School.

R. MATTHEW MONTOYA is an Associate Professor of psychology at the University of Dayton. His research interests include intergroup relations and interpersonal attraction.

*Journal of Social Issues, Vol. 72, No. 3, 2016, pp. 524–547*
doi: 10.1111/josi.12180

# A Cook's Tour Abroad: Long-Term Effects
# of Intergroup Contact on Positive Outgroup Attitudes

**David Livert**[*]

*Pennsylvania State University, Lehigh Valley*

*This mixed-methods, longitudinal study documents the short- and long-term impact of a cook's tour of Vietnam by 14 U.S. chef students. Over 3 weeks, travelers engaged in myriad intergroup interactions to experience Vietnam's cuisine and culture, exemplifying a positive intergroup orientation consistent with allophilia and xenophilia. Measures included a pretrip questionnaire, daily journal, and posttrip questionnaire, as well as participant observation. Short-term attitude change included significant increases in positive affect toward the Vietnamese, negative stereotypes, and intergroup understanding. Nearly 10 years later, the author interviewed 10 of the original trip participants. Consistent with allophilia theory, participants expressed continued affection, kinship, and enthusiasm toward the Vietnamese people and remained motivated to engage the Vietnamese culture and cuisine. Additional evidence of allophilic specificity, openness to experience, and deprovincialism is also discussed.*

Culinary tourism is an increasingly popular form of domestic and international leisure travel, due in part to what has been termed the food revolution: the striking increase in self-identified food enthusiasts, food-related media, and public concern with food production and distribution issues in the early 21st Century (Long, 2003). Cook's tours—travel undertaken to experience various dishes and food systems where they evolved—have also gained visibility through televised culinary adventurers such as Anthony Bourdain, as well as a wide range of print and digital media. Culinary professionals who engage in cook's tours share a motivation with other international culinary tourists to locate and consume cuisine that is perceived as authentic: prepared as it was originally prepared in that country (Greeley, 2009;

[*]Correspondence concerning this article should be addressed to David Livert, Department of Psychology, Pennsylvania State University, Lehigh Valley, 2809 Saucon Valley Road, Center Valley, PA 18034. [e-mail: dell1@psu.edu].

The research was partially supported through Penn State University Faculty Research Development and Faculty Travel Fund grants.

Heldke, 2003). In this endeavor, they engage in positive intergroup interactions, embodying allophilia (Pittinsky & Montoya, 2016) or xenophilia (Stürmer et al., 2013). Moreover, inquiry into a specific cuisine requires an explicitly polycultural perspective as each cuisine is embedded within a culture, yet is shaped by and, in turn, influences other cuisines (Morris, Chiu, & Liu, 2015).

Understanding a cuisine requires an exploratory stance: consuming food in a variety of settings, exploring food markets and interacting with sellers, and understanding food preparation through interaction with other cooks. Highly industrialized countries maintain extensive food distribution and preparation networks including large-scale agriculture and transportation systems, expansive retail food stores, and restaurant corporations with thousands of locations. In contrast, food production, distribution, and preparation in a country like Vietnam tend to be on a much smaller scale. Daily acquisition and consumption of food requires interaction with individual vendors or small family businesses. A cook's tour of Vietnam thus required participants to not only consume novel dishes and ingredients, but to extensively interact with locals, despite any intergroup anxiety arising from intercultural contact (Pardus, 2004).

This positive orientation toward outgroup engagement can be distinguished from other short-term intercultural experiences that may have more explicit goals (e.g., prejudice reduction, intergroup understanding) yet are structured so that such potentially positive intergroup interactions may be unintentionally avoided. Many international sojourns—particularly those developed for preexisting groups (e.g., college students, church groups)—provide limited experiences for meaningful interaction with outgroup members. Sojourners often spend considerable amounts of time traveling, eating, and lodging together. Even when interacting with local citizens (e.g., markets, pubs, or public spaces), travelers can maintain a comfortable ingroup "bubble" (Chiu, 1995; Hendrickson, Rosen, & Aune, 2011) permitting those with high levels of intergroup anxiety to experience an intercultural "free ride" through which they may avoid intergroup interaction (Plant & Devine, 2003; Stephan & Stephan, 1985). Larger groups attenuate intergroup anxiety by providing frames for interpreting ambiguous intergroup interactions, as well as providing opportunities to share emotions (Hendrickson et al., 2011), thus providing a sense of a cultural enclave or refuge (Wilkinson, 1998). These conational ingroup enclaves may offer short-term support but may hinder adaptation to a novel culture in the long run (Hendrickson et al., 2011). Although structured time in larger groups may be less anxiety-provoking, such trips have less opportunity for positive outgroup interactions and their potential impact on positive outgroup attitudes.

Group norms among culinary professionals on a cook's tour may run counter to the emergence of such an ingroup bubble. On the cook's tour described here, group members shared a strong norm of engagement with locals. Creating food memories for trip participants was an explicit goal of the tour. The tour leader, a professional chef instructor, consistently emphasized intercultural contact in which interaction with members of local communities was modeled and valued. Such group norms may shape whether experiences are evaluated as positive by the sojourner, as they are interpreted within the overall goal of learning a cuisine.

## The Trip

The travelers consisted of 14 chef students from a well-known culinary training school in the United States. All students were members of the Global Culinary Society, an extracurricular activity that required additional time and commitment. A minimum grade point average was required of Society members to qualify for the trip.

The Vietnam trip lasted 20 days. Travelers arrived in Ho Chi Minh City, and a sprawling urban center of 8 million people. They journeyed through rural regions of the south, including several days in the Mekong Delta as well as Nha Trang on the coast. Travelers then flew to the capital of Hanoi. Travelers also spent time in the rural North, including a side trip to the coastal city Ha Long and Ha Long Bay.

There was a blend of both structured activities and unstructured time. Structured activities included introductory tours of Ho Chi Minh City, Hanoi, the Mekong Delta, and Ha Long Bay with guides. Other group activities included cruises, beach picnics, and fishing trips. The group dined together roughly half the time, including "family meals" served at the hotels where the students were cooking for a scheduled dinner. Over half of the time was unstructured and un-mediated.

## Theoretical Approaches

This study draws upon the emerging body of research concerned with facilitating positive intergroup behavior and attitudes, the focus of this special issue (Siem, Stürmer, & Pittinsky, 2016). It is also informed by the more established intergroup contact paradigm (Allport, 1954; Pettigrew & Tropp, 2011), which focuses on the reduction of negative intergroup attitudes and behavior.

### Positive Intergroup Processes

In reaction to a longstanding focus on negative outgroup attitudes and their amelioration, theoretical approaches such as allophilia (Pittinsky & Montoya, 2016) and xenophilia (Barbarino & Stürmer, 2016) explore the development of positive outgroup attitudes and behavior and related outcomes. Common to these perspectives is an assumption of functional separability (Pittinsky, Rosenthal, & Montoya, 2011a): that positive and negative outgroup attitudes and behaviors constitute separate processes rather extremes of the same dimension and process (Cacioppo & Berntson, 1994). A growing body of evidence confirms this multidimensional, valence-congruent approach (Barbarino & Stürmer, 2016).

Allophilia (Pittinsky & Montoya, 2016; Pittinsky, Rosenthal, & Montoya, 2011b) provides a useful theoretical framework. Five allophilia components were employed in this study as sensitizing concepts (Miles, Huberman, & Saldana, 2013) to frame analysis of both qualitative and quantitative data collected before, during, and immediately after the trip as well as interviews conducted up to 10 years after the sojourn. The goal of this analytic approach was not deductive— a formal test of allophila theory—but rather to illustrate how allophila may emerge through a short-term experience and the lingering effects of that experience.

*Affection* is defined as positive affective orientation toward the outgroup and individual outgroup members. Individuals expressing positive outgroup affect are theorized to have a desire for reciprocal affection, such that their feelings toward the outgroup are reciprocated.

*Comfort* is a feeling of ease when interacting with outgroup members. Social interaction should be generally positive and low in negative arousal. Outgroup interactions may be characterized by initial anticipatory anxiety transitioning to ease and a sense of accomplishment.

*Kinship* entails a feeling of closeness to outgroup members. This might encompass perspective taking and/or empathy for outgroup members.

*Enthusiasm* is indicated by strong positive outgroup attitudes. During outgroup interactions, there is an overarching positive feeling about the interaction.

*Engagement* represents a tendency to seek affiliation and interaction with outgroup members. One related outcome is the desire to learn more about the outgroup.

*Allophilic Specificity versus Secondary Transfer*

Pettigrew (2009) suggested that intergroup contact may result in a secondary transfer effect through which the positive effects of intergroup contact can extend to outgroups other than the original group involved in the contact. Evidence from two important meta-analyses suggests that these secondary contact effects may be equivalent to those for the original group (Lemmer & Wagner, 2015; Pettigrew & Tropp, 2011). On the other hand, Pittinsky has argued for allophilic specificity: that the development of positive outgroup attitudes does not generalize to all outgroups (Pittinsky, 2012, p.51).

*Intergroup Contact Theory*

Originally theorized by Gordon Allport, intergroup interactions are thought to be most effective when optimal conditions are present: equal status, cooperation toward common goal, interdependence, and sanctioning of such interaction by an institution or authority. A key feature of the Vietnam trip was the planning of formal dinners in which the chef students cooked alongside Vietnamese counterparts in professional kitchens. These events were anticipated to give rise to situations which met many if not all of Allport's conditions.

*Openness to Experience*

Openness to experience has been defined as a cluster of intrapersonal traits (e.g., being imaginative, broad-minded) that can impact behavior and influence social interactions (Costa & McCrae, 1997). Individuals high in openness are more likely to be attracted to interacting with foreign people and cultures. Barbarino and Stürmer (2016) have found openness (along with extraversion) to strongly predict xenophilia. Evidence also suggests that, in the opposite direction, openness to experience may increase as a result of positive intergroup interaction. An individual's ability to step outside his or her accustomed forms of thinking may translate into a growing openness to other novel experiences and subsequent international sojourns (Cassandro & Simonton, 2010; Leung & Chiu, 2010; Martin, Katz-Buonincontro, & Livert, 2015).

*Deprovincialization*

Through positive intergroup contact experiences, individuals may cognitively reappraise their ingroup (Pettigrew, 1997). Awareness of other cultural practices and norms may provide a broader context for ingroup perspectives, resulting in a greater appreciation for differences between cultures, greater complexity when thinking about other cultures, and reduced ethnocentrism.

## Methodological Approach

One novel facet of this study is a relatively rare mixed-methods approach to intercultural contact. Quantitative data included measures of anticipatory affect, outgroup attitudes, and identity measured before and immediately after the 3-week sojourn. Qualitative data included a daily journal which documented intergroup interactions and their affective valence. The author observed the trip and maintained field notes throughout. Follow-up depth interviews with the travelers provided rich qualitative data including retrospectives of the trip as well as current outgroup attitudes and behavior.

Another contribution of this study is its time dimension. Longitudinal studies of the long-term effects of intergroup contact are rare: this represents a notable lacuna in the literature. In a recent meta-analysis of 129 studies of the effects of intergroup contact in real-world settings (Lemmer & Wagner, 2015), only a fifth included a delayed outcome measure occurring at least 1 month after the contact. Furthermore, in only 29% of those studies was the outcome measured more than 6 months later; none were more than 12 months. This study provides an important contribution to the extant research literature as it provides long-term (7 to 10 year) evidence of the impact of intercultural contact.

## Methodology

### Participants

Nine of the 14 chef students were male and five were female; they ranged in age from 19 to 28 years ($M$ age $= 21.8$, $SD = 1.42$). Twelve self-identified as white, one as Korean-American and one as Filipino-American. Although 88% had traveled outside the United States, none had previously visited Vietnam. The trip was led by a chef instructor from the culinary school as well as a New York chef/restaurant owner.

### Measures and Procedures

*Presojourn questionnaire.* An eight-page presojourn questionnaire was completed by travelers before the group departed for Vietnam and contained a variety of quantitative and qualitative measures.

Affect toward the Vietnamese was measured by an eight-item measure of positive and negative affect (e.g., proud, fearful) adopted from the PANAS-X (Watson & Clark, 1994) to which participants indicated level of agreement on a scale ranging from 1 = "extremely" to 7 = "not at all." ($\alpha = .65$ and $\alpha = .83$, for positive and negative affect, respectively). Positive and negative stereotypes of the Vietnamese (e.g., hard-working, sneaky) similarly employed a seven-point agree-disagree scale ($\alpha - .82$ and $\alpha = .72$, for positive and negative stereotypes, respectively). A measure of intergroup understanding toward the Vietnamese consisted of six Likert items (e.g., "I think I am able to see the world through the eyes of the Vietnamese") with a seven-point agree-disagree scale ($\alpha = .72$) (Stephan & Stephan, 1985).

A social identity measure of American identity was adopted from Deaux and Reids's (2000) Specific Collectivism Scale and consisted of six Likert statements (e.g., "Being an American is central to who I am") to which participants indicated their level of endorsement on a seven-point scale ($\alpha = .95$).

Additional items assessed the traveler's expectations for the trip. Graphic rating scales measured positive (not really eager to go—really looking forward to it) and negative (not at all anxious—extremely anxious) affect anticipating the trip. Accompanying open-ended questions asked what aspects of the trip the participants were most looking forward to and most worried about. Among the 14 student chefs, 10 completed the presojourn questionnaire (71%).

*Daily questionnaire.*    Vietnam sojourners completed a short questionnaire each day. Two questions measured current affective state and were asked each day "How do you feel about the Vietnam trip at the moment?" and answered on graphic rating scales ranging from "not at all happy" to "extremely happy" and "not at all anxious" to "extremely anxious." On 8 days, the questionnaire included a series of questions which asked the participant to describe an interaction with a Vietnamese citizen they experienced that day. Open-ended questions regarding the interaction included the location, number of trip sojourners present, number of Vietnamese people in the interaction, a description of the interaction, and how the sojourner felt after the interaction. These items were coded and content analyzed by the principal investigator and a research assistant. Ten chef students completed the first week of diaries (71%); six completed the second week (43%); and eight completed week 3 (57%).

*Postsojourn questionnaire.*    A final questionnaire was completed by participants during the 18-hour flight back to the United States. A number of questions were repeated from the outbound questionnaire, including measures of positive and negative affect toward and positive and negative stereotypes about the Vietnamese, intergroup understanding of the Vietnamese, and American collective identity with reliabilities similar to the pretrip questionnaire ($\alpha = .72$, $\alpha = .84$, $\alpha = .46$, $\alpha = .65$, $\alpha = .50$, $\alpha = .97$, respectively). Additional open-ended questions assessed participants' favorite recipes and foods during the trip, most interesting experiences, negative experiences, lasting memories, and greatest challenges. Thirteen chef students completed the postsojourn questionnaire (93%).

*Participant observation.*    The author traveled with the group throughout the trip and carried out extensive observations and informal conversations with trip participants.

*Posttrip follow-up interviews.*    During a period between 2012 and 2015, the author conducted a series of depth interviews with the original 14 trip participants. Participants were contacted through social media links and with the assistance of the culinary faculty member who organized the 2005 trip. A total of 10 interviews were completed, nine by telephone and one in person. The interviews were semistructured, loosely following a protocol and ranged from 35 to 65 minutes in length. Topics included memories of the trip, personal experiences since the trip, and exposure to the Vietnamese culture since the trip. Multiple interviews were also carried out with a chef instructor who was one of the trip organizers and leaders.

## Results and Discussion

### *Anticipating the Trip*

Chef students expressed strong positive and negative emotions at the trip's beginning. Mean anticipation of the trip was near the top of the scale ($M = 12.14$ cm, $SD = 0.75$). Similarly, mean anticipatory anxiety was relatively high ($M = 8.86$ cm, $SD = 4.39$). Not surprisingly, participants were looking forward to experiencing the Vietnamese cuisine ($n = 5$) but were equally looking forward to touring the markets and meeting locals ($n = 5$). Chef students were most worried about getting sick on the trip ($n = 6$).

In follow-up interviews 7 to 10 years later, chef students recalled their thoughts and feelings leading up to the trip. Pseudonyms are shown in parentheses after the quote.

> I hadn't really had much interaction with that [Vietnamese] culture at all. It wasn't really thought of besides what I learned in my textbook. (Janice)

> I was curious about using a passport, going out of the country, going somewhere where I couldn't speak the language, the culture and everything. That was my first experience traveling. (Brittany)

Many became familiar with the Vietnamese cuisine during their courses at the culinary school, which made them curious about the country, culture, and people.

> A lot of it was [interest in the trip] obviously very culinary grounded and how authentic it was. I had in my head what I thought what it was going to be like and that pretty much was what I was most curious about. (Gary)

One chef student succinctly described a mix of positive curiosity and apprehension.

> Well, for me traveling was always about discovering a new culture and luckily food is such a good way to do that. I was very curious and apprehensive about going. Other countries that I had been to, I at least spoke the same language. (Frank)

### *A Cook's Tour as Positive Engagement*

Deeper understanding of a foreign cuisine requires active engagement with that culture: experiencing indigenous ingredients, one-on-one interactions with locals and a fundamental motivation to understand local food practice. The Vietnam group was interested in food culture as embodied in practice through shopping, cooking, and eating, requiring extensive interactions with local Vietnamese. A group norm of intercultural risk taking as well as proactive engagement rapidly emerged. According to the chef instructor leading the trip:

> Cooks by nature want to share. Most cooks like to show off because they do it profes-
> sionally... The sharing component and the showoff component I think is what makes it
> so easy to travel as a cook. When I go to somewhere new I teach myself one phrase [in
> that country's language] which is "Hello, I am an American cook. Can I watch you cook?"
> Then, I get a smile, "you sit here and I will show you" and the next thing I know I am
> getting a quick lesson on the street or an invite to someone's house or restaurant. (Chef
> Instructor/Trip Leader)

Travelers encountered familiar food distribution networks in Vietnam in 2005: grocery and scattered convenience stories—particularly in tourist areas—offered many products known to Western travelers. However, the majority of food preparation and distribution was local or regional. Large open- and closed-air markets were major sources of fresh produce, fruit, and meat and fish. Thousands of street carts, roadside stands, small urban apartments, individually owned fishing boats, and even snake moonshine vendors provided the most direct route to the authentic cuisine. All of these intimate settings required American students unfamiliar with the language and culture to engage in intimate exchanges and extensive nonverbal interactions. As one student recalled in the follow-up interview:

> There was a woman that I met at a tea and coffee store and you walk into this place. I really
> tried to commit to understand their tea. I ran into this woman with 100 percent language
> barrier. This one woman was brewing all of these different types of teas by herself and
> I was tasting them with her. I would nod my head yes or no after each and it was kind
> of inquisitive. We had met so many people that opened their kitchens to us but I tell you
> what... that woman is what I remember most. I brought home a bunch of these little teas
> and coffee and each one was different and that was really special to me. I felt like I really
> got to know this woman even though we didn't share a word. (Charles)

### *Positive and Negative Informal Intergroup Interactions*

In daily diaries completed during the trip, chef students reported a total of 73 interactions with Vietnamese citizens. These interactions were classified regarding the nature of the interaction (e.g., economic exchange) and coded in terms of valence (positive or negative).

Most interactions (84%) were positive or had a positive component (Table 1). This finding parallels recent work by Graf, Paolini, and Rubin (2014) who also found positive intergroup contact experiences outnumbered negative ones across many real-life settings. It also aligns with a wider research literature on intergroup interactions, including anthropology (Siem et al., 2016). Nearly a third of the interactions concerned purchases or other economic exchanges that occurred in shops, open markets, or in hotels. Travelers had either negative or a mix of both positive and negative experiences in roughly half of these interactions. The valence of the interaction as reported by the chef student is shown in parentheses after the quote.

> They tried to sell us flowers and we kept saying no. (angry/humorous)

**Table 1.** Informal Intergroup Interactions on the Trip and Affective Valence

| Total interaction | ($n = 73$) | Positive | Neutral | Negative |
|---|---|---|---|---|
| Market/economic | | | | |
| Exchange | 23 | 16 | 1 | 11 |
| Vietnamese | | | | |
| Initiated | 8 | 7 | 0 | 1 |
| Vietnamese | | | | |
| Children | 8 | 8 | 0 | 0 |
| Acquaintance formation | | | | |
| English | 7 | 7 | 0 | 0 |
| No common | | | | |
| language | 7 | 7 | 0 | 0 |
| Seeking information | 4 | 4 | 0 | 2 |
| Restaurants | 4 | 2 | 2 | 0 |
| Observation | 3 | 3 | 0 | 0 |
| Cooking | 2 | 2 | 0 | 0 |
| Other | 7 | 5 | 0 | 3 |

*Note.* Interactions recorded in daily diaries during trip.

I walked into a store for clothes and the people that worked there followed me around curious as to what I was looking at and helping me find or pick stuff out. (excited/ positive)

They tried to get us to pay 1,000,000 dong for a fishing trip that 1) we got stranded, 2) no fish. (angry)

We bargained for a knife and drank a warm beer. The whole town came and saw us. (satisfied)

In follow-up interviews a decade later, these interactions still resonated with the sojourners.

I had an incident where I was wandering the streets by myself and went to get a massage from what looked like a legitimate massage parlor. It was weird there were like three women that were like cornering me after I paid and I tipped them really well and they wanted me to tip them more. That was one of the only bad experiences throughout. (Brittany)

Other interactions were initiated by Vietnamese citizens and involved such behaviors as touching a traveler's hair (which was blonde), spontaneously performing music, laughing at the Americans, or mistaking the Americans for Vietnamese.

We were eating – all of us between two street vendors. I and another were walking between the two when a group stopped us and asked where we were from, if we were dating, why we were here and touched my hair. (excited)

I was standing around talking with other students when a Vietnamese guy from the restaurant began speaking to me in Vietnamese. I explained to him that I was not Vietnamese but that

I am ½ Filipino. He didn't speak very good English, but he understood. He then introduced me to his Filipino friend then showed me around his restaurant, showed me fish, crab, etc. (positive)

The place we stayed, they performed a mini concert for us, playing various local instruments and singing. Everyone seemed to enjoy it. (positive)

In a number of situations, the interaction was characterized by initial acquaintance formation. They were either carried out in English, requiring the Vietnamese participant to have some knowledge of the language (the students had none), or without a common language. These interactions were uniformly rated positively.

_______ and I went and met some Vietnamese girls working at the market, we struck up a conversation because they seemed nice. (good)

They sang Vietnamese songs and we sang back. (connected with a higher being)

There was a class of Tae Kwon Do so I watched. Some of the kids started doing some breakdancing moves, so I joined in. (very pleased)

*Optimal Intergroup Contact in the Kitchen*

The chef students cooked alongside Vietnamese counterparts in professional kitchens seven times. Four of these events were formal events in Ho Chi Minh City and Hanoi held at hotels with large professional kitchens and staff. In Hanoi, the American students cooked alongside counterparts from a local cooking school specifically for assisting homeless youth. On three occasions—in Vinh Long in the Mekong Delta, Hanoi, and Hong Gai—the group took over a professional kitchen and cooked a meal for itself. This involved negotiating the space with locals and arranging for kitchen help, planning menus, and going to the local market in small teams to source the dishes, prepping and cooking, and then sharing the meal.

The four planned cooking events embodied an optimal intergroup contact setting. The American students and Vietnamese cooks (particularly the students in Hanoi) ostensibly had equal status within the kitchen: they had equivalent cooking responsibilities. There were many instances in which the Americans and Vietnamese taught each other specific techniques (e.g., how to wrap skate, make a bird's nest out of honey, or how to butcher a sea bass).

During the cooking events, American chef students and Vietnamese cooks shared the common goals of preparing dishes consistent with the chef's demo and ready to be served on time. Another common goal was learning from one another. Americans and Vietnamese were often paired at stations, imbuing many of the kitchen activities with a strong sense of interdependency as well. Another condition—normative approval of and encouragement of intergroup interaction—was an explicit component of the trip and the professional kitchen events.

Having sufficient time to become acquainted—an opportunity for acquaintance formation—has been suggested as an important additional condition to Allport's original four conditions; other studies have identified friendship formation as an important mediator of contact (Amir, 1976; Davies & Aron, 2016; Pettigrew & Tropp, 2011). Frequent language barriers in the kitchens as well as their brief duration limited the opportunities for friendship formation: no students reported in later interviews making friends with Vietnamese from the trip. However, there were opportunities for acquaintance formation with Vietnamese counterparts during various breaks and a shared meal over the 8 hours of preparation and service.

Although the intergroup interaction embodied many of the Allport conditions, the language barrier may have at times represented a negative condition. In her follow-up interview, one student recalled the challenge:

> I think especially in the dinners that we prepared while working with the staff we had to find a way to communicate because of the language barrier. We needed not only to feel welcome but I also needed them to show me and teach me things without being able to talk . . . When you have never had to work through a language barrier and then you have to, you figure out a way to communicate. (Janice)

To what degree did changes in identity salience within the intergroup contact condition potentially account for changes in outgroup attitudes? Several processes are been theorized to mediate change in intergroup interactions. These include identity decategorization (Brewer & Miller, 1984), an emphasis on intergroup identity (Hewstone & Brown, 1986), and recategorization into a superordinate category as well as dual identity salience (Gaertner & Dovidio, 2000). Observation of the cooking events suggests that the last two processes most likely applied in those settings. Salience of American and Vietnamese identities was maintained by a language barrier frequently encountered in face-to-face interactions. Quantitative data collected during the trip similarly suggest no reduction in American identity over the sojourn. However, a salient superordinate identity was equally potent in the situation: both American and Vietnamese shared an identity as trained or experienced cooks in a professional kitchen. Both groups wore chef whites and readily engaged in nonverbal communication to complete their tasks. The chef instructor/trip leader's recollection of these events echoed this shared identity:

> Cooking is a very tactile and visual thing. If we are cooks and have similar skills I don't have to talk to you. I can tap you on the shoulder and point to watch me. You will watch me cook and then you try and I will watch you cook. If there is a difference then it is accepted if we do it slightly different or I shake my head no and say watch again. (Chef Instructor/Trip Leader)

**Table 2.** Posttrip Changes in Perspectives Regarding the Vietnamese and Collective Identity

| | Pretrip | | Posttrip | | | |
| --- | --- | --- | --- | --- | --- | --- |
| | *M* | *SD* | *M* | *SD* | $W^1$ | $t^1$ |
| Affect toward the Vietnamese | | | | | | |
|   Positive affect | 5.42 | 0.91 | 6.06 | 0.43 | 32.0[*] | 2.23[†] |
|   Negative affect | 3.81 | 1.21 | 3.19 | 0.71 | 13.0 | −1.48 |
| Vietnamese stereotypes | | | | | | |
|   Positive | 6.11 | 0.72 | 6.19 | 0.53 | 23.0 | 0.34 |
|   Negative | 2.75 | 1.25 | 3.12 | 1.15 | 41.0[*] | 2.88[*] |
| Intergroup | | | | | | |
|   Understanding | 2.39 | 0.78 | 3.18 | 0.58 | 33.5[*] | 2.90[*] |
| American identity | 5.31 | 1.42 | 5.06 | 1.88 | 11.0 | −0.40 |

†$p = .056$, *$p < .05$
*Note.* $n = 9$.
[1]Given a small sample size and potential nonnormality, both Wilcoxon signed-rank tests and *t*-tests were used to compare means.

The planned cooking events closely adhered to Allport-Pettigrew's optimal conditions. A lack of opportunity for friendship formation and—more importantly—the language barrier possibly attenuated the effect of those events. On the other hand, the emergence of a superordinate identity may have facilitated the positive effects of contact: despite the challenges of language, chef students were visibly engaged and excited during the lengthy kitchen sessions.

*Short-Term Effects of Intergroup Contact*

Analysis of pre- and postsojourn questionnaires revealed significant changes in students' attitudes and perspectives regarding the Vietnamese (Table 2). Differences in means were analyzed with both nonparametric (Wilcoxin ranked-sign test) and parametric (paired *t*-test) techniques, which yielded parallel findings. Over the course of the trip, feelings toward the Vietnamese improved. Positive affect significantly increased. There was a corresponding decrease in negative affect, but this change was not statistically significant. Changes in chef students' stereotypes of the Vietnamese people were mixed. Students did not change in their endorsement of positive stereotypes, however, endorsement of negative stereotypes about the Vietnamese significantly increased.

An increase in chef students' ability to take the perspective of the Vietnamese people would be consistent with the role of empathy as a possible mediator of improved intergroup attitudes (Batson, Lishner, Cook, & Sawyer, 2005): through intergroup contact, individuals gain the ability to take on the viewpoint of outgroup. Over the course of the trip, understanding of the Vietnamese significantly increased. This finding is consistent with increased empathy, although its affective components were not measured.

Finally, collective identity as an American did not significantly change over the course of the trip. A decrease in ingroup identity would have been reflective of a process of identity decategorization or recategorization over the course of the sojourn.

*Long-Term Evidence of Allophilia toward the Vietnamese*

To what degree did the students maintain positive attitudes toward the Vietnamese people and culture as a decade passed since the trip? Evidence from the follow-up interviews are reviewed according to Pittinsky and Montoya's (2016) five facets of positive outgroup attitudes: affection, enthusiasm, comfort, kinship, and engagement.

*Affection.* As noted earlier, chef students experienced a significant increase in positive affect toward the Vietnamese over the duration of the trip; students were more likely to feel proud, enthusiastic, warm, and hopeful. There was a corresponding decrease in negative affect which was less pronounced and did not attain statistical significance. Increased positive affect toward the Vietnamese people developed in the absence of extensive prior knowledge of the country or its culture. In the follow-up interviews, a typical exchange was:

> Brian: I didn't really know much about them [Vietnamese] before I left.
>
> David: How do you feel about them now?
>
> Brian: I love them.

The former chef students expressed continued affection toward the Vietnamese; questions regarding affection toward the people typically referenced interactions during the trip.

> Definitely [felt affection], especially the children. I was going through some of the pictures and actually remembering this one little girl in particular. I think it was a little harder for some of the age groups that we interacted with. (Frank)

> I would say the most positive memory is when people were warning us that people may be apprehensive with us being American and we didn't have that at all. We were so welcomed. It was really interesting that even though this tragedy happened to them that we were still welcomed. (Melissa)

> They are some of the nicest people that I have ever met. Everyone was very pleasant. They invite you to eat food with them without even knowing you. You can't do that here. There was a woman who was cooking in her yard and she actually lived in like a hut and she offered her food to us. I did not meet one person who I thought anything negative about . . . I

think it is a very kind culture. Vietnamese are very warm and they greet you with a huge smile. (Peter)

These responses also reflected the importance of reciprocal affect: a greeting or reception was unexpectedly positive, despite language barriers (Pittinsky, 2012).

*Comfort.*     When discussing their comfort with Vietnamese people in follow-up interviews, the former chef students recalled specific interactions on the trip. Several were initially anxiety-provoking due to the language barrier or a lack of familiarity with the culture. By the end of the interaction, the traveler (and likely Vietnamese interactants) had achieved a feeling of ease. When discussing comfort with the Vietnamese, travelers typically referenced interactions which culminated in a feeling of ease, coupled with the achievement of having overcome initial hesitancy or concerns.

*Kinship.*     In the short term, the chef students felt a stronger connection with the Vietnamese people. As noted, quantitative data from the trip revealed a significant increase in intergroup understanding: the chef students felt they were more able to take the perspective of the Vietnamese after the trip. This kinship was still evident in follow-up interviews years later. Some travelers reported a sense of connection through their interaction with others in the kitchen and with the shared success of their work.

> I think regardless of whether or not you both speak English there is always that apprehension in the first hour. You don't know how they cook, if they are going to be good, if they're better than you but at the end of the service you're definitely comrades because you got through it together. (Melissa)

Others felt the connection as a result of their informal interactions on the trip.

> The people that I interacted with are just like me. We like the same music. I can't really pinpoint anything. There are a lot more similarities than differences. Especially with this generation of Vietnamese people that are my age. (Frank)

One former chef student who later had responsibility for hiring workers for all the restaurants at her hotel resort expressed a kinship with Vietnamese employees as a result of the trip:

> I felt connected to them [the Vietnamese employees] almost. I think because I had been to Vietnam before and experienced their daily life . . . We had something to communicate about. I was able to relate with them. (Janice)

Most expressed the unique experience of connecting with Vietnamese in the United States, regardless of the setting.

> Yes, whenever I meet someone from there I tell them that I have been to their country and they love talking about that with me. Just to be able to connect with someone else that has been there. (Brittany)

> I do [interact with Vietnamese currently], plenty of them. Most of them is work related. I
> have hired some of them. We have become really good friends. (Frank)

*Enthusiasm.*   Travelers continue to express enthusiasm regarding the Vietnamese people. How the Vietnamese carried out the cuisine on a daily basis was inspiring.

> [The most positive memory] would be seeing the ingredients that they used on a daily basis
> and the methods they used to get to work and leave work. They have such a huge impact
> on the cuisine with basically nothing. (Donald)

In addition to the cuisine, many chef students also expressed a sense of enthusiasm toward the Vietnamese people. Several mentioned Vietnamese immigrants in the United States:

> I think they are a wonderful group of people overall. They were very welcoming. I think
> you realize that the ones who have moved to the US are very strong because that's not easy
> for them. It is a completely different life, structure and language. I have so much respect
> for them. There was so much that I learned from them and taught me to remember that
> everyone is different. I think I owe a lot to them. (Janice)

*Engagement.*   In retrospective interviews, travelers consistently expressed a motivation to engage the Vietnamese culture and cuisine.

Three out of the 14 travelers have returned to Vietnam since the trip. At least two of them have made several return trips and one former chef student who was not interviewed was living in Vietnam during the retrospective interviews. All participants indicated a desire to return to the country and cited current career, family, and personal constraints as reasons why they had not returned as of yet.

> I keep trying to nudge Chef into doing a reunion trip. It took us so much time though to set
> up the last trip . . . I would give up my career to go back. (Brian)

All travelers indicated that they regularly ate Vietnamese food in restaurants or—if not available nearby—they cooked Vietnamese dishes.

> Yes, I eat it and I like to make it . . . At least once a month. I make a lot of different things
> at home. I don't think that experience and those flavors ever go away. It's like an itch you
> have to scratch at least for me. (Brittany)

> Yes, I still cook and eat Vietnamese food fairly often. Those flavors are definitely engraved
> in the way I like to cook and eat. I shop in Chinatown a lot. Usually when I get to cook
> what I want I always fall back to Vietnamese. It is something that is very second nature at
> this point. (Gary)

Patronizing Vietnamese restaurants provided positive outgroup interactions characterized by a perceived kinship with the staff and owners. A number indicated that they go to Vietnamese restaurants if available in their area. Eating at Vietnamese restaurants is rewarding to the former chef students in several ways. First, it provides exposure to the cuisines that they enjoy. Second, as noted above, restaurants provided a convenient way to express their unique common identity as Vietnam sojourners with direct knowledge of ingredients, preparations, quality, and the geography of the country. This occurs in the context of the food industry in the United States, an additional point of connection.

Still in the early phase of their career—the average age of respondents during the retrospective interviews was 30—most have already attained a noteworthy level of success. Two of the trip participants are now general managers of restaurants in two major U.S. cities; others are currently Executive Chef, Chef de Cuisines, or Sous Chefs. Two participants have independently opened multiple restaurants in northeast and southwest metropolitan areas. Several have hired and currently work with Vietnamese in their restaurants or hotels. For a few, acquaintances and friendships have evolved out of their shared connection. One example was shared by a traveler who has participated in the opening of several Vietnamese and Southeast Asia themed restaurants.

> Yes. I have plenty of interactions with them and past experiences. I have also hired very many people that happened to be Vietnamese. I think having been there was a nice way to relate to them and get to know them. (Gary)

*Allophilic Specificity*

To what degree did positive changes in attitudes regarding the Vietnamese generalize to other outgroups? For most, a strong positive interest in Southeastern Asia cuisine and culture has remained specific to Vietnam. Many alluded to the cuisine when answering this question.

> David: Do you feel the same way about other South East Asian cuisines such as Thai or Malaysian?

> Frank: Yeah no, I don't have quite the passion for it. I might just need to understand them better.

Two have since traveled to Southeast Asia or an Asian country other than Vietnam. One had spent extensive time cooking in China. He attributes that experience directly to the Vietnam trip and perceives a specific link between them.

> David: Can you connect for me your Vietnam and China trips?

> Gary: Yes, everything that I have been doing is Chinese but definitely with more of a Vietnamese touch. Everything pointed to China. Going to China would not have happened if it wasn't for going to Vietnam.

> David: Why didn't you go back to Vietnam?

> Gary: I think there was more to learn or more of a question with China.

Although not specifically measured by quantitative measures before and after the trip, retrospective data suggest that increased positive regard for the Vietnamese did not necessarily transfer to other outgroups.

## Openness to Experience and Deprovincialization

Reflecting on their experience, many students shared remarks suggestive of enduring changes in their orientation to novel experiences. Brittany described the trip as a transformative experience due, in part, to the blend of exhilarating engagement and anticipatory anxiety which characterized many of the trip experiences.

> I feel like at the very least this type of experience really opens you up and your decision opens you up in a better spot. You're more open to it whether you actually like it or don't like it. . . . I felt so isolated there sometimes and it scared me but exhilarated me at the same time. I don't think that I would have gotten that from somewhere like Australia, where I could understand people. I think it would have been very different. It really opened my eyes. Even Japan would have been a similar experience. I made it through and learned so much. (Brittany)

For several students, this was their first trip abroad. One may speculate that the more exotic (and daunting) Vietnamese experience likely intensified both their initial hesitancy in intergroup interactions and a sense of accomplishment once such interactions had been negotiated.

Several of the former chef students also discussed changes consistent with deprovincialization: an expanded perspective on diversity and the world outside the U.S. borders.

> Before Vietnam I traveled to Europe [which] is very much like the U.S. Vietnam prepared me to know how different the world can be. It really opened my eyes and made me think very differently. (Janice)

> Everything was fantastic, the culture, the food, it was all completely different than anything that I was used to. It made me so much more open. I'll never be the same person. Travel makes you so much more aware of culture and diversity . . . . (Melissa)

A decade later, the travelers attributed their increased openness to experience and decreased ethnocentrism to their experiences on the Vietnam trip. In some cases, they expressed the belief that these personal transformations contributed to their career success and personal development.

## A Blend of Positive and Negative Intergroup Experiences

The study's findings reveal a predominately positive experience reported both during the Vietnam sojourn as well as years later. The most negative aspects of intergroup interactions concerned economic transaction or attempts by the Vietnamese to solicit business or to beg for money. These interactions may have strengthened existing negative stereotypes which significantly increased.

The other notable negative intergroup interaction concerned the language barrier experienced when working with Vietnamese cooks. However, these interactions were embedded in a generally positive regard of those individuals and the cooking events in general. The follow-up interviews revealed consistently positive memories and reflections regarding the trip. This occurred despite the author's multiple probes of the travelers to recall challenges, frustrations, and negative experiences.

## Summary and Conclusions

Although not explicitly designed to improve outgroup attitudes, the cook's tour nevertheless had that effect. Over a 20-day sojourn in Vietnam, U.S. chef students consumed local cuisines, cooked in Vietnamese kitchens, and generally engaged the culture. Many positive intergroup interactions occurred one-on-one or in small groups despite significant language barriers. Short-term outcomes of these interactions included increased positive feelings toward and understanding. Nearly a decade later, the former chef students expressed strong positive outgroup attitudes, an increased openness to experience, and a less ethnocentric perspective. Travelers consider the trip a critical event in their personal and professional development.

### Positive Feelings and Negative Stereotypes

In the short term, chef students' positive affect toward the Vietnamese significantly increased concurrent with a significant increase in negative stereotypes of the Vietnamese. This pattern of change is most consistent with a multifaceted or tripartite view of outgroup attitudes in which distinctive affective, cognitive, and behavioral components may not necessarily be consistent with one another. The finding also aligns with a multidimensional approach to attitude components in which positive and negative outgroup affect are considered distinct dimensions (positive and negative) rather than extremes of a single dimension ranging from positive to negative (Cacioppo & Berntson, 1994; Pettigrew & Tropp, 2011). Pittinsky (2012) has argued for the functional separability of positive and negative attitudes, e.g., that intergroup interactions and other inventions that reduce negative attitudes (prejudice) are not the same ones that increase positive attitudes (xenophilia or allophilia). Consequently, an increase in both positive affect and negative stereotypes as a result of intergroup contact with the Vietnamese were likely influenced by different types of experiences on the trip. It is conceivable that the optimal intergroup interactions in professional kitchens as well as positive informal experiences with the Vietnamese promoted an increase in positive attitudes. The latter interactions may themselves have been a blend of initial anxiety and enthusiastic engagement. Similarly, increases in negative stereotypes are likely attributable to negatively valenced interactions, which tended to involve economic exchanges, unanticipated responses on the part of the Vietnamese, or frustrations with language; the trip thus provided experiences that reconfirmed the stereotypes (Pettigrew, 1997).

*Informal or Formal Interactions?*

In Pettigrew and Tropp's (2011) influential meta-analysis of intergroup contact studies, the effects of contact experiences in recreational, laboratory, and organizational settings were found to be significantly stronger than those interactions associated with travel or tourism. Overall, tourism may yield weaker contact effects as sojourners may find social buffers or ingroup bubbles that reduce intergroup anxiety and cultural shock (cf. Furnham & Bochner, 1986) in the short term, but which may attenuate long-term attitude change and development associated with the sojourn. Study abroad experiences appear to be the exception: residency in another country for an extended period of time provides opportunities for travelers to accommodate to cultural and language challenges and positively engage with others, resulting in positive intergroup contact (Pettigrew & Tropp, 2011; Stangor, Jonas, Stroebe, & Hewstone, 1996). However, these experiences are typically the length of one or two academic semesters rather than the 3 weeks' duration of the Vietnam trip.

It is unclear to what degree the joint cooking events rendered the trip more potent as an intergroup experience given that they embodied optimal intergroup contact conditions. Although students may have continued to have been cognizant of their identity as Americans, a dual identity—American/Vietnamese and Professional Cook—was likely during these interactions. Had the chef students not cooked alongside their counterparts, would the impact of the trip on positive outgroup attitudes have been lessened or have been less enduring? The data do not provide a conclusive answer to this question. As an observer of the trip, the author would argue that cooking alongside the Vietnamese counterparts provided not only the trip's most optimal intergroup contact but also a shared sense of accomplishment and positive affect at the end of the meal. This was particularly the case in Hanoi where the American students worked with Vietnamese chef students at a culinary school for homeless youth.

Finally, another facet of the trip which distinguished it from other short-term travel experiences was a norm of engagement among the chef students. There was an extremely strong commitment to the trip at the outset; only those students with a minimal grade point average and number of hours volunteering for their club were selected for attendance. All shared the motivation to engage the cuisine and culture, despite relatively little knowledge prior to the trip. The chef instructor/trip leader also provided a strong model of engagement and coping for the students. Having taken a group to Vietnam the previous year, he shared with the group examples of positive engagement and accounts of challenges overcome prior to departure. Chef students at the sociometric core of the group were consistently enthusiastic and engaged.[1] Further theoretical formulations of intergroup contact theory and allophila should take into account the norms of engagement which emerge within an ingroup during an intercultural travel experience.

Intergroup contact activities that share qualities of the cook's tour may provide optimal situations for the development of positive outgroup attitudes. These could include sporting events (playing on the same team), musical concerts (playing in the same ensemble or band), or international Habitat for Humanity-type or disaster relief experiences. All of these involve a shared task that provides a strong common identity. All of these activities are also physically embodied and may require employment of fine motor skills, which provide a more engaging situation than less embodied interactions.

*Limitations*

One limitation of this study is a relatively small sample size ($n = 14$). Among participants, 71% and 93% completed the pretrip and posttrip questionnaires, respectively, yielding only nine comparisons although statistically significant differences emerged through both parallel parametric and nonparametric tests. With a larger sample size, it is likely that the decrease in negative outgroup affect may have also attained statistical significance. Symmetric improvement in both positive and negative affective dimensions is consistent with a functional separability hypothesis associated the theoretical frameworks addressed in this special issue. On the other hand, the range of intergroup interactions experienced by travelers may have impacted both positive and negative dimensions of outgroup attitudes.

*Implications*

As with other contributions to this special issue (Siem et al., 2016), this study addresses the development and maintenance of positive outgroup attitudes and behavior as a social issue, focusing less on the reduction of prejudice and outgroup animosity. The most pertinent finding of the study is the documentation of the enduring nature of the emergent allophilia (or xenophilia) toward the Vietnamese. Trip participants also experienced long-term effects on their careers and an emerging polycultural identity (Morris et al., 2015). Implications for social policy relate to educational, government, and business interventions and programs designed to foster positive feelings toward a foreign culture. Taking a lesson from the Vietnam trip, such approaches can benefit from engaging the role of food in everyday life. Foodways are a cornerstone of culture and the highly motivated exploration of food production and distribution generated considerable one-on-one and small

---

[1] A social network analysis not discussed herein was conducted by the author during the trip.

intergroup interactions which facilitated positive attitudes among the Americans. As noted earlier, physical engagement with preparing and consuming the food of Vietnam may have also provided a potent source of feelings, food memories, and a sense of accomplishment that bolstered the emergence of allophilia and xenophilia.

*Conclusion*

This study employed a mixed methods approach to document the intergroup contact experiences during a cook's tour in terms of short- and long-term effects. Although speculative, these findings illuminate some of the strategies and activities that can promote productive, positive outgroup engagement. The trip provided chef students with an openness to experience which has infused their professional and personal lives, an affinity for the Vietnamese people, and an enduring love for the flavors of Vietnam.

# References


Allport, G. W. (1954). *The nature of prejudice*. Reading, MA: Addison-Wesley. doi: 10.2307/2573151

Amir, Y. (1976). The role of intergroup contact in change of prejudice and race relations. In P. Katz & D. A. Taylor (Eds.), *Towards the elimination of racism* (pp. 245–308). New York: Pergamon. doi: 10.1016/B978-0-08-018316-9.50016-3

Barbarino, M.-L., & Stürmer, S. (2016). Different origins of xenophile and xenophobic orientations in human personality structure: A theoretical perspective and some preliminary findings. *Journal of Social Issues, 72,* 432–449.

Batson, C. D., Lishner, D. A., Cook, J., & Sawyer, S. (2005). Similarity and nurturance: Two possible sources of empathy for strangers. *Basic and Applied Social Psychology, 27,* 15–25. doi: 10.1207/s15324834basp2701_2

Brewer, M. B., & Miller, N. (1984). Beyond the contact hypothesis: Theoretical perspectives on desegregation. In N. Miller & M. B. Brewer (Eds.), *Groups in contact: The psychology of desegregation* (pp. 291–302). Orlando, FL: Academic Press. doi: 10.1016/B978-0-12-497780-8.50019-X

Cacioppo, J. T., & Berntson, G. G. (1994). Relationship between attitudes and evaluative space: A critical review, with emphasis on the separability of positive and negative substrates. *Psychological Bulletin, 114,* 401–423. doi: 10.1037//0033-2909.115.3.401

Cassandro, V. J., & Simonton, D. K. (2010). Versatility, openness to experience, and topical diversity in creative products: An exploratory historiometric analysis of scientists, philosophers, and writers. *Journal of Creative Behavior, 44,* 1–18. doi: 10.1002/j.2162-6057.2010.tb01322.x

Chiu, M. L. (1995). The influence of anticipatory fear on foreign student adjustment: An exploratory study. *International Journal of Intercultural Relations, 19,* 1–44. doi: 10.1016/0147-1767(94)00022-P

Costa, P. T., Jr., & McCrae, R. R. (1997). Stability and change in personality assessment: The revised NEO personality inventory in the year 2000. *Journal of Personality Assessment, 68,* 86–94. doi: 10.1207/s15327752jpa6801_7

Davies, K., & Aron, A. (2016). Friendship development and intergroup attitudes: The role of interpersonal and intergroup friendship processes. *Journal of Social Issues, 72,* 489–510.

Deaux, K., & Reid, A. (2000). Contemplating collectivism. In S. Stryker, T.J. Owens, and R.W. White (Eds.), *Self, Identity, and Social Movements* (pp. 172–190). St. Paul, MN: U Minnesota Press.

Furnham, A., & Bochner, S. (1986). *Culture shock: Psychological reactions to unfamiliar environ-ments*. London: Routledge. doi: 10.2307/326456

Gaertner, S. L., & Dovidio, J. F. (2000). *Reducing intergroup bias: The common ingroup identity model*. Philadelphia, PA: Psychology Press. doi: 10.4324/9781315804576

Graf, S., Paolini, S., & Rubin, M. (2014). Negative intergroup contact is more influential, but positive intergroup contact is more common: Assessing contact prominence and contact prevalence in five Central European countries. *European Journal of Social Psychology*, *44*, 536–547. doi: 10.1002/ejsp.2052

Greeley A. (2009). Finding Pad Thai. *Gastronomica*, *9*, 78–82. doi: 10.1525/gfc.2009.9.1.78

Heldke, L. (2003). *Exotic appetites: Ruminations of a food adventurer*. New York: Routledge.

Hendrickson, B., Rosen, D., & Aune, R. K. (2011). An analysis of friendship networks, social connect-edness, homesickness, and satisfaction levels of international studies. *International Journal of Intercultural Relations*, *35*, 281–295. doi: 10.1016/j.ijintrel.2010.08.001

Hewstone, M., & Brown, R. (1986). *Contact and conflict in intergroup encounters*. Oxford: Blackwell.

Lemmer, G., & Wagner, U. (2015). Can we really reduce ethnic prejudice outside the lab? A meta-analysis of direct and indirect contact interventions. *European Journal of Social Psychology*, *45*, 152–168. doi: 10.1002/ejsp.2079

Leung, A. K.-y. & Chiu, C.-y. (2010). Multicultural experience, idea receptiveness, and creativity. *Journal of Cross-Cultural Psychology*, *41*, 723–741. doi: 10.1177/0022022110361707

Long, L. (2003). *Culinary tourism*. Lexington, KY: University of Kentucky Press. doi: 10.7202/014992ar

Martin, D., Katz-Buonincontro, J., & Livert, D. (2015). Understanding the role of openness to expe-rience in study abroad students. *Journal of College Student Development*, *56*, 619–625. doi: 10.1353/csd.2015.0067

Miles, M. B., Huberman, A. M., & Saldana, J. (2013). *Qualitative data analysis: A methods sourcebook* (3rd ed). New York: Sage. doi: 0.1080/10572252.2015.975966

Morris, M. W., Chiu, C., & Liu, Z. (2015). Polycultural psychology. *Annual Review of Psy-chology*, *66*, 631-659. doi:http://dx.doi.org.ezaccess.libraries.psu.edu/10.1146/annurev-psych-010814-015001

Pardus, M. (2004, September-November). Vietnam: A chef's tour. *The Valley Table*, 23–29.

Pettigrew, T. F. (1997). Generalized intergroup contact effects on prejudice. *Personality and Social Psychology Bulletin*, *23*, 173–185. doi: 10.1177/0146167297232006

Pettigrew, T. L. (2009). Contact's secondary transfer effect: Do intergroup contact effects spread to nonparticipating outgroups? *Social Psychology*, *40*, 55–65. doi: 10.1027/1864-9335.40.2.55

Pettigrew, T. L., & Tropp, L. R. (2011). *When groups meet: The dynamics of intergroup contact*. New York: Psychology Press. doi: 10.4324/9780203826461

Pittinsky, T. L. (2012). *Us plus them: Tapping the positive power of differences*. Boston, MA: Harvard Business Review Press. doi: 10.1111/peps.12088_6

Pittinsky, T. L., & Montoya, M. (2016). Empathic joy in positive intergroup relations. *Journal of Social Issues*, *72*, 511–523.

Pittinsky, T. L., Rosenthal, S. A., & Montoya, R. M. (2011a). Liking is not the opposite of disliking: The functional separability of positive and negative attitudes toward minority groups. *Cultural Di-versity and Ethnic Minority Psychology*, *17*, 134–143. doi: http://dx.doi.org/10.1037/a0023806

Pittinsky, T. L., Rosenthal, S. A., & Montoya, R. M. (2011b). Measuring positive outgroup attitudes: Development and validation of the Allophilia scale. In L. R. Tropp & R. K. Mallett (Eds.), *Moving beyond prejudice reduction: Pathways to positive intergroup relations* (pp. 41–60). Washington, DC: American Psychological Association. doi: 10.1037/12319-002

Plant, E. A., & Devine, P. G. (2003). The antecedents and implications of interracial anxiety. *Personality and Social Psychology Bulletin*, *29*, 790–801.

Siem, B., Stürmer, S., & Pittinsky, T. L. (2016). The psychological study of positive behavior across group boundaries: An overview. *Journal of Social Issues*, *72*, 419–431.

Stangor, C., Jonas, K., Stroebe, W., & Hewstone, M. (1996). Influence of student exchange on national stereotypes, attitudes and perceived group variability. *European Journal of Social Psychol-ogy*, *26*, 663–675. doi: 10.1002/(SICI)1099-0992(199607)26:4<663::AID-EJSP778>3.0.CO;2-6

Stephan, W. G., & Stephan, C. W. (1985). Intergroup anxiety. *Journal of Social Issues*, *41*, 157–175. doi: 10.1111/j.1540-4560.1985.tb01134.x
Stürmer, S., Benbow, A. E. F., Siem, B., Barth, M., Bodansky, A. N., & Lotz-Schmitt, K. (2013). Psychological foundations of xenophilia: The role of major personality traits in predicting favorable attitudes toward cross-cultural contact and exploration. *Journal of Personality and Social Psychology*, *105*, 832–851. doi: 10.1037/a0033488
Watson, D., & Clark, L. A. (1994). PANAS-X. *Manual for the positive and negative affect schedule*. Iowa City: IA: University of Iowa. doi: http://dx.doi.org/10.13072/midss.438
Wilkinson, S. (1998). On the nature of immersion during study abroad: Some participant perspectives. *Frontiers: The Interdisciplinary Journal of Study Abroad*, *4*, 121–138. doi: EJ608215

DAVID LIVERT is Associate Professor of Psychology at Pennsylvania State University, Lehigh Valley. His research focuses on individual and interpersonal processes within intergroup contexts, ranging from emotional management and leadership to team diversity and conflict. Many of his research studies examine social psychological processes as they unfold in the professional and home kitchens. Livert holds a PhD in Social/Personality Psychology from the City University of New York Graduate Center as well as BA and MS degrees in psychology from Vanderbilt University.

*Journal of Social Issues, Vol. 72, No. 3, 2016, pp. 548–565*
doi: 10.1111/josi.12181

# Altering Perceived Cultural and Economic Threats can Increase Immigrant Helping

**Omar K. Burhan**[*]

*Leiden University and Medan Area University*


**Esther van Leeuwen**

*Leiden University*

*We report two experimental studies in which we investigated the effects of perceived economic and cultural threat on positive interactions between a host society and immigrants. Study 1 showed that people who perceived immigrants as less of a threat to their society's economy were more willing to provide immigrants with empowerment help and less likely to expect immigrants to solve their own problems (group change). In Study 2, we found that high culturally adapted immigrant was seen as less of a threat than low culturally adapted immigrants among the low and moderate nationalists, but not among high nationalists, who viewed immigrants as threatening regardless of their cultural adaptation. Participants who perceived immigrants as culturally nonthreatening were subsequently more willing to provide immigrants with help in the form of direct assistance and less likely to expect the group to change.*

There is currently a high flow of migration of refugees from Middle Eastern and African countries such as Syria, Afghanistan, and Eritrea into Europe (Migration and migrant population statistics, 2015). Whether the reason behind asylum seeking is war, poverty, or human rights violation, the general motivation for migration is driven by the hope for better life (Tsuda, 1999). In order to achieve these dreams, immigrants need to be integrated economically and culturally into the host society (Constant, Kahanec, & Zimmermann, 2009). Successful integration, however, depends on the host society's willingness to aid

---

[*]Correspondence concerning this article should be addressed to Omar K. Burhan, Department of Social and Organizational Psychology, Leiden University, 2300 RB Leiden, the Netherlands. [e-mail: o.k.burhan@fsw.leidenuniv.nl].

The first author would like to acknowledge the support from the Indonesian Endowment Fund (LPDP), the Indonesian Ministry of Finance, under Contract Number: PRJ402/LPDP/2015.

548

immigrants in this process, for example, through providing accessible housing or hiring them for jobs. Helping immigrants to integrate could be beneficial for the immigrant themselves as well as the host society (Zimmermann, 2007). For example, immigrants' tendency for entrepreneurship means that they can contribute significantly to the provision of employment in the host country (Baycan-Levent & Nijkamp, 2009). Given the current influx of immigrants in Europe, it becomes ever more important to understand what factors promote the host society's willingness to help immigrants integrate into their society (Fleming, 2015). In the current article, we examined immigrant helping to facilitate the integration of immigrants. Specifically, we investigated whether altering perceived economic (in Study 1) or cultural challenges (in Study 2) could increase the host society's willingness to help immigrants with their integration.

## Immigrant Helping

In the present article, immigrant helping is defined as actions performed by the host society to help immigrants going with their adjustment process to the host country. Examples of immigrant helping are providing access to education and language training (Jackson & Esses, 2000). Based on Brickman et al. (1982), Jackson and Esses (2000) distinguished between three forms of immigrant helping, namely, empowerment, direct assistance, and group change. *Empowerment* is endorsed if the host society believes that both they, as host society, and the immigrants are equally responsible for any problems associated with the latter's integration, and consequently both parties are responsible for solving these problems. This form of help is partial, in which the host society and the immigrants take active part in overcoming the problems. *Direct assistance* is endorsed when the host society feels fully responsible for causing any problems with the integration process. Therefore, they feel obligated to provide a full solution to resolve the immigrants' problems. The host society would endorse *group change* when they believe that the immigrants themselves have created any problems associated with their integration. The help in group change involves the host society reminding the immigrants to take responsibility to make changes on their own.

The distinction between empowerment and direct assistance parallels what Nadler (2002) described as autonomy- and dependency-oriented helping. Autonomy-oriented helping refers to aid that encourages the recipient to become self-reliance. Dependency-oriented helping refers to aid that does not encourage self-reliance but instead renders the recipient dependent on the help provider (Halabi, Dovidio, & Nadler, 2008; Nadler, 2002). Empowerment can be considered an autonomy-oriented form of help, and as such it would stimulate immigrants to deal with immigration-related problems on their own should the problems reoccur. Direct assistance is a dependency-oriented form of help that renders immigrants unable to sustain themselves should the host society cease giving aid. From a

long-term perspective, it should be clear that empowerment helping is more beneficial to both the immigrants and the host society than direct assistance or group
change. It is the aim of the present study to examine factors that would affect the
host society's willingness to provide immigrants with empowerment type of help.

## Perceived Threats and Immigrant Helping

Given the desirability of providing empowerment help to immigrants, the
question now becomes what factors promote or hinder the host society's willingness to provide this form of help, as compared to direct assistance or group
change. In this article, we focused on the role of perceived threat. Perceived threat
refers to the degree to which threats are subjectively perceived to exist by group
members (in this case, the host society) by the presence of outgroup (in this case,
immigrants: Stephan & Mealy, 2011). Stephan and Mealy distinguished threats
into two basic forms: realistic and symbolic. Realistic threats refer to tangible
threats (e.g., threat toward the host society's economic resources, power), while
symbolic threats are more abstract (e.g., threat toward the host society's cultural
values ways of life). As will be further discussed, these two types of perceived
threats can determine whether the natives of a host society welcome or oppose
immigrants, which would consequently affect their willingness to help immigrants
with their integration.

*Perceived Economic Threat*

In terms of realistic threat, prior research suggests that the fear that immigrants
would take away the jobs of the natives population is generally associated with
opposition toward immigration (Facchini & Mayda, 2012; Hanson, Scheve, &
Slaughter, 2008). It is within this context (labor market competition) that Jackson
and Esses (2000) examined their immigrant helping model. Their research showed
that perceived economic competition did not have a significant impact on the host
society's endorsement of direct assistance, but it did attenuate the willingness to
empower immigrants, and increase the likelihood of group change. They postulated
that this effect occurred because immigrants' competition over economic resources
threatens the economic well-being of native members of the host society, who view
the immigrants' gain as their loss. The study by Jackson and Esses suggests that
the host society would be willing to help immigrant as long as immigrants are not
perceived to affect the labor market of the host society.

*Perceived Cultural Threat*

In terms of symbolic threat, research suggests that natives of a host society
would be more willing to accept immigrants if they believe that immigrants will not

change the host society's cultural values and way of life (Card, Dustmann, & Preston, 2005; Hainmueller & Hiscox, 2010). Indeed, the acculturation literature also demonstrates a clear preference among natives of a host society for immigrants to adapt to the host society's culture (Breugelmans, van de Vijver, & Schalk-Soekar, 2009; Verkuyten & Martinovic, 2006). Immigrants who are culturally very different from the host society are more likely to be perceived as threatening, but when these immigrants are perceived to be adapting to the host society's culture, the level of threat declines (Rohmann, Florack, & Piontkowski, 2006). Moreover, immigrants that are seen as unthreatening to the host society's culture elicit more positive attitudes among members of the host society (Stephan, Renfro, Esses, Stephan, & Martin, 2005). Fortunately, immigrants often possess high endorsement of multicultural attitudes, which entails that they are willing to adapt to the host society's culture to a meaningful extent (Arends-Tóth & van de Vijver, 2003; Breugelmans et al., 2009; Verkuyten & Martinovic, 2006). However, while immigrants may be exerting effort to adapt to the host society's culture, the host society may not necessarily see these efforts (Navas et al., 2005). From this point of view, it is plausible that making salient the immigrants' effort to adapt to the host society's culture could be a way to alter the host society's perception of threats of immigrants. Consequently, it can be expected that immigrants who are viewed as making an effort to adapt to the host society's culture would be more likely to receive help (empowerment or direct assistance) and less likely to be admonished (group change) than immigrants who are viewed as not making this adaptation effort.

## Nationalism

We argue that an important moderator in this context is nationalism. Nationalism is part of the general concept of national identity. It describes an individual's feelings such as liking and pride, and their preference for and perceived superiority of the nation (Dekker, Malova, & Hoogendoorn, 2003). It is characterized by the need to keep the nation uncontaminated by the presence of other groups (Blank & Schmidt, 2003; Davidov, 2010). Nationalists tend to perceived outsiders (e.g., immigrants) as threatening; hence, they are more likely to oppose immigrants to acquire national citizenship (Raijman, Davidov, Schmidt, & Hochman, 2008). Prior research has shown that nationalism is associated with xenophobia, welfare chauvinism, exclusionism, and general anti-immigration attitudes (Mieriņa & Koroļeva, 2015). Indeed, nationalists movements, such as Pegida in Germany or Britain First in Great Britain, have publicly expressed their opposition toward immigration, in their point of view the presence of immigrants, especially Muslim immigrants are imminent threat for the nation (Dostal, 2015; see also "Britain First," 2015).

## The Present Studies

In the present research, we examined immigrant helping (empowerment, direct assistance, and group change) as influenced by perceived economic threat and perceived cultural threat. We examined these types of threat in two separate studies. In Study 1, we manipulated the context of economic threat and examined its impact on the host society's willingness to help immigrants. In Study 2, we manipulated the context of cultural threat and likewise examined its impact on the host society's preference to help immigrants. We expected that low perceived (economic or cultural) threat would be associated with a higher willingness to help immigrants. In both studies, we also considered the role of nationalism, for which we expected that high nationalists would be more likely to perceive immigrants as threatening, regardless of the context of economic or cultural threat. Consequently, immigrant helping would be more likely exhibited by members of the host society who possess low degree of nationalism.

## Study 1: Economic Threat

The goal of Study 1 was to examine whether altering perceived economic threat could increase the host society's willingness to help immigrants. The 2008 European Social Survey suggests that a large number of natives believe that immigrants are receiving more social welfare benefit than the natives of the host society (Dustmann & Frattini, 2014). Natives who experience more exposure to immigrants' fiscal pressure (e.g., perceiving immigrants having much access to public services) are more likely to oppose immigration (Hanson, Scheve, & Slaughter, 2007). We used this context of fiscal pressure in Study 1, in which participants were informed about either low or high fiscal pressure that immigrants put to the society. We expected that perceived economic threat would be lower in the low fiscal pressure condition compared to the high fiscal pressure condition (Hypothesis 1a). We further expected that low nationalists would be less likely to perceive immigrants as threatening than high nationalists (Hypothesis 1b). Social identity theory postulates that high in-group identifiers place more value on their group than low identifiers (Tajfel & Turner, 1979). Although not the same as nationalism, consequences of identification often mirror those of nationalism due to the fact that they both reflect an attachment to a group or nation (Rothi, Lyons, & Chryssochoou, 2005). We thus expected that the manipulation of fiscal pressure would affect perceived economic threat more strongly among high nationalists compared to low nationalists (Hypothesis 1c). Subsequently, we expected that the interaction of fiscal pressure and nationalism would affect empowerment (Hypothesis 2a) and group change (Hypothesis 2b) indirectly via perceived economic threat.

*Method*

   *Participants.*    Participants were 50 native Dutch students (19 males, 31 females), who were equally distributed across two conditions (low vs. high fiscal pressure). On average, participants were 21 years old ($SD = 4.99$). They participated either for course credit or €2.50 payment.

   *Procedure.*    Upon arrival in the laboratory, participants were led to a cubicle with an envelope containing the manipulation, questionnaire, and the instruction of the study. To ensure anonymity, participants were asked to put all the study materials back into the envelope upon completion, before returning it to the experimenter.

   Participants first completed a measure of nationalism. Next, they read an editorial that had ostensibly appeared on a reputable news website (Editorial 1). The editorial informed participants about common problems faced by immigrants (Turkish and Moroccans) in the Netherlands (e.g., "In primary school, the achievement of Turkish and Moroccans are almost 2.5 years behind those of native pupils....27 per cent of Moroccans and 21 per cent of Turkish in the Netherlands are unemployed, as opposed to 9 per cent of the native Dutch....").

   After completing an attentional check, participants read Editorial 2, which also ostensibly appeared on a reputable news website. In the *low fiscal pressure condition*, the article described how the Dutch government spends a substantial amount of its social welfare budget on the native Dutch (e.g., "...natives are most likely to receive social benefits"). In the *high fiscal pressure condition*, Native Dutch was replaced by immigrants ("...Turkish and Moroccans are twice as likely to received social benefits..."). Following another attention check, we assessed participants' perceived economic threat, the willingness to empower immigrants (empowerment helping), and the belief that immigrants are responsible for their own life improvement (group change). Participants were subsequently thanked, paid, and debriefed.

   *Measures.*    Unless stated otherwise, all items were presented as statements for which participants were asked to indicate their agreement on five point scales ($1 = $ *not at all*, $5 = $ *very much*). Scales were created by averaging the items. We assessed nationalism with two items from Davidov's (2010) nationalism and constructive patriotism scale ("The world would be a better place if people from other countries were more like the Dutch," "Generally speaking, the Netherlands is a better country than most other countries"; $\alpha = .67$). Three separate items assessed whether participants had paid sufficient attention to Editorial 1 (e.g., "What are the average annual incomes of the Turkish and Moroccans?"). Attention to Editorial 2 was checked with two items (e.g., "According to editorial 2, what is the heavy burden on the Dutch economy?"). Perceived economic threat was measured with five items (e.g., "Unemployed immigrants are exploiting the Netherlands welfare system"; "Immigrants will become a burden to Dutch society"; $\alpha = .76$). The measurements of empowerment and group change were adopted from Jackson and Esses (2000). The empowerment scale consisted of five items (e.g., "People should help the immigrants to overcome the barriers they face in adjusting to life in the Netherlands," "People should help immigrants to help themselves adjust to the Netherlands"; $\alpha = .83$). The group change scale consisted of 10 items ("The immigrants way of life causes their adjustment problems, so they should look to the Dutch way of life for help with adjusting," "Immigrants can adjust to the Netherlands, they just have to be willing to work at it"; $\alpha = .83$).[1]

*Results*

*Perceived economic threat.* We hypothesized that participants in the high fiscal pressure condition would perceive immigrants as more threatening to their economic resources (Hypothesis 1a) than participants in the low fiscal pressure condition, that nationalism would be positively related to the extent to which immigrants were perceived as a threat (Hypothesis 1b), and that the effect of fiscal pressure on perceived economic threat would be moderated by nationalism (Hypothesis 1c). To test these hypotheses, we conducted a regression analysis, in which fiscal pressure (coded: $0 =$ low fiscal pressure, $1 =$ high fiscal pressure), nationalism (mean centered), and their interaction term were entered as predictors of perceived economic threat. Neither fiscal pressure ($B = 0.01$, $t = 0.02$, $p = .982$), nor nationalism ($B = 0.66$, $t = 1.82$, $p = .075$), or their interaction term ($B = -0.28$, $t = -1.22$, $p = .230$) predicted perceived economic threat. In contrast to the proposed hypotheses (Hypotheses 1a–1c), the results did not show evidence that fiscal pressure and nationalism affected natives' perceived economic threat.

*Empowerment and group change.* We regressed empowerment on fiscal pressure, nationalism, and their interaction term. Fiscal pressure ($B = -0.01$, $t = -0.01$, $p = .990$), nationalism ($B = -0.37$, $t = -1.03$, $p = .311$), and their interaction term ($B = 0.14$, $t = 0.61$, $p = .546$) did not significantly predict empowerment. We also regressed group change on fiscal pressure, nationalism, and their interaction term. Fiscal pressure ($B = -0.21$, $t = -1.30$, $p = .201$), nationalism ($B = -0.20$, $t = -0.63$, $p = .531$), and their interaction term ($B = 0.26$, $t = 1.34$, $p = .187$) also did not significantly impact group change. These analyses showed no evidence that fiscal pressure and nationalism influenced natives' preference to endorse empowerment or group change to immigrants.

---

[1]One participant was omitted from further analysis for answering two of the three check items of Editorial 1 incorrectly.

Although perceived economic threat was not affected by the manipulation of fiscal pressure or by nationalism, perceived economic threat did significantly correlate with both empowerment ($r = -.38, p = .007$) and group change ($r = .55, p = .001$). This means that natives who reported low perceived economic threat were more likely to endorse empowerment, and less likely to abandon immigrants (group change), compared to natives who reported high perceived economic threat.

*Discussion*

The results showed meaningful relationships between perceived economic threat and immigrant helping. Specifically, in support of Hypotheses 2a and 2b, less perceived economic threat was associated with an increased willingness to empower immigrants, and with a reduced preference to admonish immigrants to solve their problems on their own (group change). However, in contrast to Hypotheses 1a–1c, there was no evidence that perceived economic threat in the present study was affected by the manipulation of fiscal pressure, nor by nationalism, or their interaction.

It is possible that the manipulation of fiscal pressure was ineffective in changing perceptions of economic threat in this sample because our participants had a relatively high educational background. In Europe, negative sentiments toward immigrants due to economic competition are inconsistent (Card et al., 2005; Hainmueller & Hopkins, 2014). Fear toward immigrants is more prevalent among the unemployed, retirees, elders, and lower income workers, but not among the young or the highly educated (Constant et al., 2009). As all our participants were university students, they may not have been overly concerned about fiscal pressure since most of them probably were not paying income tax at the time of the study. Moreover, a study conducted among highly educated people showed that it is not fear related to economic well-being that creates anti-immigration attitudes, but fear that the host population's culture or ways of life will be altered by the presence of immigrants (Hainmueller & Hiscox, 2007). Bearing in mind that participants in our study were mainly young and highly educated native Dutch, fiscal pressure might not be the most relevant type of threat for them. Cultural threat, on the other hand, as was the focus of Study 2, might be more relevant to this particular sample.

## Study 2: Cultural Threat

The goal of Study 2 was to examine how perceived cultural threat affects the host society's willingness to help immigrants. According to the acculturation literature, immigrants often endorse a multicultural ideology (Arends-Tóth & van de Vijver, 2003; Verkuyten & Martinovic, 2006). The multicultural ideology entails that immigrants are willing to adapt their culture as means of accommodating the culture of the host society (Breugelmans et al., 2009). We used this context of cultural adaptation in Study 2 and expected that high cultural adaptation of immigrants would lead natives to view immigrants as less of a threat than low cultural adaptation (Hypothesis 1a). Following Study 1, we expected that high nationalists would be more likely to perceived immigrants as a threat than low nationalists (Hypothesis 1b). We also expected that the effect of immigrants' cultural adaptation on perceived threat would be moderated by nationalism, such that cultural adaptation would affect perceived cultural threat more strongly among low nationalists compared to high nationalists (Hypothesis 1c). Subsequently, we expected that the interaction of cultural adaptation and nationalism would affect empowerment (Hypothesis 2a) and group change (Hypothesis 2b) indirectly via perceived economic threat.

In addition to help in the form of empowerment or group change, we also incorporated help in the form of direct assistance (Jackson & Esses, 2000). Empowerment help is partial, which means that it rests on the assumption that the host society as provider and immigrants as recipients shares resources to solve the problem. Empowerment help would fail if immigrants did not possess the resources needed to contribute. For example, looking at the current immigrant crisis in Europe, on their arrivals, immigrants (or refugees) are limited in their ability to take care of their own basic needs (e.g., shelter, food). In such cases, immigrants rely heavily on the host society for assistance. Direct assistance implies a full provision of aid that does not require the recipient to contribute. While direct assistance fulfills the recipients' needs in full, it also renders them dependent on the help provider (Halabi et al., 2008; Nadler, 2002). However, it may nonetheless be a basic requirement for empowerment. For example, it would not make much sense to provide language training (empowerment) to immigrants if they are struggling to fulfill their basic needs for food and shelter. Given that direct assistance is often a costly type of help, particularly since it implies a continued dependency of the help recipients (Jackson & Esses, 2000), it can also be regarded as a more "sacrificing" type of help in certain circumstances. Therefore, we expected the interaction of cultural adaptation and nationalism would also affect direct assistance indirectly via perceived economic threat (Hypothesis 2c).

*Method*

*Participants.*     Participants were 52 native Dutch students (24 males, 28 females). On average, participants were 20 years old ($SD = 2.26$). They participated either for course credit or a 2.50 Euro payment. The design of the study was a between subjects design, in which participants were assigned into either low or high cultural adaptation.

*Procedure.*     Study 2 was similar to Study 1, with some adjustments. After assessing nationalism, participants read Editorial 1 (the same as in Study 1) about problems related to immigrants' job employment and education. Then, they read Editorial 2, which described ethnic minorities' (Turkish and Moroccans) low (e.g., "... their preference to wear their own clothing, such as headscarves, to perform religious rituals, to continue speaking their own language, and to live in general accordance with their Islamic faith") versus high (e.g., "... willingness to tolerate the absence of typical Islamic clothing such as headscarves, a good command of Dutch language, and live in general accordance to Dutch culture") willingness to adapt to the Dutch culture. After a check of the effectiveness of the manipulation, we assessed perceived cultural threat, empowerment, group change, and direct assistance.

*Measures.*     All answers were assessed on five-point scales ($1 = $ *not at all*, $5 = $ *very much*), and scales were created by averaging the items. The manipulation was checked with two items ("According to the article, to what extent do the Turkish and Moroccans immigrants wish to preserve their tradition?"; "To what extent do the Turkish and Moroccans immigrants wish to conform to the Dutch culture?"; $r = .87, p = .001$). We assessed nationalism ($\alpha = .62$), empowerment ($\alpha = .76$), and group change ($\alpha = .87$) with the same items as in Study 1. Direct assistance was assessed with five items taken from Jackson and Esses (2000; e.g., "Immigrants faced the problems of adjustment that aren't their fault, so the Dutch government should provide programs to help them adjust", "It should be made easier for the immigrants to adjust to the Netherlands, because their adjustment problems are the responsibility of the Dutch society"; $\alpha = .78$).[2]

*Results*

*Checks*     An independent samples t-test showed that participants in the high cultural adaptation condition ($M = 4.00$, $SD = 0.72$) perceived immigrants as more willing to adapt to Dutch culture than participants in the low cultural adaptation condition ($M = 1.71$, $SD = 0.55$), $t(54) = 13.33, p = .001$. This shows that the manipulation was successful.

---

[2]We conducted a principal component analysis with Varimax rotation on the immigrant helping items in Studies 1 and 2. Both analyses showed that the items corresponded to the intended separate constructs (Study 1: group change eigenvalue $= 3.72$, empowerment eigenvalue $= 2.23$; Study 2: group change eigenvalue $= 4.65$, direct assistance eigenvalue $= 2.68$, empowerment eigenvalue $= 2.27$). Overall, the factor analyses showed very similar results to those reported by Jackson and Esses (2000).

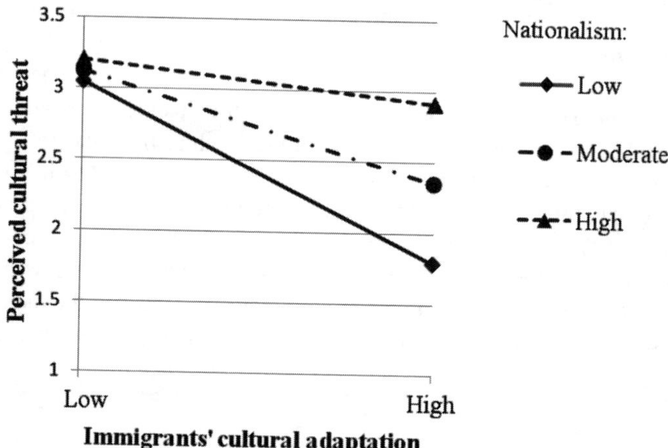


**Fig. 1.** The effect of immigrants' cultural adaptation on perceived cultural threat among natives with low, moderate, and high levels of nationalism.

*Perceived cultural threat.*     We conducted a regression analysis, in which cultural adaptation (coded $0 =$ low cultural adaptation, $1 =$ high cultural adaptation), nationalism (mean centered), and their interaction term were entered as predictors of perceived cultural threat. Supporting Hypothesis 1a, cultural adaptation ($B = -0.75, t = -4.13, p = .001$) uniquely predicted perceived cultural threat. High culturally adapted immigrants were perceived as less threatening than low culturally adapted immigrants. In contrast to Hypothesis 1b, there was no significant main effect of nationalism on perceived cultural threat ($B = -0.43$, $t = -1.38, p = .17$). However, in line with Hypothesis 1c, the interaction term was significant ($B = 0.52, t = 2.62, p = .012$). Simple slope analyses showed that the effect of cultural adaptation on perceived cultural threat was significant among participants with low ($-1$ $SD$; $B = -1.25, t = -4.86, p = .001$) and moderate ($M$; $B = -0.77, t = -4.25, p = .001$) nationalism, but not among those who were high in nationalism ($+1$ $SD$; $B = 0.87, t = -1.13, p = .264$). As depicted in Figure 1, participants in the low cultural adaptation condition perceived immigrants as threatening regardless of their level of nationalism. However, in line with Hypothesis 1c, in the high cultural adaptation condition, perceived cultural threat tended to be lower among low nationalists compared to high nationalists.

*Empowerment.*     We conducted a regression analysis in which cultural adaptation, nationalism, and their interaction term were entered as predictors of empowerment. Neither cultural adaptation ($B = 0.052, t = 0.32, p = .750$), nor nationalism ($B = -0.52$, $t = -0.82$, $p = .072$), or the interaction term ($B = 0.32$, $t = 1.81$, $p = .076$) significantly predicted empowerment. Although the interaction between nationalism and cultural adaptation was not significant, as stated in Hypothesis 2a, it is still possible that they affect group change *indirectly* through perceived cultural threat. We therefore tested whether the indirect interaction effect of cultural adaptation and nationalism on group change was mediated by perceived cultural threat. To this end, we conducted a mediated moderation analysis using PROCESS, model 8 (see Hayes, 2013). The analysis showed that low perceived cultural threat was marginally associated with empowerment ($B = -0.24$, $t = -1.92$, $p = .060$). However, the index of the moderated mediation was $-.13$, 95% CI $=-.42$ to $.043$. In contrast to Hypothesis 2a, the fact that zero was not included in the 95% confidence interval indicated that the interaction of cultural adaptation and nationalism did not indirectly affected empowerment via perceived cultural threat.

*Group change.*     Group change was regressed on cultural adaptation, nationalism, and their interaction term. The effects of cultural adaptation ($B = -0.36$, $t = -2.18$, $p = .034$) was significant. Natives were more likely to endorse group change to the low culturally adapted than high culturally adapted immigrants. The direct effects of nationalism ($B = -0.23$, $t = -0.82$, $p = .419$) and the interaction term ($B = 0.31$, $t = 1.73$, $p = .090$) on group change were not significant. We subsequently tested whether the indirect interaction effect of cultural adaptation and nationalism on group change was mediated by perceived cultural threat. To this end, we conducted a mediated moderation analysis using PROCESS, model 8 (see Hayes, 2013). The analysis showed that perceived cultural threat had a unique effect on group change ($B = 0.47$, $t = 4.20$, $p = .001$), indicating that less perceived cultural threat was associated with less preference for group change. Furthermore, the indirect effect of the interaction between nationalism and cultural adaptation on group change was significant, as indicated by the fact that zero was not included in the 95% confidence interval ($.25$, 95% CI $= 0.09$–$0.50$). In line with Hypothesis 2b, decreased in perceived cultural threat as affected by the interaction of cultural adaptation and nationalism indirectly reduced natives' preference for group change.

*Direct assistance.*     We conducted a regression analysis in which cultural adaptation, nationalism, and the interaction term as predictors of direct assistance. The effect of cultural adaptation was significant ($B = 0.43$, $t = 2.07$, $p = .044$). High culturally adapted immigrants were more likely to received direct assistance than low culturally adapted immigrants. Nationalism ($B = -0.32$, $t = -0.89$, $p = .375$) and their interaction ($B = 0.17$, $t = 0.74$, $p = .465$) did not significantly predict direct assistance. We also test whether the interaction of cultural adaptation and nationalism indirectly affected direct assistance, with perceived threat acted as mediator. We conducted a moderated mediation analysis using PROCESS, model 8 (see Hayes, 2013). The analysis showed that low perceived cultural threat was associated with more endorsement of direct assistance ($B = -0.50$, $t = -3.33$, $p = .002$). Furthermore, in line with Hypothesis 2c, the index of the moderated mediation was $-.26$, 95% CI $= -0.59$ to $-0.05$, indicating a significant mediation. In line with Hypothesis 2c, decreased in perceived cultural threat as affected by the interaction of cultural adaptation and nationalism indirectly increased natives' willingness to endorse direct assistance.

*Discussion*

In Study 2, we demonstrated the impact of cultural adaptation of immigrants and its interaction with nationalism on the extent to which natives perceived immigrants as a threat to their culture and way of life. Consistent with Hypothesis 1a, we found that participants were less likely to view immigrants as a threat when these immigrants were portrayed as highly adapted to participants' culture. In line with Hypothesis 1c, this was especially prominent among participants who possessed a low to moderate level of nationalism. However, for participants with a high level of nationalism, immigrants were always seen as a threat to their culture, regardless of their purported level of cultural adaptation. In support of Hypotheses 2b and 2c, the perception of cultural threat, as affected by immigrants' cultural adaptation and participants' degree of nationalism, subsequently affected participants' willingness to provide direct assistance and to endorse group change.

Unexpectedly, we found only modest support for the idea that low perceived cultural threat increases natives' preference to provide immigrants with empowerment help. This might due to our particular sample, which consisted of highly educated students. According to research in political ideology, higher levels of education are associated with more social liberalism (Feldman & Johnston, 2014). Equal allocation of economy, politics, and other legal rights to all members of a society are the core of the social liberalism ideology (Bierbrauer & Klinger, 2002). Considering the fact that empowerment is a way to equalize the disparity between the host society and immigrants, participants in our research may have been motivated to maintain consistency with their political ideology, and the exemption of immigrants from such rights would be inconsistent with this ideology.

## General Discussion

The present studies contribute to our understanding of factors that can promote immigrant helping. We investigated how perceived threat, either to the nation's economy or to its culture, can impact the host society's willingness to help immigrants. In Study 1, we showed that low perceived economic threat was associated with more willingness to empower immigrants, and a lower likelihood to abandon immigrants by arguing that they should solve their problems by themselves (i.e., group change). In Study 2, we showed how the context of immigrants' cultural adaptation affected low nationalists' (but not high nationalists') belief that immigrants pose a threat to their cultural values and way of life. Participants who did not perceive immigrants as threatening their cultural values or way of life were subsequently more willing to provide these immigrants with direct assistance, and less inclined to reproach these immigrants, compared to participants who did perceive immigrants as a threat to their culture.

In Study 2, we found that perceived cultural threat decreased participants' willingness to provide immigrants with help in the form of direct assistance. This result may appear to contradict prior findings in which threat to in-group identity increased the provision of so-called dependency-oriented help, which is similar to direct assistance in many ways (Halabi et al., 2008; Nadler, Harpaz-Gorodeisky, & Ben-David, 2009; see also Cunningham & Platow, 2007). However, further examination of the data showed that there was a substantial correlation between empowerment and direct assistance ($r = .42, p = .002$), while both direct assistance ($r = -.26, p = .065$) and empowerment ($r = -.07, p = .613$) had no significant correlation with group change. This suggests that instead of viewing empowerment and direct assistance as opposites of the same continuum (running from autonomy/empowerment to dependency/direct assistance helping), our participants viewed the two types of help as distinct, but related forms of helping. It is also interesting that both participants in the low ($M = 3.88$, $SD = 0.68$) and high ($M = 3.91$, $SD = 0.49$) cultural adaptation condition strongly endorsed empowerment help (i.e., mean scores were above the scale midpoint in both conditions). This high endorsement of empowerment help, and the fact that the provision of direct assistance involves more resources than empowerment (Jackson & Esses, 2000), suggests that direct assistance should not be interpreted as a form of strategic helping, as dependency-oriented help often is (e.g., Halabi et al., 2008; Nadler et al., 2009). Instead, direct assistance appears to reflect participants' genuine willingness to help immigrants improve their lives.

Several limitations of our studies need to be addressed. First, the numbers of participants in both studies were quite low considering the analyses we reported in the present article. Such a relatively low sample size may be prone to failures to reject a false null hypothesis (type II error: Petratis, Dunham, & Niewiarowski, 1996). Future studies should therefore employ a larger sample size to avoid this issue. Second, we used vignettes to manipulate fiscal and cultural threat in our studies. This approach is useful for examining topics that are sensitive or difficult to experimentally manipulate (Hughes, 1998). However, a potential drawback of vignettes is that they are sometimes not realistic enough to stimulate participants' level of immersion to the vignette context (Aguinis & Bradley, 2014). Third, participants in our studies were university students. As indicated in Study 1, university students may experience economic threat differently from natives who, for example, have a fulltime job and a family to support. It is thus imperative that future research investigates perceptions of economic threat among a more mature, nonstudent sample.

Based on our findings, several suggestions can be made to policy makers and other professionals who wish to encourage immigrant helping. First, our research suggests that highlighting immigrants' effort to adapt to the cultural values of the host society is an effective way to promote natives' willingness to help immigrants. This might be accomplished by promoting positive contact between members of the host society and the immigrants (see Pettigrew, 1998). Such contact can be facilitated, for example, through the promotion of polyculturalism (Rosenthal and Levy, 2016). Another approach is by promoting positive cross-group friendships (see Davies and Aron, 2016) that could increase the host society's awareness of immigrants' effort to adapt to the host society's culture. The effort taken by immigrants, in turn, may be perceived by the host society as a reflection of the immigrants' appreciation of and respect for the host society's culture. As suggested by Montoya and Pinter (2016), emphasizing out-group (i.e., immigrants') values as congruent with the in-group's interests can be an effective way to promote positive intergroup relations.

Second, it is important to consider ways of promoting immigrant helping by taking levels of nationalism into account. Specifically, in Study 2, nationalism acted as a moderator of the effect of cultural adaptation on perceived cultural threat. Participants with a high level of nationalism consistently viewed immigrants as a threat to their culture, regardless of the immigrants purported level of cultural adaptation. The problematic role of nationalism may be caused by the high nationalists' tendency to perceive immigrants as outsiders (Dekker et al., 2003; Schatz, Staub, & Lavine, 1999). Based on insights from the common in-group identity model (Gaertner & Dovidio, 2000), encouraging the host population to categorize immigrants as part of their nation may improve the host society's attitudes and behavior toward the immigrants. Indeed, previous research also suggested that the perception of a common group identity may effectively improve the host society's attitude toward immigrants, which may increase the willingness to help immigrants with various problems (Esses, Dovidio, Jackson, & Armstrong, 2001).

It may also be fruitful to consider ways of transforming nationalism to more benign forms of attachment. For example, nationalism may be altered by promoting the counterconcept of nationalism, that is, constructive patriotism (Blank & Schmidt, 2003). While nationalism refers to a blind idealization of one's own nation, constructive patriotism is characterized by the rejection of idealization and the willingness to acknowledge the nation's weaknesses, such that it enables high constructive patriots to engage in critical and constructive actions to improve the nation (Davidov, 2010). One way to elevate constructive patriotism is by promoting civic engagement that would increase people's concern and knowledge toward the society, which, in turn, would promote the engagement of solving various problems faced by the society (Richey, 2011).

# References


Aguinis, H., & Bradley, K. J. (2014). Best practice recommendations for designing and implementing experimental vignette methodology studies. *Organizational Research Methods, 17*, 351–371. doi: 10.1177/1094428114547952

Arends-Tóth, J., & van de Vijver, F. J. R. (2003). Multiculturalism and acculturation: Views of Dutch and Turkish-Dutch. *European Journal of Social Psychology, 33*, 249–266. doi: 10.1002/ejsp.143

Baycan-Levent, T., & Nijkamp, P. (2009). Characteristics of migrant entrepreneurship in Europe. *Entrepreneurship & Regional Development, 21*, 375–397. doi: 10.1080/08985620903020060

Bierbrauer, G., & Klinger, E. W. (2002). Political ideology, perceived threat, and justice towards immigrants. *Social Justice Research, 15*, 41–52. doi: 10.1023/A:1016045731732

Blank, T., & Schmidt, P. (2003). National identity in a united Germany: Nationalism or patriotism? An empirical test with representative data. *Political Psychology, 24*, 289–312. doi: 10.1111/0162-895X.00329

Breugelmans, S. M., van de Vijver, F. J. R., & Schalk-Soekar, S. G. S. (2009). Stability of majority attitudes toward multiculturalism in the Netherlands between 1999 and 2007. *Applied Psychology, 58*, 653–671. doi: 10.1111/j.1464-0597.2008.00368.x

Brickman, P., Rabinowitz, V. C., Jurgis, K. J., Coates, D., Cohn, E., & Kidder, L. (1982). Models of helping and coping. *American Psychologist, 37*, 368–384. doi: 10.1037/0003-066X.37.4.368

Britain First. (2015). Retrieved November 28, 2015, from http://www.britainfirst.org/

Card, D., Dustmann, C., & Preston, I. (2005). *Understanding attitudes to immigration: The migration and minority module of the first European social survey* (CReAM Discussion Paper Series No. 0503). Retrieved November 28, 2015, from Centre for Research and Analysis of Migration website: http://www.cream-migration.org/publ_uploads/CDP_03_05.pdf

Constant, A. F., Kahanec, M., & Zimmermann, K. F. (2009). Attitudes towards immigrants, other integration barriers, and their veracity. *International Journal of Manpower, 30*, 5–14. doi: 10.1108/01437720910948357

Cunningham, E., & Platow, M. J. (2007). On helping lower status out-groups: The nature of the help and the stability of the intergroup status hierarchy. *Asian Journal of Social Psychology, 10*, 258–264. doi: 10.1111/j.1467-839X.2007.00234.x

Davies, K., & Aron, A. (2016). Friendship development and intergroup attitudes: The role of interpersonal and intergroup friendship processes. *Journal of Social Issues, 72*, 489–510.

Davidov, E. (2010). Nationalism and constructive patriotism: A longitudinal test of comparability in 22 countries with the ISSP. *International Journal of Public Opinion Research, 23*, 88–103. doi: 10.1093/ijpor/edq031

Dekker, H., Malova, D., & Hoogendoorn, S. (2003). Nationalism and its explanations. *Political Psychology, 24*, 345–376. doi: 10.1111/0162-895X.00331

Dostal, G. M. (2015). The Pegida movement and German political culture: Is right-wing populism here to stay? *The Political Quarterly 86*, 523–531. doi: 10.1111/1467-923X.12204

Dustmann, C., & Frattini, T. (2014). The fiscal effects of immigration to the UK. *Economic Journal, 124*, 593–643. doi: 10.1111/ecoj.12181

Esses, V. M., Dovidio, J. F., Jackson, L. M., & Armstrong, T. L. (2001). The immigration dilemma: The role of perceived group competition, ethnic prejudice, and national identity. *Journal of Social Issues, 57*, 389–412. doi: 10.1111/0022-4537.00220

Facchini, G., & Mayda, A. M. (2012). Individual attitudes towards skilled migration: An empirical analysis across countries. *World Economy, 35*, 183–196. doi: 10.1111/j.1467-9701.2011.01427.x

Feldman, S., & Johnston, C. (2014). Understanding the determinants of political ideology: Implications of structural complexity. *Political Psychology, 35*, 337–358. doi: 10.1111/pops.12055

Fleming, M. (2015, September 22). UNHCR outlines proposal to manage refugee and migration crisis in Europe ahead of EU Summit. Retrieved from http://www.unhcr.org/56015ba86.html

Gaertner, S. L., & Dovidio, J. F. (2000). *Reducing intergroup bias: The common ingroup identity model*. Philadelphia: Psychology Press.

Hainmueller, J., & Hiscox, M. J. (2007). Educated preferences: Explaining attitudes toward immigration in Europe. *International Organization, 61*, 399–442. doi: 10.1017/S0020818307070142

Hainmueller, J., & Hiscox, M. J. (2010). Attitudes toward highly skilled and low-skilled immigration: Evidence from a survey experiment. *American Political Science Review, 104*, 1–24. doi: 10.1017/S0003055409990372

Hainmueller, J., & Hopkins, D. J. (2014). Public attitudes toward immigration. *Annual Review of Political Science, 17*, 225–249. doi: 10.1146/annurev-polisci-102512-194818

Halabi, S., Dovidio, J. F., & Nadler, A. (2008). When and how do high status group members offer help: Effects of social dominance orientation and status threat. *Political Psychology, 29*, 841–858. doi: 10.1111/j.1467-9221.2008.00669.x

Hanson, G. H., Scheve, K., & Slaughter, M. J. (2007). Public finance and individual preferences over globalization strategies. *Economics & Politics, 19*, 1–33. doi: 10.1111/j.1468-0343.2007.00300.x

Hanson, G. H., Scheve, K., & Slaughter, M. J. (2008). Individual preferences over high-skilled immigration in the United States. In J. Bhagwati & G. Hanson (Eds.), *Skilled migration today: Prospects, problems, and policies* (pp. 24–44). New York: Council on Foreign Relations Press.

Hayes, A. F. (2013). *Introduction to mediation, moderation, and conditional process analysis: A regression-based approach*. New York: Guilford Press.

Hughes, R. (1998). Considering the vignette technique and its application to a study of drug injecting and HIV risk and safer behaviour. *Sociology of Health & Illness, 20*, 381–400. doi: 10.1111/1467-9566.00107

Jackson, L. M., & Esses, V. M. (2000). Effects of perceived economic competition on people's willingness to help empower immigrants. *Group Processes and Intergroup Relations, 3*, 419–435. doi: 10.1177/1368430200003004006

Mieriņa, I., & Koroļeva, I. (2015). Support for far right ideology and anti-migrant attitudes among youth in Europe. *Sociological Review, 63*, 183–205. doi: 10.1111/1467-954X.12268

Migration and migrant population statistics. (2015, May). Retrieved from http://ec.europa.eu/eurostat/statistics-explained/index.php/Migration_and_migrant_population_statistics

Montoya, R. M., & Pinter, B. (2016). A model for understanding positive intergroup relations using the ingroup-favoring norm. *Journal of Social Issues, 72*, 584–600.

Nadler, A. (2002). Inter-group helping as power relations: Maintaining or challenging social dominance between groups through helping. *Journal of Social Issues, 58*, 487–502. doi: 10.1111/1540-4560.00272

Nadler, A., Harpaz-Gorodeisky, G., & Ben-David, Y. (2009). Defensive helping: Threat group identity, ingroup identification, status stability, and common group identity as determinants of intergroup help-giving. *Journal of Personality and Social Psychology, 97*, 823–34. doi: 10.1037/a0015968

Navas, M., Garcia, M. C., Sánchez, J., Rojas, A. J., Pumeras, P., & Fernández, J. S. (2005). Relative acculturation extended model (RAEM): New contributions with regard to the study of acculturation. *International Journal of Intercultural Relations, 29*, 21–37. doi: 10.1016/j.ijintrel.2005.04.001

Petratis, P. S., Dunham, A. E., & Niewiarowski, P. H. (1996). Inferring multiple causality: The limitations of path analysis. *Functional Ecology, 10*, 421–431. doi: 10.2307/2389934

Pettigrew, T. F. (1998). Intergroup contact theory. *Annual Review of Psychology, 49*, 65–85. doi: 10.1146/annurev.psych.49.1.65

Raijman, R., Davidov, E., Schmidt, P., & Hochman, O. (2008). What does a nation owe non-citizens? National attachments, perception of threat and attitudes towards granting citizenship rights in a comparative perspective. *International Journal of Comparative Sociology, 49*, 195–220. doi: 10.1177/0020715208088912

Richey, S. (2011). Civic Engagement and patriotism. *Social Science Quarterly, 92*, 1044–1056. doi: 10.1111/j.1540-6237.2011.00803.x

Rohmann, A., Florack, A., & Piontkowski, U. (2006). The role of discordant acculturation attitudes in perceived threat: An analysis of host and immigrant attitudes in Germany. *International Journal of Intercultural Relations, 30*, 683–702. doi: 10.1016/j.ijintrel.2006.06.006

Rosenthal, L., & Levy, S. R. (2016). Endorsement of polyculturalism predicts increased positive intergroup contact and friendship across the beginning of college. *Journal of Social Issues, 72,* 472–488.

Rothi, D. M., Lyons, E., & Chryssochoou, X. (2005). National attachment and patriotism in a European nation: A British study. *Political Psychology, 26,* 135–155. doi: 10.1111/j.1467-9221.2005.00412.x

Schatz, R. T., Staub, E., & Lavine, H. (1999). On the varieties of national attachment: Blind versus constructive patriotism. *Political Psychology, 20,* 151–174. doi: 10.1111/0162-895X.00140

Stephan, W. G., Renfro, C. L., Esses, V. M., Stephan, C. W., & Martin, T. (2005). The effects of feeling threatened on attitudes toward immigrants. *International Journal of Intercultural Relations, 29,* 1–19. doi: 10.1016/j.ijintrel.2005.04.011

Stephan, W. G., & Mealy, M. D. (2011). Intergroup threat theory. In T. Nelson (Ed.), *The encyclopedia of peace psychology* (pp. 309–332). Oxford, UK: Blackwell Publishing Ltd. doi: 10.1002/9780470672532.wbepp139

Tajfel, H., & Turner, J. C. (1979). An integrative theory of intergroup conflict. In W. G. Austin & S. Worchel (Eds.), *The social psychology of intergroup relations* (pp. 33–47). Monterey, CA: Brooks-Cole.

Tsuda, T. (1999). The motivation to migrate: The ethnic and sociocultural constitution of the Japanese-Brazilian return-migration system. *Economic Development and Cultural Change, 48,* 1–31. doi: 10.1086/452444

Verkuyten, M., & Martinovic, B. (2006). Understanding multicultural attitudes: The role of groups status, identification, friendship, and justifying ideologies. *International Journal of Intercultural Relations, 30,* 1–18. doi: 10.1016/j.ijintrel.2005.05.015

Zimmermann, K. F. (2007). The economic of migrant ethnicity. *Journal of Population Economics, 20,* 487–494. doi: 10.1007/s00148-007-0155-6

OMAR K. BURHAN completed his MSc in Social Psychology at the VU University Amsterdam, the Netherlands, in 2011. He then worked at the University of Sumatera Utara from 2011 to 2015. As of 2015, he is pursuing his PhD at Leiden University, the Netherlands, for which he received an Indonesian Endowment Fund. He has also been affiliated with Medan Area University, Indonesia, since 2013.

ESTHER VAN LEEUWEN is an Assistant Professor in social and organizational psychology at Leiden University, the Netherlands. She completed her PhD, in which she investigated group-based reactions to mergers, at that same university in 2001. Since then, she has worked at the department of social and organizational psychology of VU University Amsterdam, the Netherlands, until 2014. Her current research interests are in the field of positive intergroup relations, with an emphasis on intergroup helping. Combining experimental laboratory research with field studies, she has investigated a range of factors that can affect the willingness to help, or to seek help from, members of another group.

*Journal of Social Issues, Vol. 72, No. 3, 2016, pp. 566–583*
doi: 10.1111/josi.12182

# The Power to be Moral: Affirming Israelis' and Palestinians' Agency Promotes Prosocial Tendencies across Group Boundaries

**Ilanit SimanTov-Nachlieli and Nurit Shnabel**[*]
*Tel-Aviv University*

**Samer Halabi**
*Tel-Aviv-Yaffo Academic College*

*Based on recent extensions of the needs-based model of reconciliation, we argue that in conflicts characterized by mutual transgressions, such as the Israeli–Palestinian conflict, group members prioritize their agency-related over morality-related needs. Optimistically, however, two studies conducted among Israeli Jews (Study 1) and West Bank Palestinians (Study 2) found that addressing group members' pressing need for agency by affirming their in-group's strength, competence, and self-determination brought their moral considerations to the fore, leading to stronger prosocial tendencies across group boundaries. These studies suggest that group members need to feel secure and agentic in order to allow their otherwise unprioritized moral needs to come into play. Practically, our insights regarding the positive effects of agency affirmation can be used in the planning of interventions by dialog group facilitators, mediators, or group leaders who wish to encourage members to relinquish some power in order to exhibit greater morality toward their out-group.*

One of the main messages of the present volume is that due to the widespread conception of groups as inherently "tribal" (Hawkins, 1997), as well as the influence of historical events such as the Second World War, the traditional focus of social psychological theorizing and research has been on negative intergroup processes, while positive intergroup processes remained relatively overlooked (Siem,

---

[*]Correspondence concerning this article should be addressed to Nurit Shnabel, School of Psychological Sciences, Tel-Aviv University, Ramat Aviv, Tel-Aviv 69978, Israel. [e-mail: shnabeln@post.tau.ac.il].

Ilanit SimanTov-Nachlieli and Nurit Shnabel made equal contribution to this paper.

Stürmer, & Pittinsky, 2016). Also evident in related disciplines such as anthropology (Fry, 2006), this predominantly negative view of intergroup relations has overshadowed key processes such as attraction and curiosity for foreign cultures, as well as intergroup helping and cooperation (Siem et al., 2016; Tropp & Mallett, 2011).

One of the resulting lacunae has to do with the role of morality in intergroup relations (Leach, Ellemers, & Barreto, 2007). Indeed, prominent social psychological theories designed to provide a general framework for understanding intergroup relations, including social dominance theory (Sidanius & Pratto, 1999), group position theory (Blumer, 1958), and realistic group conflict theory (LeVine & Campbell, 1972), have stressed groups' competition over status, dominance, power, and control over valued resources at the expense of groups' need for morality. Even when this theorizing did acknowledge groups' moral motives and behavior, these have often been viewed as subservient to the need for power and dominance rather than reflecting an authentic motivation. For example, Saguy, Dovidio, and Pratto (2008) found that in a situation of intergroup contact between Ashkenazi and Mizrahi Jews, Ashkenazi Jews (representing the advantaged group) preferred to talk about the commonalities rather than the differences between the groups. This preference was interpreted as a strategic attempt to obscure group-based power inequality by fostering a false sense of harmony. However, an alternative explanation—that Ashkenazi Jews' preference reflected a genuine wish to behave in a communal way toward the Mizrahi group—has not been examined (see Shnabel & Ullrich, 2013, for a discussion of this research).

This relative deemphasizing of group members' authentic need for morality may be partially responsible for these theories' failure to satisfactorily account for the phenomenon of "solidarity-based collective action" (Becker, 2012), namely, advantaged group members' readiness to act to promote the just cause of other groups, even at the expense of their own group's power and privilege (e.g., Harth, Kessler, & Leach, 2008). A striking illustration of this possibility is the growing recognition of animal rights (e.g., Singer, 1975) and related legislation.

Arguably, group members have a genuine need for morality, with evolutionary roots in nonhuman primates (de Waal, 2006), which is not just of disguising their "real" motivation for power. In line with this argument, Leach et al. (2007) demonstrated in a series of studies that morality was perceived by group members as the most important dimension of their in-group's identity—essential to their pride in and psychological distance from or closeness to it. They concluded that "recognizing the importance of morality to in-group membership may be an important first step toward understanding its importance in intergroup relations" (Leach et al. 2007, p. 248).

The needs-based model of reconciliation (Nadler & Shnabel, 2008), the theoretical framework that guides the present research, integrates Leach et al.'s (2007) theorizing with the more traditional social psychological emphasis on power-related needs. Our framework suggests that group members have both morality- and power-related needs. Yet, the degree to which each of these needs influences group members' tendency to behave prosocially across group boundaries is determined by their in-group's role (victim vs. perpetrator) within the given social context. We now turn to a detailed review of this model, which seeks to explain the dynamics between conflicting groups.

## The Needs-Based Model of Reconciliation: An Overview

The "Big Two" theory (Abele & Wojciszke, 2013) suggests that there are two fundamental content dimensions along which group members perceive their own and other groups: the *agency* dimension, representing traits such as power, competence, influence, and self-determination; and the *moral–social* dimension (also called the communion dimension), representing traits such as morality, warmth, and trustworthiness (see also Fiske, Cuddy, & Click, 2007). Building on this theorizing, the needs-based model argues that transgressions cause asymmetric threats to the identities of victim and perpetrator groups (SimanTov-Nachlieli, Shnabel, & Nadler, 2013). Victims, who feel inferior in terms of power, control, and honor (Scheff, 1994), experience threat to their agentic identity. In contrast, perpetrators experience threat to their moral identity, and are concerned with being excluded by other groups due to their breaching of common moral standards (Tavuchis, 1991).

Importantly, based on the argument that when a given in-group–out-group distinction is salient, people define themselves in terms of prototypical attributes of their in-group rather than in terms of their individual characteristics (Turner, Hogg, Oakes, Reicher, & Wetherell, 1987), group members may experience these identity threats due to historical or contemporary events in which their in-group has been involved, regardless of their personal involvement. For example, U.S. Americans may experience threat to the agency dimension of their identity when reminded of 9/11, and threat to the morality dimension when reminded of Hiroshima—even if they had no personal role in these events.

The needs-based model further posits that because group members wish to maintain their in-group's positive identity (Tajfel & Turner, 1986), experiencing identity threats brings about different motivational states among members of victim and perpetrator groups. Victims experience a need to restore their sense of agency (i.e., respect and ability to determine their outcomes). Consequently, they often exhibit heightened power-seeking behavior (Foster & Rusbult, 1999) and even take vengeance as a means to restore status and agency (Frijda, 1994). Perpetrators, by contrast, experience the need to restore their positive moral identity and regain acceptance in the community from which they feel potentially excluded due to their wrongdoings. Sometimes, perpetrators cope with their culpability through moral disengagement (i.e., minimizing the severity of the harm done or blaming the victims for bringing it upon themselves; Bandura, 1990). Yet, perpetrators' need to gain moral–social acceptance may also lead them to seek forgiveness (Shnabel & Nadler, 2008) and show heightened helping behavior toward others, including their victims (Dovidio, Piliavin, Schroeder, & Penner, 2006).

Finally, the needs-based model argues that restoring the agentic and moral identities of victim and perpetrator groups may address these group members' unmet needs and thus open them for reconciliation. Supporting this argument, a message from Jewish representatives that conveyed moral acceptance toward Germans at the opening of the Berlin Holocaust memorial was found to increase German participants' readiness to reconcile with the Jews, whereas a message from German representatives that conveyed empowerment toward Jews (e.g., acknowledgment of their right for self-determination) increased Jewish participants' readiness to reconcile with Germans. Positive messages that failed to address group members' specific identity-related needs (i.e., an empowering message for Germans, or a message conveying moral–social acceptance for Jews) were relatively ineffective in promoting conciliatory tendencies (Shnabel, Nadler, Ullrich, Dovidio, & Carmi, 2009).

While the German–Jewish relations represent a context in which the roles of victims and perpetrators are clear-cut, many conflicts, including the Israeli–Palestinian conflict, are characterized by mutual transgressions (Bar-Tal, 2013), even if not on the same scales. A recent research that explored conflicts characterized by such blurred, "dual" social roles (SimanTov-Nachlieli & Shnabel, 2014) revealed that when Israeli Jews were reminded of incidents in which their in-group was victimized by Palestinians, they experienced enhanced motivation to restore their in-group's agency (expressing greater wish for a "strong Israel") and showed less prosocial tendencies toward Palestinians (e.g., willingness to provide humanitarian aid to Gaza). When they were reminded of incidents in which their in-group victimized Palestinians, on the other hand, they experienced enhanced motivation to restore their in-group's moral identity (expressing greater wish for a "moral Israel") and showed more prosocial tendencies. When reminded of incidents of both victimization and perpetration, Israeli Jews experienced heightened needs for both agency and morality; in terms of behavior, however, they exhibited reduced prosocial tendencies, resembling participants in the victim rather than the perpetrator condition.

This finding, which was replicated in other contexts (see SimanTov-Nachlieli & Shnabel, 2014), suggests that in conflicts characterized by mutual transgressions, group members' agency-related needs exert more influence on their ultimate behavior than their morality-related needs. Nevertheless, this should not be viewed as contradicting Leach et al.'s (2007) theorizing regarding the role of moral motivations. Rather, consistent with the logic of Maslow's (1943) classical model of human needs, we theorized that once conflicting group members' pressing need for agency is addressed through an affirmation of their in-group's agency, their morality-related needs would come to fore and exert greater influence on their behavior. This hypothesis is consistent with findings that individuals who enjoyed greater agency exhibited less aggressive behavior following transgressions (Warburton, Williams, & Cairns, 2006). It is also consistent with findings that the experience of power predicted more altruistic behavior when one's care for moral issues (i.e., "moral identity") was strong (DeCelles, DeRue, Margolis, & Ceranic, 2012)—as is the case in dual conflicts in which group members wish to restore their in-group's moral identity (SimanTov-Nachlieli & Shnabel, 2014). The present research tested this theorizing in the context of the dual Israeli–Palestinian conflict.

## The Present Research

Despite the extreme power asymmetry between Israeli Jews and Palestinians (e.g., Palestinians are subjected to Israeli occupation in the West Bank), the conflict between these groups may be viewed as dual because both sides have transgressed against each other and often compete over the status of the conflict's "real" victim (Shnabel & Noor, 2012). While this duality leads Palestinians and Israelis to experience the needs to restore both their agency and morality (Shnabel, Halabi, & Noor, 2013), addressing one need comes, or is perceived to come, at the expense of the other. To illustrate, Israel's attacks on Gaza may prove its power superiority but impair its moral identity, whereas restraint may bolster Israel's morality but be viewed as eroding its strength and deterrence; a similar "damned if you do, damned if you don't" catch characterizes the Palestinians' (in)actions.

Tragically, because the conflict poses an acute threat to Palestinians' and Israeli Jews' security (Bar-Tal, 2013), they often feel entitled to behave aggressively toward each other (Klar, Schori-Eyal, & Klar, 2013). However, we theorized that Israelis and Palestinians are relatively inattentive to moral considerations not because they simply do not at all care about being moral toward the out-group (i.e., perceive it to be outside the "scope of justice"; Clayton & Opotow, 2003), but rather because they are preoccupied with their agency-related need to feel that their in-group is a powerful social actor able to control its outcomes. In line with this reasoning, the present research tested the hypothesis that addressing Israelis' (Study 1) and Palestinians' (Study 2) pressing need for agency by reminding them of their in-group's strength, competence, and resilience would increase their willingness to relinquish the misuse of power for the sake of moral considerations, leading to prosocial behavior across group boundaries.

Our theorizing was based on Sherman, Kinias, Major, Kim, and Prenovost's (2007) research, which extended self-affirmation theory (Cohen & Sherman, 2014; Steele, 1988) to the group level. Sherman et al. (2007) demonstrated that the negative effects of identity threat on group members' motivation, attitudes, and behavior may be alleviated by affirming the positive aspects of their in-group's identity

(see also Derks, Scheepers, Van Laar, & Ellemers, 2011; Gunn & Wilson, 2011).
Building on this research, as well as on findings that such affirmations effectively
promote prosocial tendencies in conflict contexts only if they focus on the *specific*
identity dimension impaired due to the transgression (Woodyatt & Wenzel, 2014),
we developed an *agency affirmation*. This affirmation exposed group members
to short texts that highlight their in-group's agentic identity, namely, its strength,
competence, resilience, and control over outcomes. We predicted that Israelis and
Palestinians whose in-group's agency was affirmed would show greater willingness to relinquish the use of power for the sake of moral considerations, and that
this, in turn, would lead to greater prosocial tendencies across group boundaries.

In addition, we tested the effect of a *moral threat* manipulation on Israeli
Jews' and Palestinians' mutual prosocial tendencies. Based on previous findings
suggesting that group members view morality as the most important dimension
in their in-group's identity (Leach et al., 2007) and may respond to threats to
their in-group's morality by increased helping tendencies (Dovidio et al., 2006),
such a threat could be assumed to increase Israelis' and Palestinians prosociality.
An alternative prediction, however, was that the exposure to moral threat would
fail to affect Israelis' and Palestinians prosociality because the experience of
such threat (e.g., boycott initiatives against one's in-group due to its immoral
acts; condemnations of terror attacks) becomes chronic in intractable conflicts
(Bar-Tal, 2013). As conflicting group members become inured to such threats
(Bleich, Gelkopf, & Solomon, 2003), they might become unresponsive and resort
to their "habituated course of action" (Bar-Tal, 2001, p. 620) even in response
to new inputs. This habituated response to moral threats was illustrated in a
speech by Israeli Prime Minister Binyamin Netanyahu: "There is a new campaign
against us ... but this is not new. Boycott campaigns against Jews have always
existed" ("Netanyahu: Boycott campaign is anti-Semitic," 2014). We therefore had
a bidirectional prediction pertaining to the effect of moral threat on prosociality.
Importantly, finding that agency affirmation—but not moral threat—increased
prosociality would support our theorizing regarding the need to address conflicting
groups' pressing need for agency before their moral needs can come into play.

## Study 1

Israeli Jewish participants were randomly assigned to one of four experimental
conditions using a 2 (moral threat [yes, no]) × 2 (agency-affirmation [yes, no])
between-subjects design. Following the experimental manipulation, participants
reported their readiness to relinquish power for the sake of moral considerations,
as well as their prosocial tendencies toward Palestinians. While we expected the
main effect of moral threat (to which group members may have become habituated)
to be either positive or null, we predicted a positive main effect for the agency-
affirmation condition, such that agency affirmation would increase participants'

willingness to relinquish power for the sake of moral considerations, which would, in turn, increase their prosocial tendencies toward Palestinians.

*Method*

*Participants.*     One-hundred-and-seven Israeli Jewish students registered in the subject pool of a large Israeli university. To avoid disproportionate influence of outlying observations (McClelland, 2000), three outliers (with studentized residuals > 2.5) were excluded. Hence, the final sample included 104 participants (71 women, $M_{age} = 25.35$, $SD = 3.19$; 35.7% rightists, 35.5% leftists, 28.8% centrists).

*Materials and procedure.*     In response to online materials, the participants provided demographic information including political orientation (1 = *radically rightist* to 7 = *radically leftist*) and were then randomly assigned to one of four conditions. Participants assigned to the agency-affirmation condition read a text that affirmed Israel's agency (see Derks et al., 2011, for group affirmation through the reading of short texts):

> Israel is considered one of the strongest nations in the world. [ . . . ] Israel's military industries develop advanced technologies that contribute to its security, strength and resilience. [ . . . ] It ranks first in terms of economic viability and crisis resilience, and in investment in research and development. Seven Israelis have won the Nobel Prize for their contributions to humanity, and Israeli medical and agricultural developments are a source of pride and strength [ . . . ].

In the moral-threat condition, participants were exposed to a text challenging Israel's morality:

> Every nation needs a moral compass that will guide its actions. [ . . . ] Israel must act ethically toward the Palestinians, otherwise we might find ourselves denying who we are and crumbling from the inside because of the loss of faith in our righteousness, as well as outcast from the outside. [ . . . ] While in the past Israel had been perceived as moral, since the 80s (the First Intifada) this image was greatly tarnished [ . . . ].

The agency-affirmation-and-moral-threat condition combined both texts, whereas the control condition included none.

We next administered the dependent measures, which used a seven-point Likert scales (1 = *not at all* to 7 = *very much*). Following manipulation checks confirming text comprehension, participants indicated their agreement with two items measuring their willingness to relinquish power for morality (e.g., "Israel must give up its power superiority in order to be just and fair with the Palestinians," $r(104) = .59$, $p < .001$). The purpose of these items was to capture participants' actual readiness to make sacrifices in terms of power superiority out of moral considerations (rather than for other reasons, such as the ineffectiveness of using power). Finally, six items measured participants' prosocial behavioral tendencies

**Table 1.** Covariate Corrected Means and Standard Errors (in Parentheses) for Studies 1 and 2

| | No affirmation | | Agency affirmation | |
|---|---|---|---|---|
| | No threat | Moral threat | No threat | Moral threat |
| Study 1 (Israeli Jews) | ($n = 28$) | ($n = 25$) | ($n = 26$) | ($n = 25$) |
| Prosocial tendencies | 4.07a (.173) | 4.17a (.182) | 4.41ab (.180) | 4.62b (.182) |
| Relinquish power for morality | 3.11a (.226) | 3.06a (.238) | 3.33ab (.235) | 3.81b (.238) |
| | No affirmation | | Agency affirmation | |
| | No threat | Moral threat | No threat | Moral threat |
| Study 2 (West Bank Palestinians) | ($n = 17$) | ($n = 14$) | ($n = 17$) | ($n = 12$) |
| Prosocial tendencies | 4.47a (.301) | 4.70a (.331) | 5.13a (.301) | 5.25a (.358) |
| Relinquish power for morality | 3.35a (.449) | 3.89ab (.495) | 4.44b (.449) | 4.21ab (.535) |

toward Palestinians (e.g., "Israel must provide humanitarian aid to Gaza"; "Israel must invest substantial financial resources for the betterment of the Palestinians"; $\alpha = .83$). Upon completion, participants were thanked and debriefed.

*Results*

Given the strong association between political orientation and behavioral tendencies toward Palestinians (a leftist orientation significantly increased prosociality, $p < .001$), we controlled for political orientation in all analyses reported below. This allowed us to isolate the experimental conditions' unique effect on prosocial tendencies. Means and standard errors of the dependent variables are presented in the upper part of Table 1.

A two-way ANOVA revealed the predicted main effect of agency affirmation: affirmed participants showed greater prosociality, $F(1,99) = 4.80, p = .031, \eta_p^2 = .046$. The main effect of moral threat was nonsignificant, $F(1,99) = 0.79, p = .376, \eta_p^2 = .008$, as was the two-way interaction, $F(1,99) = 0.09, p = .761, \eta_p^2 = .001$. An additional ANCOVA revealed that affirmed participants showed greater willingness to relinquish power for morality, $F(1,99) = 4.25, p = .042, \eta_p^2 = .041$. Again, the main effect of moral threat was nonsignificant, $F(1,99) = 0.89, p = .348, \eta_p^2 = .009$, as was the interaction, $F(1,99) = 1.25, p = .267, \eta_p^2 = .012$. Figure 1 presents the results of a bootstrapping mediation analysis (1,000 resamples): as predicted, the indirect effect of agency affirmation on prosociality through willingness to relinquish power for morality was significant, $b = .05, SE = .03, 95\%$ CI [0.005, 0.147].

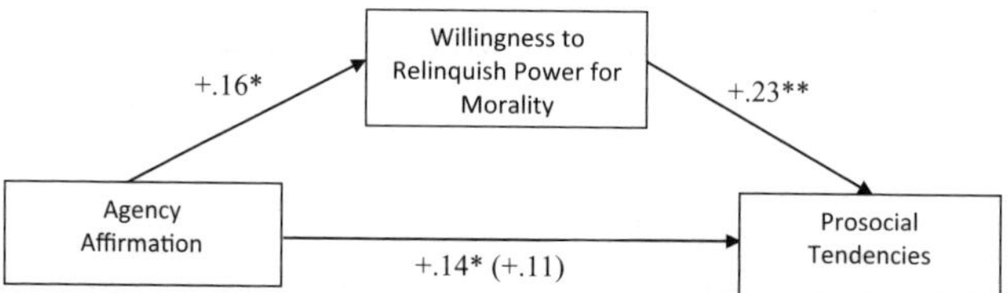


**Fig. 1.** Mediation model with agency-affirmation (i.e., the experimental manipulation, coded such that: 0 = no affirmation, 1 = agency affirmation) as the independent variable, relinquish-power-for-morality as the mediator, and prosocial tendencies as the dependent variable (Study 1). Standardized regression coefficients (betas) are presented. For the path between agency affirmation and prosocial tendencies, the coefficients outside and inside parentheses represent total and direct effects, respectively. Coefficients with one or two asterisks indicate beta weights significance level of $p < .05$ or $p < .01$, respectively. The indirect effect was significant (see Study 1's Results).

## *Discussion*

Study 1 revealed a positive effect of agency affirmation on Israeli Jews' prosocial tendencies toward Palestinians. Moreover, in line with our theorizing, this effect was mediated by increased readiness to give up some power out of moral considerations. In addition, consistent with previous theorizing that parties involved in an intractable conflict become habituated to moral threats (Bar-Tal, 2013), our threat manipulation failed to promote prosociality. As always with null effects, this failure might stem from various methodological limitations, such as lack of sufficient statistical power or the manipulation's weakness. For example, perhaps, extreme moral threats (e.g., images in which in-group members torture out-group members, as in the Abu-Ghraib photos) would have led to stronger prosocial tendencies even in the absence of agency affirmation. Thus, while our findings should not necessarily be interpreted as proving the ineffectiveness of moral threats, they should be viewed as demonstrating the effectiveness of agency affirmation in increasing Israeli Jews' prosociality toward Palestinians.

## Study 2

Although Study 1 supported our hypothesis, it was important to show that its results did not stem from the unique status of Israelis as the stronger party in the conflict. Therefore, Study 2 was designed to test our theorizing among Palestinians who, as the weaker party, might be less susceptible to agency affirmation. Moreover, because Palestinians are often perceived as the victim group—a social role associated with superior morality (Shnabel & Noor, 2012)—they may experience a comparatively less pressing need to restore their moral identity. Thus, even if their agency is successfully affirmed, they might fail to respond by increasing their attentiveness to moral considerations as in the Israeli group.

Demonstrating the effectiveness of agency affirmation among Palestinians was also important for establishing that the increase in prosociality following such affirmation reflects group members' genuine moral considerations, rather than impression management concerns. Specifically, members of dominant groups sometimes help their out-group strategically, as a means to boost their image as kind and moral while at the same time reasserting their dominance (Nadler, Halabi, & Harpaz-Gorodeisky, 2009). If so, it is possible that the heightened prosociality observed among affirmed Israeli Jews in Study 1 reflected a "noblesse oblige" response, whose real purpose was to reassert their superiority. This possibility, however, would not account for an increase in prosociality among Palestinians who were never dominant to begin with.

*Method*

*Participants.* Sixty-one Palestinian students from the West Bank were recruited to participate in an online study in exchange for payment. One outlier (studentized residuals > 2.5) was excluded. Hence, the final sample included 60 participants (24 women, $M_{age} = 24.66$, $SD = 4.45$; 73.4% were religious, 6.7% secular, 16.7% neutral, and 3.2% have not indicated their religiosity).

*Materials and procedure.* The design and procedure were identical to Study 1; materials and measures were translated to Arabic and adjusted to the Palestinian context. Participants were randomly assigned to the four experimental conditions. The text in the agency-affirmation condition affirmed the Palestinians' strength, self-determination, and resilience:

> The Palestinian people are known worldwide for resiliency and inner strength. The Palestinian nation is strong and cohesive, standing firm in the face of many challenges. The Palestinian economy is on the rise. [ ... ] Palestinians have growing intellectual and cultural influence, as the number of Palestinian intellectuals, athletes, lecturers and scientists in universities gradually increases [ ... ].

The text in the moral-threat condition read:

> Every nation needs a moral compass that will guide its actions. Despite the occupation and oppression the Palestinians must act ethically toward the Israelis, otherwise we might find ourselves denying who we are and crumbling from the inside because of the loss of faith in the legitimacy of the struggle, as well as outcast from the outside. [ ... ] While in the past the Palestinian people had been perceived as moral, since the 2000s (the Second Intifada) this image was greatly tarnished [ ... ].

The agency-affirmation-and-moral-threat condition combined both texts, whereas the control condition included none. Following the manipulation checks for text comprehension, two items measured participants' willingness to give up the misuse of power out of moral considerations (e.g., ""Even at the cost of relinquishing the use of force, the Palestinian people must act morally toward the

Jews," $r(60) = .56, p < .001$). Six items measured participants' prosociality (e.g., "Palestinians should not hesitate to provide logistical support to Israel in cases of natural disasters such as the Mount Carmel fire"; "The Palestinian Authority must help Israel in environmental projects such as waste and sewage treatment," $\alpha = .74$).[1] Upon completion, participants were thanked and debriefed.

*Results and Discussion*

Means and standard errors are presented in the lower part of Table 1. A two-way ANOVA revealed a marginally significant agency-affirmation effect on prosociality, such that affirmed Palestinians tended to exhibit greater prosocial tendencies, $F(1,56) = 3.47$, $p = .062$, $\eta_p^2 = .060$.[2] The effect of moral threat, $F(1,56) = 0.30$, $p = .582$, $\eta_p^2 = .005$, and the two-way interaction, $F(1,56) = 0.03$, $p = .867$, $\eta_p^2 < .001$, were nonsignificant. The effect of agency affirmation on willingness to relinquish power for morality was in the expected direction, yet failed to reach significance, $F(1,56) = 2.11, p = .121, \eta_p^2 = .036$. The effect of moral threat, $F(1,56) = 0.10, p = .732, \eta_p^2 = .002$, and the two-way interaction, $F(1,56) = 0.64, p = .427, \eta_p^2 = .011$, were nonsignificant. Figure 2 presents the results of a bootstrapping (1,000 resamples) mediation analysis. Importantly, the indirect effect of agency affirmation on prosociality through relinquish-power-for-morality was significant, $b = .10$, $SE = .08$, 95% CI [0.004, 0.317]. These findings demonstrate the generalizability of the effectiveness of agency affirmation across two groups who face substantially different circumstances.

## General Discussion

Two studies demonstrated that whereas moral threats did not influence participants' prosocial tendencies, the affirmation of Israeli Jews' (Study 1) and

---

[1] Due to the power asymmetry between Israelis and Palestinians, we used different items to measure the two dependent variables in the two groups (e.g., it made no sense to ask Palestinians about their willingness to provide humanitarian aid to Israel). Despite the difference in operationalization, the dependent measures for both groups were conceptually similar.

[2] The marginality of the total agency-affirmation effect on prosociality may be due to the small sample size, which interferes with the ability to replicate results across studies (Schimmack, 2012). We could not proceed with data collection due to a dramatic exacerbation of the conflict, which was expected to critically affect participants' response set. One approach to boost statistical power (see Schimmack, 2012) was to collapse the data across Studies 1 and 2 ($N = 164$). When the two studies were entered into a single analysis, a clear pattern supporting our hypotheses emerged, such that the main effect of agency affirmation on both prosociality, $F(1,156) = 6.55$, $p = .011$, $\eta_p^2 = .040$, and readiness to relinquish power for morality, $F(1,156) = 5.77$, $p = .017$, $\eta_p^2 = .036$, was significant, as was the indirect effect of agency affirmation on prosociality through readiness to relinquish power for morality, $b = .13, SE = .06$, 95% CI [.026, .253].

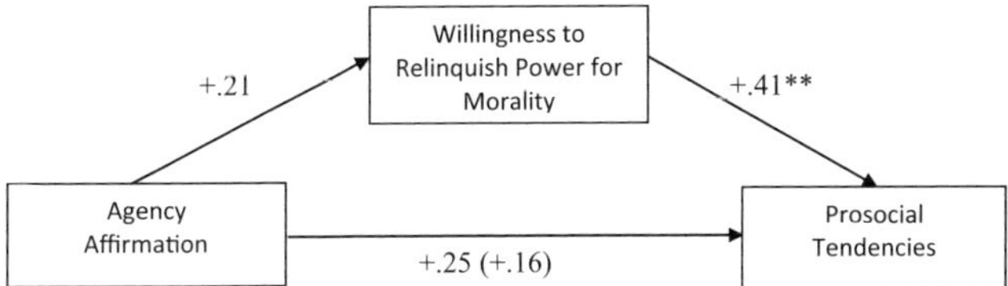


**Fig. 2.** Mediation model with agency affirmation (i.e., the experimental manipulation, coded such that: 0 = no affirmation, 1 = agency affirmation) as the independent variable, relinquish-power-for-morality as the mediator, and prosocial tendencies as the dependent variable (Study 2). Standardized regression coefficients (betas) are presented. For the path between agency affirmation and prosocial tendencies, the coefficients shown outside and inside parentheses represent total and direct effects, respectively. Coefficients with two asterisks indicate beta weights significance level of $p < .001$. Note that the current approach to mediation (e.g., Preacher & Hayes, 2004) argues that a significance test of the product term $a*b$ ($a$ denoting the path from the independent variable to the mediator, and $b$ denoting the path from the mediator to the dependent variable) addresses mediation more directly than the series of separate significance tests proposed by Baron and Kenny (1986), which increase the risk of Type II error. That is, rejecting the null hypothesis that $a*b = 0$ is sufficient for establishing mediation, even when paths $a$ and/or $c$ (denoting the path from the independent variable to the dependent variable) are not significant (see also MacKinnon, 2000 and Shrout & Bolger, 2002 for the argument that a significant total effect is not necessary for mediation to occur). Therefore, the significant indirect effect found in Study 2 is sufficient to establish mediation, even though the effect of agency affirmation on willingness to relinquish power and prosocial tendencies failed to reach significance—likely due to lack of sufficient statistical power (see Footnote 2).

Palestinians' (Study 2) in-group agency allowed their morality-related needs and considerations to come to fore, leading to stronger mutual prosocial tendencies. The conclusion derived from these studies—that group members need to feel secure and agentic before their morality-related needs can come to the fore—is consistent with the finding of Burhan and van Leeuwen (2016) that the removal of perceived threat is a prerequisite for fostering support and hospitality toward immigrants among host society members. Our conclusion is also consistent with Leach et al.'s (2007) argument that in its emphasis on power-related needs in intergroup relations, traditional social psychological theorizing has overlooked the importance of morality. As mentioned in the Introduction, Leach and colleagues have urged social psychologists to explore the role of morality in intergroup relations. Consistent with this call, the present research aimed to reach a better understanding of the conditions under which group members' moral needs can be mobilized to promote positive intergroup relations, even in the context of an intractable conflict.

From a broader theoretical perspective, the current research extends the existing research on intergroup helping, which has typically focused on factors located either in the nature of relations between groups that provide and receive help, or in the help recipients' identity as perceived by help providers. To illustrate the former, the intergroup-helping-as-status relations model (e.g., Nadler & Halabi, 2015) has examined how the security of the status relations between groups (the extent to which group disparity is perceived as stable and legitimate; Tajfel & Turner, 1986) affects the type of help (autonomy- vs. dependency-oriented) in-group members choose to offer to or are willing to accept from out-group members. As for the latter, Lotz-Schmitt, Siem, and Stürmer (2015) examined how group members' prosocial behavior toward an out-group member in need is influenced by evaluations of his or her trustworthiness, competence, and sociability. The contribution of the present work lies in underscoring the importance of *internal processes of identity restoration* among help providers. Our work suggests that regardless of the out-group's characteristics (e.g., the extent to which its members are perceived as trustworthy) or the nature of relations with it (e.g., the extent to which intergroup hierarchy is perceived as stable), the extent to which group members perceive their *own identity* to be secure critically affects their prosocial tendencies.

Our findings have also major practical implications. First, the insights about the positive effects of agency affirmation can be used in the planning of interventions such as dialog groups (i.e., encounters between members of conflicting groups in educational settings), designed to open adversarial groups to reconciliation. Existing interventions often stress the importance of empathy. For example, interventions based on the contact hypothesis (see Davies & Aron, 2016; Paolini, Wright, Dys-Steenbergen, & Favara, 2016) encourage cross-group friendship because they promote outcomes such as empathy, warmth, and positive regard for the out-group (see the outcome variables examined by Davies & Aron, 2016). Also, Pittinsky and Montoya (2016) pointed to the potential role of empathic joy experienced as the result of taking the out-group members' perspective in promoting positive intergroup relations; and Maoz and Bar-On (2002) developed the to reflect and trust (TRT) intervention highlighting mutual recognition of suffering (empathic sorrow) among members of conflicting groups such as Jews and Germans. Without detracting from the importance of empathy, we argue that interventions that focus exclusively on the facilitation of empathic joy or sorrow might leave the conflicting group members' pressing need for agency unmet. Hence, their empathy and moral concern toward the out-group, even if successfully increased due to the intervention, could fail to translate into prosociality. Thus, existing interventions may benefit from affirming the agency of participants' in-group as a central or at least additional aspect in their programs.

In addition, expressions of empathy and recognition of suffering are effective in bringing about reconciliation only when offered by representatives of the conflicting out-group (Harth & Shnabel, 2015), whereas the agency-affirmation intervention does not require such direct dialog between the conflicting groups. This is an important advantage because direct intergroup communication is often difficult to achieve in contexts of intractable conflicts (Bar-Tal, 2013). Thus, agency affirmation can be a useful tool for mediators who try to convince group leaders to promote conflict resolution and peace. Affirming their in-group's agency can also be used by the group leaders themselves, if they seek to encourage their groups to relinquish control, influence, strength, or dominance for the sake of being fair and moral toward their out-group.

Agency affirmation can also be implemented in restorative justice procedures—practices that focus on rectifying relationships damaged by violent transgressions, rather than on punishing the perpetrators (Wachtel & McCold, 2001) and may include structured encounters between the victims and the perpetrators and the latter's involvement in determining, or at least influencing, the appropriate punishment and/or compensation. These practices are used in international peacemaking tribunals such as the South African Truth and Reconciliation Commission (TRC) as well as in the criminal justice system, schools, social services, and communities (Boyes-Watson, 2008). Our findings suggest that empowering and affirming the victims' agency as part of these procedures may, at least to some extent, provide them with "the power to forgive" and thus contribute to their success.

Despite its potential implications, the current research is not without limitations. One methodological limitation is that participants in the four conditions were exposed to different lengths of text. Another limitation is that the outcome variables were self-reported measures, rather than actual behavior such as peace activism. An even more critical limitation is that an implicit assumption that underlies our work is that group members perceive out-group members as entitled to (at least) basic human rights. However, in contexts of mass, violence members of the conflicting out-group are often subjected to "moral exclusion and dehumanization," as they are perceived to be "outside the scope of justice, barred from the protections of community membership" (Janoff-Bulman & Werther, 2008, p. 148; see also Clayton & Opotow, 2003, and Wenzel, 2000, for the link between categorization processes and perceptions of justice and morality). In such contexts, bringing morality to the fore—the process facilitated by the agency affirmation—cannot be expected to promote prosocial tendencies toward the conflicting out-group. On the contrary, behaving prosocially toward the out group might be interpreted as immoral (e.g., as betrayal of the in-group). If so, perhaps, among extremely radical group members who exclude out-group members from "the scope of justice," agency affirmation would lead to increased *antisocial* tendencies toward the out-group. This possibility should be examined in the future research.

Bearing in mind the bounding conditions of our conclusions, the present research found positive effects for agency affirmation, among both Jews and Palestinians. Based on these findings, and in the spirit of this special issue, we propose that even in the context of a prolonged and hopelessly intractable conflict characterized by cycles of mutual violence, addressing conflicting groups' need for agency has the potential of stopping the downward spiral of aggression (Staub, 2003) and foster prosocial behavior across group boundaries.

# References


Abele, A. E., & Wojciszke, B. (2013). The Big Two in social judgment and behavior. *Social Psychology*, *44*, 61–62. doi: 10.1027/1864-9335/a000137

Bandura, A. (1990). Selective activation and disengagement of moral control. *Journal of Social Issues*, *46*, 27–46. doi: 10.1111/j.1540-4560.1990.tb00270.x

Baron, R. M., & Kenny, D. A. (1986). The moderator-mediator variable distinction in social psychological research: Conceptual, strategic, and statistical considerations. *Journal of Personality and Social Psychology*, *51*, 1173–1182. doi: 10.1037/0022-3514.51.6.1173

Bar-Tal, D. (2001). Why does fear override hope in societies engulfed by intractable conflict, as it does in the Israeli society? *Political Psychology*, *22*, 601–627. doi: 10.1111/0162-895X.00255

Bar-Tal, D. (2013). *Intractable conflicts: Psychological foundations and dynamics*. Cambridge, England: Cambridge University Press.

Becker, J. C. (2012). Virtual special issue on theory and research on collective action in the European Journal of Social Psychology. *European Journal of Social Psychology*, *42*, 19–23. doi: 10.1002/ejsp.1839

Bleich, A., Gelkopf, M., & Solomon, Z. (2003). Exposure to terrorism, stress-related mental health symptoms, and coping behaviors among a nationally representative sample in Israel. *The Journal of the American Medical Association*, *290*, 612–620. doi: 10.1001/jama.290.5.612

Blumer, H. (1958). Race prejudice as a sense of group position. *Pacific Sociological Review*, *1*, 3–7. doi: 10.2307/1388607

Boyes-Watson, C. (2008). *Peacemaking circles and urban youth: Bringing justice home*. St. Paul, MN: Living Justice Press.

Burhan, O. K., & van Leeuwen, E. (2016). Altering perceived cultural and economic threats can increase immigrant helping. *Journal of Social Issues*, *72*, 548–565.

Clayton, S., & Opotow, S. (2003). Justice and identity: Changing perspectives on what is fair. *Personality and Social Psychology Review*, *7*, 298–310. doi: 10.1207/S15327957PSPR0704_03

Cohen, G. L., & Sherman, D. K. (2014). The psychology of change: Self-affirmation and social psychological intervention. *Annual Review of Psychology*, *65*, 333–371. doi: 10.1146/annurev-psych-010213-115137

Davies, K., & Aron, A. (2016). Friendship development and intergroup attitudes: The role of interpersonal and intergroup friendship processes. *Journal of Social Issues*, *72*, 489–510.

DeCelles, K. A., DeRue, S. D., Margolis, J. D., & Ceranic, T. L. (2012). Does power corrupt or enable? When and why power facilitates self-interested behavior. *Journal of Applied Psychology*, *97*, 681–689. doi: 10.1037/a0026811

Derks, B., Scheepers, D., Van Laar, C., & Ellemers, N. (2011). The threat vs. challenge of car parking for women: How self- and group affirmation affect cardiovascular responses. *Journal of Experimental Social Psychology*, *47*, 178–183. doi:10.1016/j.jesp.2010.08.016

de Waal, F. B. M. (2006). Morally evolved: Primate social instincts, human morality, and the rise and fall of "veneer theory". In J. Ober & S. Macedo (Eds.), *Primates and philosophers: How morality evolved* (pp. 1–58). Princeton, NJ: Princeton University Press.

Dovidio, J. F., Piliavin, J. A., Schroeder D. A., & Penner, L. (2006). *The social psychology of prosocial behavior*. Mahwah, NJ: Lawrence Erlbaum Associates Publishers.

Fiske, S. T., Cuddy, A. J. C, & Click, P. (2007). Universal dimensions of social cognition: Warmth and competence. *Trends in Cognitive Sciences*, *11*, 77–83. doi: 10.1016/j.tics.2006.11.005

Foster, C. A., & Rusbult, C. E. (1999). Injustice and powerseeking. *Personality and Social Psychology Bulletin*, *25*, 834–849. doi: 10.1177/01461672990250070006

Frijda, N. H. (1994). The lextalionis: On vengeance. In S. H. M. Van Goozen, N. E. Van de Poll, & J. A. Sergeant (Eds.), *Emotions: Essays on emotion theory* (pp. 263–289). Hillsdale, NJ: Lawrence Erlbaum.

Fry, D. P. (2006). *The human potential for peace: An anthropological challenge to assumptions about war and violence*. New York: Oxford University Press.

Gunn, G. R., & Wilson, A. E. (2011). Acknowledging the skeletons in our closet: The effect of group affirmation on collective guilt, collective shame, and reparatory attitudes. *Personality and Social Psychology Bulletin*, *37*. doi: 10.1177/0146167211413607

Harth, N. S., Kessler, T., & Leach, C. W. (2008). Advantaged group's emotional reactions to intergroup inequality: The dynamics of pride, guilt, and sympathy. *Personality and Social Psychology Bulletin, 34*, 115–129. doi:10.1177/0146167207309193

Harth, N. S, & Shnabel, N. (2015). Third-party intervention in intergroup reconciliation: The role of neutrality and common identity with the other conflict party. *Group Processes & Intergroup Relations, 18*, 676–695. doi:10.1177/1368430215583151

Hawkins, M. (1997). *Social darwinism in European and American thought, 1860-1945: Nature as model and nature as threat.* Cambridge, UK: Cambridge University Press.

Janoff-Bulman, R., & Werther, A. (2008). The social psychology of respect: Implications for delegitimization and reconciliation. In A. Nadler, T. Malloy, & J. D. Fischer (Eds.), *Social Psychology of inter-group reconciliation: From violent conflict to peaceful coexistence* (pp. 145–171). Cambridge: Cambridge University Press.

Klar, Y., Schori-Eyal, N., & Klar, Y. (2013). The "Never Again" State of Israel: The emergence of the holocaust as a core feature of Israeli identity and its four incongruent voices. *Journal of Social Issues, 69*, 125–143. doi: 10.1111/josi.12007

Leach, C. W., Ellemers, N., & Barreto, M. (2007). Group virtue: The importance of morality (vs. competence and sociability) in the positive evaluation of in-groups. *Journal of Personality and Social Psychology, 93*, 234–249. doi: 10.1037/0022-3514.93.2.234

LeVine, R. A., & Campbell, D. T. (1972). *Ethnocentrism: Theories of conflict, ethnic attitudes and group behavior.* New York, NY: Wiley.

Lotz-Schmitt, K., Siem, B., & Stürmer, S. (2015). Empathy as a motivator of dyadic helping across group boundaries – The dis-inhibiting effect of the recipient's perceived benevolence. *Group Processes and Intergroup Relations.* Advance online publication. doi: 10.1177/1368430215612218

Maoz, I., & Bar-On, D. (2002). From working through the Holocaust to current ethnic conflicts: Evaluating the TRT group workshop in Hamburg. *Group, 26*, 29–48. doi: 10.1023/A:1015595027902

Maslow, A. H. (1943). A theory of human motivation. *Psychological Review, 50*, 370-396.

McClelland, G. H. (2000). Nasty data: Unruly, ill-mannered observations can ruin your analysis. In H. T. Reis & C. M. Judd (Eds.), *Handbook of research methods in social and personality psychology* (pp. 393–411). Cambridge: Cambridge University Press.

MacKinnon, D. P. (2000). Contrasts in multiple mediator models. In J. S. Rose, L. Chassin, C. C. Presson, & S. J. Sherman (Eds.), *Multivariate applications in substance use research* (pp. 141–160). Mahwah, NJ: Erlbaum.

Nadler, A., & Halabi, S. (2015). Helping relations and inequality between individuals and groups. In M. Mikulincer, P. R. Shaver, J. F. Dovidio, & J. A. Simpson (Eds.), *APA handbook of personality and social psychology, Volume 2: Group processes* (pp. 371–393). Washington, DC: American Psychological Association.

Nadler, A., Halabi, S., & Harpaz-Gorodeisky, G. (2009). Intergroup helping as status organizing processes: Implications for intergroup misunderstandings. In S. Demoulin, J. P. Leyens, & J. F. Dovidio (Eds.), *Intergroup misunderstandings: Impact of divergent social realities* (pp. 311–331). Washington, DC: Psychology Press

Nadler, A., & Shnabel, N. (2008). Intergroup reconciliation: The instrumental and socio- emotional paths and the need based model of socio-emotional reconciliation. In A. Nadler, T. Malloy, & J. D. Fisher (Eds.), *Social psychology of intergroup reconciliation* (pp. 37–56). New York, NY: Oxford University Press.

Netanyahu: Boycott campaign is anti-Semitic (February 18, 2014). *Middle East Monitor.* Retrieved from https://www.middleeastmonitor.com/news/middle-east/9817-netanyahu-boycott-campaign-is-anti-semetic.

Paolini, S., Wright, S., Dys-Steenbergen, O., & Favara, I. (2016). Self-expansion and intergroup contact: Expectancies and motives to self-expand lead to greater interest in outgroup contact and more positive intergroup relations. *Journal of Social Issues, 72*, 450–471.

Pittinsky, T. L., & Montoya, R. M. (2016). Empathic joy in positive intergroup relations. *Journal of Social Issues, 72*, 511–523.

Preacher, K. J., & Hayes, A. F. (2004). SPSS and SAS procedures for estimating indirect effects in simple mediation models. *Behavior Research Methods, Instruments, & Computers, 36*, 717–731. doi:10.3758/BF03206553

Saguy, T., Dovidio, J. F., & Pratto, F. (2008). Beyond contact: Intergroup contact in the context of power relations. *Personality and Social Psychology Bulletin, 34*, 432–445. doi: 10.1177/0146167207311200

Scheff, T. J. (1994). *Bloody revenge: Emotions, nationalism and war.* Boulder, CO: Westview Press.

Schimmack, U. (2012). The ironic effect of significant results on the credibility of multiple-study articles. *Psychological Methods, 17*, 551–566. doi: 10.1037/a0029487

Sherman, D. K., Kinias, Z., Major, B., Kim, H. S., & Prenovost, M. (2007). The group as a resource: Reducing biased attributions for group success and failure via group affirmation. *Personality and Social Psychology Bulletin, 33*, 1100–1112. doi: 10.1177/0146167207303027

Shnabel, N., Halabi, S., & Noor, M. (2013). Overcoming competitive victimhood and facilitating forgiveness through re-categorization into a common victim or perpetrator identity. *Journal of Experimental Social Psychology, 49*, 867–877. doi: 10.1016/j.jesp.2013.04.007

Shnabel, N., & Nadler, A. (2008). A needs-based model of reconciliation: Satisfying the differential emotional needs of victim and perpetrator as a key to promoting reconciliation. *Journal of Personality and Social Psychology, 94*, 116–132. doi: 10.1037/0022-3514.94.1.116

Shnabel, N., Nadler, A., Ullrich, J., Dovidio, J. F., & Carmi, D. (2009). Promoting reconciliation through the satisfaction of the emotional needs of victimized and perpetrating group members: The needs-based model of reconciliation. *Personality and Social Psychology Bulletin, 35*, 1021–1030. doi: 10.1177/0146167209336610

Shnabel, N., & Noor, M. (2012). Competitive victimhood among Jewish and Palestinian Israelis reflects differential threats to their identities: The perspective of the needs-based model. In K. J. Jonas & T. Morton (Eds.), *Restoring civil societies: The psychology of intervention and engagement following crisis* (pp. 192–207). Malden, MA: Wiley-Blackwell.

Shnabel, N., & Ullrich, J. (2013). Increasing intergroup cooperation toward social change through the restoration of advantaged and disadvantaged groups' positive identities. *Journal of Social and Political Psychology, 1*, 216–238. doi: 10.5964/jspp.v1i1.187

Shrout, P. E., & Bolger, N. (2002). Mediation in experimental and nonexperimental studies: New procedures and recommendations. *Psychological Methods, 7*, 422–445. doi: 10.1037//1082-989X.7.4.422

Sidanius, J., & Pratto, F. (1999). *Social dominance: An intergroup theory of social hierarchy and oppression.* New York, NY: Cambridge University Press.

Siem, B., Stürmer, S., & Pittinsky, T.L. (2016). The psychological study of positive behavior across group boundaries: An overview. *Journal of Social Issues, 72*, 419–431.

SimanTov-Nachlieli, I., & Shnabel, N. (2014) Feeling both victim and perpetrator: Investigating duality within the needs-based model. *Personality and Social Psychology Bulletin, 40*, 301–314. doi: 10.1177/0146167213510746

SimanTov-Nachlieli, I., Shnabel, N., & Nadler, A. (2013). Individuals' and groups' motivation to restore their impaired identity dimensions following conflicts: Evidence and implications. *Social Psychology, 44*, 129–137. doi: 10.1027/1864-9335/a000148

Singer, P. (1975). *Animal liberation: A new ethics for our treatment of animals.* New York, NY: Random House.

Staub, E. (2003). Notes on cultures of violence, cultures of caring and peace, and the fulfillment of basic human needs. *Political Psychology, 24*, 1–21.

Steele, C. M. (1988). The psychology of self-affirmation: Sustaining the integrity of the self. In L. Berkowitz (Ed.), *Advances in experimental social psychology* (Vol. *21*, pp. 261–302). San Diego, CA: Academic Press.

Tajfel, H., & Turner, J. C. (1986). The social identity theory of inter-group behavior. In S. Worchel & L. W. Austin (Eds.), *Psychology of intergroup relations.* Chicago: Nelson-Hall.

Tavuchis, N. (1991). *Mea culpa: A sociology of apology and reconciliation.* Stanford, CA: Stanford University Press.

Tropp, L. R., & Mallett, R. K. (Eds.). (2011). *Moving beyond prejudice reduction: Pathways to positive intergroup relations.* Washington, DC: American Psychological Association.

Turner, J. C., Hogg, M. A., Oakes, P. J., Reicher, S. D., & Wetherell, M. S. (1987). *Rediscovering the social group: A self-categorization theory.* Oxford, England: Blackwell.
Wachtel, T., & McCold, P. (2001). Restorative justice in everyday life. In H. Strang & J. Braithwaite (Eds.), *Restorative justice in civil society.* New York: Cambridge University Press.
Warburton, W. A., Williams, K. D., & Cairns, D. R. (2006). When ostracism leads to aggression: The moderating effects of control deprivation. *Journal of Experimental Social Psychology, 42,* 213–220. doi: 10.1016/j.jesp.2005.03.00
Wenzel, M. (2000). Justice and identity: The significance of inclusion for perceptions of entitlement and the justice motive. *Personality and Social Psychology Bulletin, 26,* 157–176. doi: 10.1177/0146167200264004
Woodyatt, L., & Wenzel, M. (2014). A needs-based perspective on self-forgiveness: Addressing threat to moral identity as a means of encouraging interpersonal and intrapersonal restoration. *Journal of Experimental Social Psychology, 50,* 125–135. doi: 10.1016/j.jesp.2013.09.012

ILANIT SIMANTOV-NACHLIELI received her PhD in Social Psychology from Tel-Aviv University. She is currently a postdoctoral fellow at the Guilford Glazer Faculty of Business and Management at Ben-Gurion University. Her research focuses on the facilitation of interpersonal and intergroup conflicts. In her postdoctoral research, she extends her work to the organizational behavior and negotiation domains.

NURIT SHNABEL received her PhD from Tel-Aviv University. After completing her postdoctoral studies as a Fulbright Exchange Scholar at Yale University, she joined the School of Psychological Sciences at Tel-Aviv University in 2010. Her work focuses on the needs-based model of reconciliation, a theoretical framework for understanding the dynamics between victims and perpetrators, which was awarded by the International Association for Conflict Management (IACM). In addition, she has facilitated encounters between adversarial groups in Israel.

SAMER HALABI received his PhD from Haifa University. He joined the department of behavioral sciences at Tel-Aviv-Yaffo Academic College after completing his postdoctoral studies at University of Connecticut. His research focuses on intergroup helping processes. In particular, building on intergroup relations theories, he investigates the consequences of receiving, seeking, and giving help for members of low- and high-status groups. His more recent research examines reconciliation processes, exploring the effects of trust, willingness to reconcile, and apology on intergroup helping processes.

*Journal of Social Issues, Vol. 72, No. 3, 2016, pp. 584–600*
*doi: 10.1111/josi.12183*

# A Model for Understanding Positive Intergroup Relations Using the In-Group-Favoring Norm

**R. Matthew Montoya**[*]
*University of Dayton*

**Brad Pinter**
*The Pennsylvania State University, Altoona*

*We present a model of intergroup relations focused on the role of the in-group-favoring norm as capable of facilitating positive intergroup relations. We begin by defining the in-group-favoring norm and describing how it affects self-evaluations and evaluations of out-group members. We then outline how positive intergroup relations may result via the implementation of specific techniques fundamental to the in-group-favoring norm, including emphasizing the value of interactions with the out-group, establishing cooperative intergroup norms, and establishing superordinate goals. In so doing, we discuss how classic moderators of intergroup relations, including leadership, guilt, and in-group norms are facilitators of positive intergroup relations once in-group interests are considered.*

Considerable research has proposed that group norms are primarily responsible for an array of intergroup atrocities ranging from terrorism (Louis & Taylor, 2002), racial discrimination, and segregation (Rutland, Cameron, Milne, & McGeorge, 2005), to warfare (Cohen, Montoya, & Insko, 2006). Whereas such accounts emphasize the negative consequences of group norms, the goal of this article is to specify and describe a model of intergroup relations based on a group-level norm that can explain not only negative, but also positive, intergroup outcomes. More specifically, we elaborate on how the in-group-favoring norm can produce both negative and positive evaluations of, and behavior toward, in-group and out-group members. In this article, we begin by discussing the definition, origin, and defining characteristics of the in-group-favoring norm. Second, we

---

[*]Correspondence concerning this article should be addressed to R. Matthew Montoya, Department of Psychology, University of Dayton, 300 College Park, Dayton, OH 45469, USA. [e-mail: matt.montoya@udayton.edu].

outline different strategies for how the in-group-favoring norm can be harnessed to facilitate more positive intergroup relations.

## What Is the In-Group-Favoring Norm?

The in-group-favoring norm is a group-level norm that motivates and orients behavior in the intragroup and intergroup context by directing group members to first consider the interests of the in-group. Tajfel (1970) was among the first to propose the existence of such a norm. Specifically, Tajfel originally interpreted the intergroup competitiveness observed in the early minimal group studies as deriving from a learned "generic norm" that dictates that a group member "act in a manner that discriminates against the out-group and favors the in-group" (pp. 98–99). Years later, Rabbie and Lodewijkx (1994) similarly proposed that in-group favoritism developed from a normative in-group schema that includes beliefs that the in-group's needs should precede the out-group's needs.

The in-group-favoring norm is broader in scope and distinct from research that focuses on situation-specific norms. Jetten, Spears, and Manstead (1996), for example, manipulated the presence of a situation-specific group norm that directed group members to act either cooperatively or competitively with an out-group. In contrast to such studies (e.g., Jetten, Spears, & Manstead, 1997), the in-group-favoring norm is hypothesized to be present in any group context, regardless of local imperatives. Furthermore, and as discussed later, in situations in which a specific group norm is available to guide group members, the in-group-favoring norm is hypothesized to promote the expression of that group norm in ways that service group interests (Allison, 1992; Campbell, 1975; Louis, Taylor, & Douglas, 2005). In further contrast to research focused on specific group-level norms, the in-group-favoring norm is most commonly investigated via individual variability in adherence to the in-group-favoring norm (e.g., Montoya & Pittinsky, 2013) or via laboratory manipulations of whether group members believe that they are accountable to their fellow group members (e.g., Wildschut, Insko, & Gaertner, 2002).

The in-group-favoring norm has been hypothesized to be a result of evolutionary processes. According to this view, living in a group context offered humans a survival advantage via shared resources, common defense from outsiders, and communal child-rearing (Caporael & Brewer, 1991). Given this evolutionary landscape, individuals adhered to group norms and supported the group's interests to avoid the reputation as a free rider and rejection from the group (Yamagishi, Jin, & Miller, 1998; Yamagishi & Mifune, 2008), either of which would lower inclusive fitness. From this perspective, norms developed as a means by which fitness is maximized by ensuring the fulfillment of basic survival needs (Kameda, Takezawa, & Hastie, 2005). Consistent with this evolutionary analysis, researchers have proposed that the norm to consider the interests of their group members was an adaptation that not only maximized group members' fitness, but also fostered harmonious intragroup relations and enhanced the viability of the group as a whole (Montoya & Pittinsky, 2013).

## Defining Characteristics of the In-Group-Favoring Norm

We begin by outlining the defining characteristics of an in-group-favoring norm-based approach to intergroup relations, specifically, (i) the norm's operation on mere group membership, (ii) how the norm can predict self-evaluations in the intergroup context, and (iii) the ability of the norm to account for positive and negative intergroup relations.

*Fundamental to Group Membership*

An in-group-favoring norm-based approach submits that mere categorization activates generalized expectations that bias group members' evaluations and behavior in favor of the in-group. Campbell (1958) was the first to propose that any one of several intragroup characteristics, including similarity, common fate, and propinquity, was sufficient to generate the experience of "groupness." Importantly, such group membership is also sufficient to facilitate cooperation among in-group members (e.g., Brewer & Kramer, 1986; Gaertner & Schopler, 1998) and instigate favoritism toward fellow in-group members (Gaertner, Iuzzini, Witt, & Oriña, 2006). Similarly, Wilder (1986) described a processes by which on exposure to the group, individuals follow a "social script" that dictates that they are to favor the in-group. Hertel and Kerr (2001) also proposed that in-group scripts are activated by mere group membership and dictates that group members are to favor the in-group (Kerr & Hertel, 1998, as cited in Hertel & Kerr, 2001). These views are also consistent with Yamagishi et al.'s (1998) "group heuristic," which states that there is a group-level rule that becomes active "by default" in the mere presence of the group and states that group members should be willing to interact and freely exchange goods and outcomes with fellow group members.

Laboratory evidence supports the view that the in-group-favoring norm becomes active once the group context becomes salient. Walton, Cohen, Cwir, and Spencer (2012), for instance, found that "mere belonging" to a group produced motivation to complete group-relevant goals. Montoya and Pittinsky (2008) went further to demonstrate that the in-group-favoring norm and group membership—and not the degree to which a group member identified with the group—predicted behavior in the intragroup and intergroup context.

Interestingly, activation of the in-group-favoring norm may even occur in even more minimal intergroup conditions than proposed by Tajfel (1970), such as those described in the literature on implicit partisanship (Greenwald, Pickrell, & Farnham, 2002; Pinter & Greenwald, 2004). Pinter and Greenwald (2011), for instance, revealed that simply asking participants to memorize the names of people assigned to their same group category resulted in greater attraction and biased monetary allocations, with these effects having similar magnitude as those observed with traditional group categorization-induction techniques.

*In-Group-Favoring Norm Adherence Predicts Self-Evaluations*

A model of intergroup relations based on the in-group-favoring norm outlines predictions regarding how a group member evaluates himself/herself. Specifically, other peoples' approval and acceptance is considered to be an important source of self-esteem (e.g., Leary & Baumeister, 2000), and one critical determinant of acceptance is whether a group member adheres to the norms of the group. Yamagishi and Mifune (2008) forwarded a similar view, proposing that evaluations of in-group members result from determining whether they adhered to and supported the in-group's norms. In line with this reasoning, Leary, Cottrell, and Philips (2001) proposed that being a good group member was the key to sustaining one's self-esteem.

The link between self-esteem, norm adherence, and in-group acceptance is supported by both experimental (e.g., Leary et al., 2001) and correlational (Postmes & Branscombe, 2002) research. Vickers, Abrams, and Hogg (1988), for example, demonstrated that participants who followed an in-group's cooperative norm in a minimal group context reported higher self-esteem than those who did not follow the norm. Alternatively, Vickers et al. (1985, as cited in Abrams & Hogg, 1988) reported that group members experienced lower self-esteem when they violated a cooperative intergroup norm.

In addition, research on stigmatized groups indicates that self-esteem is maintained by in-group acceptance despite negative comparisons with other groups. For instance, although there may be a negative perception of African Americans by non-African Americans, African Americans tend to have higher self-esteem compared to their non-African American counterparts (Gray-Little & Hafdahl, 2000). One possible explanation for these findings comes from Postmes and Branscombe (2002), who in a study of in-group and out-group acceptance among African American participants, found that in-group acceptance ameliorated the adverse consequences of stigmatization. Such findings are consistent with theorizing regarding the in-group-favoring norm, such that being accepted by one's group is critical to one's self-esteem, and provides a separate pathway to self-esteem maintenance independent of intergroup comparisons.

*In-Group-Favoring Norm Predicts Out-Group Behavior*

Although the in-group-favoring norm has been repeatedly invoked to justify conflict and antagonism toward out-groups (e.g., Spini, Elcheroth, & Fasel, 2008), closer inspection of the various definitions of the in-group-favoring norm indicates that the norm does not necessarily promote out-group antagonism. Whereas Tajfel's (1970) defined his "generic norm" as dictating that group members favor the in-group by both biasing behavior toward the in-group *and* by discriminating against out-groups, Rabbie and Lodewijkx's (1994) definition only proposed favoritism for the in-group. Wildschut et al. (2002) defined the in-group-favoring norm similarly, stating that group members "should take into account the interest of one's own group before taking into account the interests of other groups" (p. 977). Importantly, empirical evidence supports Wildschut et al.'s and Rabbie and Lodewijkx's definition, such that group members are primarily motivated to benefit the in-group rather than to harm the out-group. Specifically, in studies in which in-group evaluations can be assessed independently of out-group evaluations, behaviors that benefit the in-group are generally preferred over those that harm the out-group (Brewer, 1999; Mummendey et al., 1992). This is also consistent with research that concludes that adherence to the in-group-favoring norm leads to maximization of the in-group's absolute outcomes rather than maximizing the relative differences between groups (Insko, Kirchner, Pinter, Efaw, & Wildschut, 2005).

The focus on absolute outcomes, rather than on relative outcomes, is consistent with other research (e.g., Abrams, 1994; Hogg, 2007) that suggests that a competitive out-group orientation is not fait accompli. Indeed, there is considerable evidence that the processes that are associated with dislike are different from those associated with liking (e.g., Barbarino & Stürmer, 2016; Pittinsky, Rosenthal, & Montoya, 2011). From the in-group-favoring norm-based perspective, as a default, group members should be indifferent from out-groups that cannot materially facilitate or hinder the in-group's outcomes. Such indifference is the proposed explanation for (i) a majority of monetary allocations during intergroup allocation tasks being fair or equitable in nature (e.g., Mummendey et al., 1992), (ii) the finding that group categorization does not necessarily produce more out-group derogation (Brewer, 1979), and (iii) the lack of conflict between distinct natural groups of 172 Western American Indian tribes (Jorgensen, 1980).

However, the in-group-favoring norm does hypothesize the presence of negative intergroup responses when competition is viewed as best supporting the interests of the group. Unfortunately, multiple group-level processes tilt intergroup orientations to be competitive, particularly in the minimal group context. For example, competitive behavior, compared to cooperative behavior, is more likely to be perceived as linked to the group's interests (Wildschut, Pinter, Vevea, Insko, & Schopler, 2003) and individuals expect other group members to have a competitively self-interested orientation (Epley, Caruso, & Bazerman, 2006). These processes provide the foundation for adherence to the in-group-favoring norm in the minimal group context to default to greater intergroup competition (Wildschut et al., 2002).

Importantly, the focus on absolute outcomes indicates that positive intergroup relations can result when the out-group is perceived as a pathway to maximizing outcomes and/or when group-level norms are cooperative. Although competitive intergroup norms are common, not all groups have a group-level norm that dictates competitiveness. A cooperative group norm is associated with some professions (e.g., nurses, Oaker & Brown, 1986; forest rangers, Hall, Schneider, & Nygren, 1970), and those who adhere strongly to the in-group-favoring norm are expected to adhere more closely to group-level norms. In a laboratory demonstration of these processes, Montoya and Pittinsky (2013) gave participants a group norm to act either cooperatively or competitively with an out-group, and then provided participants with an opportunity to allocate money to the in-group and out-group. They found that individuals who adhered strongly to the in-group-favoring norm were particularly likely to follow the group norm; whether it was cooperative or competitive—when it was competitive, those participants who adhered closely to the in-group-favoring norm were more competitive, but when it was cooperative, they were descriptively more cooperative.

It is important to note that from this approach, intergroup cooperation or competition results from group members' desire to be "a good group member." In other words, intergroup competition results from an intragroup pressure to be viewed favorably by fellow in-group members. Whereas traditional approaches have framed competition as originating from intergroup processes, the in-group-favoring norm approach emphasizes the importance of adherence to group-level norms to acceptance and self-evaluations. The importance of group member's considerations regarding acceptance can be observed from studies that explore group members' group-level decisions that could (or could not) be evaluated by other group members. Wildschut et al. (2002), for instance, had participants who play a single-trial prisoner's dilemma game (PDG) as part of a three-person group interacting with another group. They manipulated whether participants believed that they would discuss their individual PDG votes with their fellow group members after their votes had been cast (public condition) or not (private condition). The researchers proposed that group members in the public condition should feel more accountable to their group members and feel more concerned with taking into consideration the outcomes of the in-group. As expected, in the public condition, compared with the private condition, group members expressed more concern with maximizing their group's outcomes, and as a result, competed more with the other group. Similarly, Ben-Yoav and Pruitt (1984) found that when group representatives were accountable to their group, they were more cooperatively motivated when cooperation was seen as beneficial to the group's interests, but when cooperation was not seen as beneficial, they were less cooperative. Such findings support the contention that the public/private manipulation affected group members' behavior due to concerns regarding acceptance/rejection from fellow group members.

## Harnessing the In-Group-Favoring Norm to Facilitate Positive Intergroup Relations

In this section, we discuss several pathways by which the in-group-favoring norm can be used to promote positive intergroup relations. First, we describe how intergroup relations are enhanced by emphasizing the value that may result from interactions with an out-group. Second, we discuss how the establishment of in-group norms that focus on intergroup cooperation can facilitate positive intergroup relations. And finally, we discuss how superordinate goals, rather than superordinate identities, provide the most direct pathway to positive intergroup relations. For each pathway, we include a discussion of specific policy and program recommendations that would facilitate the impact of the in-group-favoring norm. Finally, and when available, we also include a discussion of how predictions of an in-group-favoring norm-based approach differ from predictions of other theories of intergroup relations.

### Emphasizing the Value of Interactions with the Out-Group

One pathway by which intergroup relations can be improved via the in-group-favoring norm is by emphasizing the value of interactions with the out-group. Although a tactic centered on emphasizing the benefits of cooperating with the out-group appears obvious, considerable research has proposed that even seemingly cooperative intergroup relations generate intergroup hostilities. Social identity theory (Tajfel & Turner, 1979), for example, posits that individuals' social identities are derived from their group memberships. Group members are generally motivated to maintain a positive social identity and in so doing, maintain and enhance individual self-esteem (for other motives, see Hogg, 2007). Social identity theory further submits that group members compare their group to other relevant groups and are motivated to view their group favorably (i.e., positive distinctiveness via metacontrast; Tajfel & Turner, 1985). Deschamps and Brown (1983), for instance, concluded that even cooperative relations produce identity threats that fuel intergroup hostilities.

In contrast to placing an emphasis on intergroup comparisons, the in-group-favoring norm perspective emphasizes that cooperative relations are possible due to the importance of adherence to group-level norms for gaining acceptance from fellow group members. To capitalize on the relation between the in-group-favoring norm and cooperation, social programs may emphasize the beneficial outcomes that may accrue from cooperative relations with the out-group. As noted by Paolini and colleagues (Paolini, Wright, Dys-Steenbergen, & Favara, 2016), the benefits that may result from positive intergroup relations may be tangible (e.g., better monetary outcomes) or intangible (self-expansion). The aforementioned study by Montoya and Pittinsky (2013) is particularly relevant: Participants were not competitive with an out-group to bolster self-esteem, but rather they responded to whichever situation-specific norm was operating. Participants who adhered most strongly to the in-group-favoring norm were the most likely to conform to cues to the in-group's interests, whether that was manifested as cooperation or competition. Clearly, whatever self-esteem concerns participants had were tied closely to the normative demands of the particular cooperation/competition group situation and resulted in more cooperation when cooperation was seen as beneficial.

Two additional areas of inquiry are relevant for considering strategies for emphasizing the value of interactions with the out-group. First, research has explored the influence of patriotism on evaluations of in-group and out-group members (e.g., Staub, 1997). This work has specifically focused on the degree to which citizens attach themselves to their country and makes the distinction between blind patriotism and critical patriotism. Blind patriotism refers to the degree to which citizens experience an "unquestioning" positive evaluation of the country and its actions and policies. Alternatively, critical patriotism assesses the degree to which individuals support their country with the goal of enhancing the welfare of the nation. Critical patriotism mirrors sentiments that comprise the in-group-favoring norm construct, as both constructs emphasize the desire to maximize the group's interests independent of the degree to which group members identify with the nation. Importantly, critical patriotism is negatively related to fears regarding the nation's uniqueness and distinctiveness, but also with fears of heterogeneity and loss of national distinctiveness. Importantly, constructive patriotism (which is analogous to critical patriotism) predicts attitudes oriented toward cooperative policies with other nations (Henderson-King, Henderson-King, & Hathaway, 2010) and predicts proimmigration and multicultural views (Spry & Hornsey, 2007). Such research provides evidence for the relation between an in-group-favoring orientation and cooperative behavior: If group members can perceive cooperative behavior as beneficial to the group, group members—particularly those who adhere strongly to the in-group-favoring norm—support intergroup cooperation.

Research that identifies differences in cultural worldviews provides a second domain for considering strategies for emphasizing the value of interactions with the out-group. Specifically, research has made a distinction between individualistic and collectivistic societies. According to Hofstede (1991), individualistic societies are oriented toward the individual as a unique entity with loose connections to the group, in which an individual's identity is based on autonomy and personal accomplishment (see also Hofstede, 1980). Alternatively, collectivism emphasizes an individual's place in a structured relational network with interpersonal bonds among group members (Triandis, 1995). Relevant to the current approach, cultures can be further categorized by their vertical versus horizontal orientations. Important to processes that mirror the in-group-favoring norm, in horizontal-collectivist societies, people emphasize interdependence with other in-group members and orient toward equality with other in-group members (Erez & Earley, 1987).

In principle, there is a high degree of correspondence between the values of the in-group-favoring norm and horizontal collectivists, as they are both interested in prioritizing the in-group's goals and the well-being of group members without identification with the in-group or the desire to positively distinguish the group (Triandis & Gelfand, 1998). Soh and Leong (2002), for example, concluded that horizontal collectivism is associated with beliefs in universalism (protecting and tolerance for all people) and conformity (the restraint of action that may harm others). In addition, Turel and Connelly (2012) found that collectivists were more focused on collaboration and had a greater concern for others. Furthermore, and analogous to the aforementioned findings regarding the in-group-favoring norm, collectivists in a competitive context were the most competitive, but in a cooperative context, they were descriptively the most cooperative (Chatman & Barsade, 1995). Similarly, Chen, Wasti, and Triandis (2007) revealed that the degree to which participants identified with a collectivistic orientation moderated the relation between cooperative/competitive group norm and intergroup cooperation, such that participants who identified strongly with collectivism were the most cooperative when a cooperative group norm was present. Such findings provide additional evidence that constructs analogous to the in-group-favoring norm can facilitate intergroup cooperation when group members perceive a benefit from cooperation.

After the value of positive intergroup relations is made salient, a simple manipulation of asking group members to consider "what is best for your group" is hypothesized to be associated with not only more cooperation, but with higher self-esteem. The jigsaw classroom (Aronson, Blaney, Sikes, Stephan, & Snapp, 1975), for example, involves creating small student led interdependent workgroups, in which each student is asked to study one topic before presenting that topic to the larger group. Research is consistent in showing that this technique is effective at not only reducing prejudice, but also boosting self-efficacy and self-esteem (Aronson & Yates, 1983). From the perspective of the in-group-favoring norm, prejudice falls because positive intergroup relations are seen as beneficial to the in-group's interests, and bolstered self-esteem results from adherence to the in-group's norms. Perhaps, counterintuitively, after making cooperative relations salient, asking students to "consider the interests of your group" is expected to generate more concerns regarding the welfare of in-group members, and thus produce more positive relations and self-esteem.

## Establish a Group Norm to Cooperate with the Out-Group

As noted earlier, the importance of group-level norms to guide group members' actions has received considerable empirical attention. From the in-group-favoring norm perspective, cooperative relations result when group members view cooperative interactions as facilitating the in-group's interests. In other words, when in-group members perceive cooperative intergroup behavior as profitable, they are predicted to become more motivated to cooperate, as positive intergroup relations are viewed as bolstering the group's (and one's own) interests (Pruitt & Kimmel, 1977; Rabbie, Schot, & Visser, 1989). Importantly, there is laboratory support for the hypothesis that the in-group-favoring norm does moderate group norms, with evidence suggesting that emphasizing the importance of cooperation produces more cooperation between groups (Montoya & Pittinsky, 2013).

The importance of establishing a group norm is particularly apparent in studies of social inclusion (vs. exclusion). For example, in a case study of the methods used by Bulgarian leaders to end the deportation of their Jewish citizens in the years before World War II, Reicher, Cassidy, Wolpert, Hopkins, and Levine (2006) revealed how leaders motivated intergroup cooperation by producing rhetoric that made salient social norms emphasizing inclusiveness. Similarly, Tropp and Mallett (2011) proposed that school systems may generate norms of inclusion that can facilitate children's interest in friendships with out-group members. Relatedly, in the domain of bullying, Perkins, Craig, and Perkins (2011) produced a reduction in bullying attitudes after presenting students with normative information regarding bullying. More broadly, these processes should operate in any of a number of situations, whether it is the school playground, negotiation table, or local discotheque. In each case, presenting in-group members with clear expectations about the group's standards is not only expected to result in more positive intergroup outcomes, but clear expectations with the salience of the in-group's interests should moderate the degree of positivity.

*Guilt enhances the effects of group norms.* The influence of guilt on the development of positive intergroup relations requires specific discussion. Guilt, given its nature as a moral emotion (Tangney, 2003), increases adherence to norms (e.g., Bandura, Barbaranelli, Caprara, & Pastorelli, 1996), particularly when norm-relevant behavior can be evaluated by other group members (Tangney & Dearing, 2002). Accordingly, guilt should predict adherence to the in-group-favoring norm, such that guilt-prone group members should act competitively in the intergroup context to ensure that they behave consistently with the in-group's norm. Consistent with this premise, Wildschut and Insko (2006) found that group members were more competitive when group members were aware of their intergroup choices (public) than unaware (private), but only for those participants high in guilt. Similarly, Cohen et al. (2006) found that relative to guilt-prone group members who were instructed to remain objective, guilt-prone group members who were instructed to empathize with their in-group were more competitive with the out-group.

Such effects may be magnified in contexts in which leaders control the group decision making. Pinter et al. (2007; Experiment 2) compared leaders in an intergroup mixed-motive setting who were either accountable or unaccountable to their group members. Results revealed that high guilt-proneness produced more competition for those leaders who were accountable, but reduced competition for unaccountable leaders. Pinter et al. proposed that the greater competition for high-guilt leaders resulted from the salience of the in-group-favoring norm (via thinking about how their group members might respond), whereas the reduced competition for the high-guilt unaccountable leaders resulted from the relative salience of the individual's own motives (which in the case of interindividual interactions is cooperative; Wolf et al., 2009). Such results indicate that to promote positive interactions, researchers must not only consider the dynamics of intergroup processes, but also the complexities associated with individual difference variables.

*Establish superordinate goals, Not superordinate identities.*     A commonly theorized mechanism for the enhancement of intergroup relations is to produce or make salient a superordinate identity. From the perspective of the common in-group identity model (Gaertner & Dovidio, 2000), conflict is likely when group members clearly categorize intergroup relations as "us" versus "them." It is only when group members recategorize an out-group as part of the in-group can positive "intergroup" relations occur (i.e., via recategorization). One implication is that individual group members must reduce their identification with their "home" group or must identify with a superordinate group before positive intergroup relations can occur (Gaertner, Mann, Dovidio, Murrell, & Pomare, 1990).

However, research has also revealed that greater in-group identification can be associated with *more* favorable intergroup relations and that strong identification with the superordinate group is unnecessary for positive intergroup relations. Brown and colleagues (Brown & Williams, 1984; Oaker & Brown, 1986), for example, found that in a cooperative context, the more group members identified with their group, the more they liked and demonstrated favoritism toward the out-group. Similarly, Montoya and Pittinsky (2011) experimentally manipulated the cooperative/competitive relations between groups and the degree to which group members identified with the group. Consistent with expectations, highly identified group members who engaged in cooperative relations with the out-group had the most positive out-group evaluations (also see Montoya & Pittinsky, 2016).

Given that threats to one's social identity are hypothesized to result when either cooperation or competition is present, it is reasonable to question whether superordinate identities, versus superordinate goals, are more effective in generating positive intergroup relations. A resolution to the question may rely on changing the focus of the question from "superordinate identity versus superordinate goal" to "amount of available information." From the in-group-favoring norm perspective, group members are oriented toward maximizing self-interest and group interest, and do so by evaluating the degree to which out-groups are evaluated as positively/negatively affecting in-group members (see also Sherif,

Harvey, White, Hood, & Sherif, 1961). In this light, evaluating the relative importance of "superordinate goals" versus "superordinate identities" can be viewed as subsumed under a drive to understand the positivity/negativity of the relations between groups. Categorical information ("in-group member" or "out-group member") informs group members of what actions to take, with the expectation that in-group members will be cooperative (e.g., Yamagishi & Mifune, 2008) and uncertainty regarding how out-group members will respond. Thus, in minimal contexts, the only available information is the categorical information of group membership; and as discussed earlier, when intergroup decisions are based on mere category information, group members tend to perceive out-group members as competitively oriented (e.g., Pemberton, Insko, & Schopler, 1996). Importantly, as the amount of information about the out-group grows, the less competitive intergroup relations become (Wilder & Simon, 1998; Wildschut et al., 2003). In other words, as intergroup relations develop, more information regarding the relative interests/goals of out-groups becomes available that makes it possible for superordinate goals, relative to superordinate identities, to be the driving force behind the enhancement of intergroup relations. In this way, to facilitate positive intergroup relations via the in-group-favoring norm, interventions should focus on making salient superordinate goals, as goals are more direct at informing group members as to what is "good for the group." For example, Pinto, Pinto, and Prescott (1993) revealed that the competitive relations in the context of the health care industry were attenuated by a focus on superordinate goals, a focus that produced both enhanced intergroup task performance and enjoyment with the intergroup task.

## Conclusion

We contend that the in-group-favoring norm—the expectation that group members first consider the interests of fellow group members—can promote the degree to which intergroup relations are positive. Despite the apparent contradiction that an orientation toward one's own group members can be beneficial to intergroup relations, we presented three pathways by which the norm can result in more positive intergroup relations. Specifically, we proposed that the in-group-favoring norm can be harnessed to improve intergroup relations via (i) emphasizing the value of interactions with the out-group, (ii) establishing an in-group norm to cooperate with the out-group, and (iii) establishing a superordinate goal.

## References

Abrams, D. (1994). Social self-regulation. *Personality and Social Psychology Bulletin, 20*, 473–483. doi: 10.1177/0146167294205004

Abrams, D., & Hogg, M. A. (1988). Comments on the motivational status of self-esteem in social identity and intergroup discrimination. *European Journal of Social Psychology, 18*, 317–334. doi: 10.1002/ejsp.2420180403

Allison, P. D. (1992). Cultural relatedness under oblique and horizontal transmission rules. *Ethology & Sociobiology, 13*, 153–169. doi: 10.1016/0162-3095(92)90031-x

Aronson, E., & Yates, S. (1983). Cooperation in the classroom: The impact of the jigsaw method on inter-ethnic relations, classroom performance and self-esteem. In H. Blumberg & P. Hare (Eds.), *Small groups* (pp. 119–139). London: John Wiley & Sons.

Aronson, E., Blaney, N., Sikes, J., Stephan, C., & Snapp, M. (1975). Busing and racial tension: The jigsaw route to learning and liking. *Psychology Today, 8*, 43–50.

Bandura, A., Barbaranelli, C., Caprara, G. V., & Pastorelli, C. (1996). Mechanisms of moral disengagement in the exercise of moral agency. *Journal of Personality and Social Psychology, 71*, 364–374. doi: 10.1037/0022-3514.71.2.364

Barbarino, M.-L. & Stürmer, S. (2016). Different origins of xenophile and xenophobic tendencies in human personality structure: A theoretical perspective and some preliminary findings. *Journal of Social Issues.*

Ben-Yoav, O., & Pruitt, D. (1984). Accountability to constituents: A two-edged sword. *Organizational Behavior & Human Performance, 34*, 283–295. doi: 10.1016/0030-5073(84)90040-0

Brewer, M. B. (1979). In-group bias in the minimal intergroup situation: A cognitive-motivational analysis. *Psychological Bulletin, 86*, 307–324. doi: 10.1037/0033-2909.86.2.307

Brewer, M. B. (1999). The psychology of prejudice: Ingroup love or outgroup hate? *Journal of Social Issues, 55*, 429–444. doi: 10.1111/0022-4537.00126

Brewer, M. B., & Kramer, R. M. (1986). Choice behavior in social dilemmas: Effects of social identity, group size, and decision framing. *Journal of Personality and Social Psychology, 50*, 543–549. doi: 10.1037/0022-3514.50.3.543

Brown, R., & Williams, J. (1984). Group identification: The same thing to all people? *Human Relations, 37*, 547–564. doi: 10.1177/001872678403700704

Campbell, D. T. (1958). Common fate, similarity, and other indices of the status of aggregates of persons as social entities. *Behavioral Science, 3*, 14–25. doi: 10.1002/bs.3830030103

Campbell, D. T. (1975). On the conflicts between biological and social evolution and between psychology and moral tradition. *American Psychologist, 30*, 1103–1126. doi: 10.1037/0003-066x.30.12.1103

Caporael, L. R., & Brewer, M. B. (1991). Reviving evolutionary psychology: Biology meets society. *Journal of Social Issues, 47*, 187–195. doi: 10.1111/j.1540-4560.1991.tb01830.x

Chatman, J. A., & Barsade, S. G. (1995). Personality, organizational culture, and cooperation: Evidence from a business simulation. *Administrative Science Quarterly, 40*, 423–443. doi: 10.2307/2393792

Chen, X. P., Wasti, S. A., & Triandis, H. C. (2007). When does group norm or group identity predict cooperation in a public goods dilemma? The moderating effects of idiocentrism and allocentrism. *International Journal of Intercultural Relations, 31*, 259–276. doi: 10.1016/j.ijintrel.2006.02.004

Cohen, T. R., Montoya, R. M., & Insko, C. A. (2006). Group morality and intergroup relations: Cross-cultural and experimental evidence. *Personality and Social Psychology Bulletin, 32*, 1559–1572. doi: 10.1177/0146167206291673

Deschamps, J. C., & Brown, R. (1983). Superordinate goals and intergroup conflict. *British Journal of Social Psychology, 22*, 189–195. doi: 10.1111/j.2044-8309.1983.tb00583.x

Erez, M., & Earley, P. C. (1987). Comparative analysis of goal-setting strategies across cultures. *Journal of Applied Psychology, 72*, 658–665. doi: 10.1037/0021-9010.72.4.658

Epley, N., Caruso, E., & Bazerman, M. H. (2006). When perspective taking increases taking: Reactive egoism in social interaction. *Journal of Personality and social Psychology, 91*, 872–889. doi: 10.1037/e633962013-094

Gaertner, L., Iuzzini, J., Witt, M., & Oriña, M. (2006). Us without them: Evidence for an intragroup origin of positive in-group regard. *Journal of Personality and Social Psychology, 90*, 426–439. doi: 10.1037/0022-3514.90.3.426

Gaertner, L., & Schopler, J. (1998). Perceived ingroup entitativity and intergroup bias: An interconnection of self and others. *European Journal of Social Psychology, 28*, 963–980.

Gaertner, S. L., & Dovidio, J. F. (2000). *Reducing intergroup bias: The common ingroup identity model.* Philadelphia: Psychology Press/Taylor & Francis.

Gaertner, S. L., Mann, J. A., Dovidio, J. F., Murrell, A. J., & Pomare, M. (1990). How does cooperation reduce intergroup bias? *Journal of Personality and Social Psychology*, *59*, 692–704. doi: 10.1037/0022-3514.59.4.692

Gray-Little, B., & Hafdahl, A. R. (2000). Factors influencing racial comparisons of self-esteem: A quantitative review. *Psychological Bulletin*, *126*, 26–54. doi: 10.1037/0033-2909.126.1.26

Greenwald, A. G., Pickrell, J. E., & Farnham, S. D. (2002). Implicit partisanship: Taking sides for no reason. *Journal of Personality and Social Psychology*, *83*, 367–379. doi: 10.1037/0022-3514.83.2.367

Hall, D. T., Schneider, B., & Nygren, H. T. (1970). Personal factors in organizational identification. *Administrative Science Quarterly*, *15*, 176–190. doi: 10.2307/2391488

Henderson-King, E., Henderson-King, D., & Hathaway, L. (2010). Group favoritism and support for government policies as a function of patriotic orientation and perceived threat. *Revue Internationale de Psychologie Sociale*, *3*, 235–266.

Hertel, G., & Kerr, N. L. (2001). Priming in-group favoritism: The impact of normative scripts in the minimal group paradigm. *Journal of Experimental Social Psychology*, *37*, 316–324. doi: 10.1006/jesp.2000.1447

Hofstede, G. (1980). *Culture's consequences: International differences in work-related values*. Newbury Park, CA: Sage.

Hofstede, G. (1991). *Cultures and organizations: Software of the mind*. London: McGraw-Hill.

Hogg, M. A. (2007). Uncertainty-identity theory. *Advances in Experimental Social Psychology*, *39*, 69–126.

Insko, C. A., Kirchner, J. L., Pinter, B., Efaw, J., & Wildschut, T. (2005). Interindividual-intergroup discontinuity as a function of trust and categorization: The paradox of expected cooperation. *Journal of Personality and Social Psychology*, *88*, 365–385. doi: 10.1037/0022-3514.88.2.365

Jetten, J., Spears, R., & Manstead, A. S. R. (1996). Strength of identification and intergroup differentiation: The influence of group norms. *European Journal of Social Psychology*, *27*, 603–609.

Jetten, J., Spears, R., & Manstead, A. S. R. (1997). Strength of identification and intergroup differentiation: The influence of group norms. *European Journal of Social Psychology*, *27*, 603–609.

Jorgensen, J. G. (1980). *Western Indians. Comparative environments, languages, and cultures of 172 Western American Indian tribes*. San Francisco: Freeman.

Kameda, T., Takezawa, M., & Hastie, R. (2005). Where do social norms come from? The example of communal sharing. *Current Directions in Psychological Science*, *14*, 331–334. doi: 10.1111/j.0963-7214.2005.00392.x

Kerr, N. L., & Hertel, G. (1998). *Effects of spontaneously perceived in-group norms on allocations in the minimal intergroup paradigm*. Unpublished data.

Leary, M. R., & Baumeister, R. F. (2000). The nature and function of self-esteem: Sociometer theory. *Advances in Experimental Social Psychology*, *32*, 1–62. doi: 10.1016/s0065-2601(00)80003-9

Leary, M. R., Cottrell, C. A., & Philips, M. (2001). Deconfounding the effects of dominance and social acceptance on self-esteem. *Journal of Personality and Social Psychology*, *81*, 898–909. doi: 10.1037/0022-3514.81.5.898

Louis, W. R., & Taylor, D. M. (2002). Understanding the September 11 terrorist attack on America: The role of intergroup theories of normative influence. *Analyses of Social Issues and Public Policy*, *2*, 87–100. doi: 10.1111/j.1530-2415.2002.00029.x

Louis, W. R., Taylor, D. M., & Douglas, R. L. (2005). Normative influence and rational conflict decisions: Group norms and cost-benefit analyses for intergroup behavior. *Group Processes and Intergroup Relations*, *8*, 355–374. doi: 10.1177/1368430205056465

Montoya, R. M., & Pittinsky, T. L. (2008). *The role of the norm of group interest to determine self-esteem in the intergroup context*. Unpublished manuscript.

Montoya, R. M., & Pittinsky, T. L. (2011). When increased group identification leads to outgroup liking and cooperation: The role of trust. *The Journal of Social Psychology*, *151*, 784–806. doi: 10.1080/00224545.2010.538762

Montoya, R. M., & Pittinsky, T. L. (2013). Individual variability in adherence to the norm of group interest predicts outgroup bias. *Group Processes & Intergroup Relations*, *16*, 173–191. doi: 10.1177/1368430212450523

Montoya, R. M., & Pittinsky, T. L. (2016). Bounded rationality's account for the influence of group identification on ingroup favoritism: A field investigation using Jewish and Arab populations in Israel. *Basic and Applied Social Psychology, 38.* Advance online publication. doi: 10.1080/01973533.2016.1180295

Mummendey, A., Simon, B., Dietze, C., Grünert, M., Haeger, G., Kessler, S., Lettgen, S., & Schäferhoff, S. (1992). Categorization is not enough: Intergroup discrimination in negative outcome allocation. *Journal of Experimental Social Psychology, 28,* 125–144. doi: 10.1016/0022-1031(92)90035-i

Oaker, G., & Brown, R. (1986). Intergroup relations in a hospital setting: A further test of social identity theory. *Human Relations, 39,* 767–778.

Paolini, S., Wright, S., Dys-Steenbergen, O., & Favara, I. (2016). Self-expansion and intergroup contact: Expectancies and motives to self-expand lead to greater interest in outgroup contact and more positive intergroup relations. *Journal of Social Issues.*

Pemberton, M. B., Insko, C. A., & Schopler, J. (1996). Memory for and experience of differential competitive behavior of individuals and groups. *Journal of Personality and Social Psychology, 71,* 953–966. doi: 10.1037/0022-3514.71.5.953

Perkins, H. W., Craig, D. W., & Perkins, J. M. (2011 Using social norms to reduce bullying: A research intervention among adolescents in five middle schools. *Group Processes & Intergroup Relations, 14,* 703–722. doi 10.1177/1368430210398004

Pinter, B., & Greenwald, A. G. (2004). Exploring implicit partisanship: Enigmatic (but genuine) group identification and attraction. *Group Processes & Intergroup Relations, 7,* 283–296. doi: 10.1177/1368430204046112

Pinter, B., & Greenwald, A. G. (2011). A comparison of minimal group induction procedures. *Group Processes and Intergroup Relations, 14,* 81–98. doi: 10.1177/1368430210375251

Pinter, B., Insko, C. A., Wildschut, T., Kirchner, J., Montoya, R. M., & Wolf, S. (2007). Reduction of interindividual-intergroup discontinuity: The role of leader accountability and proneness to guilt. *Journal of Personality and Social Psychology, 93,* 250–265. doi: 10.1037/0022-3514.93.2.250

Pinto, M. B., Pinto, J. K., & Prescott, J. E. (1993). Antecedents and consequences of project team cross-functional cooperation. *Management Science, 39,* 1281–1297. doi: 10.1287/mnsc.39.10.1281

Pittinsky, T. L., Rosenthal, S. A., & Montoya, R. M. (2011). Liking is not the opposite of disliking: The functional separability of positive and negative attitudes toward minority groups. *Cultural Diversity and Ethnic Minority Psychology, 17,* 134–143. doi: 10.1037/a0023806

Postmes, T., & Branscombe, N. R. (2002). Influence of long-term racial environmental composition on subjective well-being in African Americans. *Journal of Personality and Social Psychology, 83,* 735–751. doi: 10.1037/0022-3514.83.3.735

Pruitt, D. G., & Kimmel, M. J. (1977). Twenty years of experimental gaming: Critique, synthesis, and suggestions for the future. *Annual Review of Psychology, 28,* 363–392.

Rabbie, J. M., & Lodewijkx, H. F. (1994). Conflict and aggression: An individual-group continuum. In B. Markovsky, J. O'Brien, & K. Heimer (Eds.), *Advances in group processes, Vol. 11* (pp. 139–174). Greenwich, CT: JAI Press.

Rabbie, J. M., Schot, J. C., & Visser, L. (1989, July). *Instrumental intragroup co-operation and intergroup competition in the minimal group paradigm.* Paper presented at the Social Identity Conference, University of Exeter, Exeter, Great Britain.

Reicher, S., Cassidy, C., Wolpert, I., Hopkins, N., & Levine, M. (2006). Saving Bulgaria's Jews: An analysis of social identity and the mobilisation of social solidarity. *European Journal of Social Psychology, 36,* 49–72. doi: 10.1002/ejsp.2420240408

Rutland, A., Cameron, L., Milne, A., & McGeorge, P. (2005). Social norms and self-presentation: Children's implicit and explicit intergroup attitudes. *Child Development, 76,* 451–466. doi: 10.1111/j.1467-8624.2005.00856.x

Sherif, M., Harvey, O. J., White, B. J., Hood, W. R., & Sherif, C. W. (1961). *Intergroup conflict and cooperation: The Robbers Cave experiment.* Norman, OK: University Book Exchange.

Soh, S., & Leong, F. T. (2002). Validity of vertical and horizontal individualism and collectivism in Singapore relationships with values and interests. *Journal of Cross-Cultural Psychology, 33,* 3–15. doi: 10.1177/0022022102033001001

Spini, D., Elcheroth, G., & Fasel, R. (2008). The impact of group norms and generalization of risks across groups on judgments of war behavior. *Political Psychology, 29*, 919–941. doi: 10.1111/j.1467-9221.2008.00673.x

Spry, C., & Hornsey, M. (2007). The influence of blind and constructive patriotism on attitudes toward multiculturalism and immigration. *Australian Journal of Psychology, 59*, 151–158.

Staub, E. (1997). Blind versus constructive patriotism: Moving from embeddedness in the group to critical loyalty and action. In D. Bar-Tal & E. Staub (Eds.), *Patriotism: In the lives of individuals and nations. Nelson-Hall series in psychology* (pp. 213–228). Chicago, IL: Nelson-Hall Publishers.

Tajfel, H. (1970). Experiments in intergroup discrimination. *Scientific America, 223*, 96–102.

Tajfel, H., & Turner, J. C. (1979). An integrative theory of intergroup conflict. In W. G. Austin & S. Worchel (Eds.), *The social psychology of intergroup relations* (pp. 33–47). Monterey, CA: Brooks/Cole.

Tajfel, H., & Turner, J. C. (1985). The social identity theory of intergroup behavior. In S. Worchel & W. G. Austin (Eds.), *Psychology of intergroup relations* (2nd ed., pp. 7–24). Chicago: Nelson-Hall.

Tangney, J. P. (2003). Self-relevant emotions. In M. R. Leary & R. F. Tangney (Eds.), *Handbook of self and identity* (pp. 384–400). New York: Guilford press.

Tangney, J. P., & Dearing, R. L. (2002). *Shame and guilt*. New York: Guilford.

Triandis, H. C. (1995). *Individualism and collectivism*. Boulder, CO: Westview.

Triandis, H. C., & Gelfand, M. J. (1998). Converging measurement of horizontal and vertical individualism and collectivism. *Journal of Personality and Social Psychology, 74*, 118–128. doi: 10.1037/0022-3514.74.1.118

Tropp, L. R., & Mallett, R. K. (Eds.) (2011). *Moving beyond prejudice reduction: Pathways to positive intergroup relations*. Washington, DC: American Psychological Association.

Turel, O., & Connelly, C. E. (2012). Team spirit: The influence of psychological collectivism on the usage of e-collaboration tools. *Group Decision and Negotiation, 21*, 703–725. doi: 10.1007/s10726-011-9245-7

Vickers, E., Abrams, D., & Hogg, M. A. (1988). *The influence of social norms on discrimination in the minimal group paradigm*. Unpublished manuscript.

Vickers, E., Abrams, D., & Hogg, M. A. (1985). *The influence of social norms on discrimination in the minimal group paradigm*. Unpublished manuscript.

Walton, G. M., Cohen, G. L., Cwir, D., & Spencer, S. J. (2012). Mere belonging: The power of social connections. *Journal of Personality and Social Psychology, 102*, 513–532. doi: 10.1037/a0025731

Wilder, D. A. (1986). Social categorization: Implications for creation and reduction of intergroup bias. *Advances in Experimental Social Psychology, 19*, 291–355. doi: 10.1016/s0065-2601(08)60217-8

Wilder, D. A., & Simon, B. (1998). Categorical and dynamic groups: Implication for social perception and intergroup behavior. In C. Sedikides, J. Schopler, & C. Insko (Eds.), *Intergroup cognition and intergroup behavior* (pp. 27–44). Mahwah, NJ: Erlbaum.

Wildschut, T., & Insko, C. A. (2006). A paradox of intergroup morality: Social psychology as empirical philosophy. In P. A. M. Van Lange (Ed), *Bridging social psychology: Benefits of transdisciplinary approaches* (pp. 377–384). Mahwah, NJ: Erlbaum.

Wildschut, T., Insko, C. A., & Gaertner, L. (2002). Intragroup social influence and intergroup competition. *Journal of Personality and Social Psychology, 82*, 975–992. doi: 10.1037/0022-3514.82.6.975

Wildschut, T., Pinter, B., Vevea, J. L., Insko, C. A., & Schopler, J. (2003). Beyond the group mind: A quantitative review of the interindividual-intergroup discontinuity effect. *Psychological Bulletin, 129*, 698–722. doi: 10.1037/0033-2909.129.5.698

Wolf, S. T., Kirchner, J. L., Cohen, T. R., Rea, A., Montoya, R. M., & Insko, C. A. (2009). Reducing intergroup conflict through the consideration of future consequences. *European Journal of Social Psychology, 39*, 831–841. doi: 10.1002/ejsp.592

Yamagishi, T., Jin, N., & Miller, A. S. (1998). In-group bias and culture of collectivism. *Asian Journal of Social Psychology, 1*, 315–328. doi: 10.1111/1467-839x.00020

Yamagishi, T., & Mifune, N. (2008). Does shared group membership promote altruism? Fear, greed, and reputation. *Rationality and Society, 20*, 5–30. doi: 10.1177/1043463107085442

R. MATTHEW MONTOYA is an Associate Professor of Psychology at the University of Dayton. His research interests include intergroup relations and interpersonal attraction.

BRAD PINTER is an Associate Professor of Psychology at The Pennsylvania State University, Altoona. His research interests concern intergroup attitudes and behavior.

*Journal of Social Issues, Vol. 72, No. 3, 2016, pp. 601–613*
*doi: 10.1111/josi.12184*

# The Historical and Relational Contexts of the Study of Positive Behaviors across Group Boundaries

Arie Nadler[*]

*Tel Aviv University and The Academic College of Society and Arts*

*The article begins by placing the present emphasis against the background of developments in two fields of social psychological research: intergroup relations and prosocial behavior. This interest in cross-group positive behaviors emanates, partly at least, from developments in Social Psychology the sociocultural environment in which it has developed. Subsequently, the meaning of positive behavior is considered within a specific intergroup relational context. From a broad perspective, intergroup relations are positive, neutral, or negative. Negative relations can be characterized by direct violence or structural violence. Allophilia and xenophilia are seen as most appropriate in relatively neutral relational contexts, social change in contexts of structural violence, and the healing conflict-related psychological scars in direct violence. A final section discusses three possible future research directions: Effects of power relations, in-group identity, and Internet-based interactions on cross-group positive behaviors. A discussion of the important implications of the research concludes this article.*

Positive behavior between individuals and groups is a stage on which people's needs for interdependence with others, and independence from them are expressed (Nadler, 2012a). Caring for others and showing an interest in them represents solidarity within or between group boundaries, whereas dependency on them constitutes social inequality in interpersonal and intergroup relations (Nadler, 2015; Nadler & Halabi, 2015). The present volume centers its attention on cross-group positive behaviors as the expressions solidarity and benevolence across group boundaries. This research on intergroup helping is anchored in two fields of social psychology: research on prosocial behavior and intergroup

*Correspondence concerning this article should be addressed to Arie Nadler, Department of Psychology, Tel Aviv University, Ramat-Aviv, 69978, Israel. [e-mail: arie@freud.tau.ac.il].

Preparation of this manuscript was supported by the German Science Foundation (Grant number LE12603/3-2).*

relations. This concluding article begins by considering the present volume as it relates to these two fields of research, continues to discuss how a specific relational intergroup context (e.g., conflict involving direct or structural violence, Galtung, 1969) determines the meaning of what constitutes positive intergroup behaviors. This discussion of the relational intergroup context addresses the other side of positive intergroup behaviors: a potential expression of intergroup inequality. The article continues to suggest future research directions, and concludes by considering the implications of research on positive intergroup behaviors for diverse contexts of intergroup relations.

## Intergroup Relations and Prosocial Behavior: Two Relevant Fields of Social Psychological Research

### Research on Intergroup Relations

The present focus on positive intergroup behaviors draws from the long tradition of research on the social psychology of intergroup relations. Yet, the contents of the present volume depart from much of this past research that has viewed intergroup relations through "dark glasses" of prejudice, discrimination, conflict, and competition (Siem, Stürmer, & Pittinsky, 2016; Stürmer et al., 2013). One reason for the dominance of this pessimistic view in past research is that when social psychology was created, in the first half of the 20th century, the emphasis in the broad discipline of psychology was on the negative, maladjusted, and pathological aspects of human behavior. In its early days, social psychology emulated this pessimistic outlook. One expression of this is the fact that the title of the first major journal in social psychology was the *Journal of Abnormal and Social Psychology*. This title changed to the current title of *Journal of Personality and Social Psychology* only in 1965.

A second reason for this pessimistic view of intergroup relations is that the field of social psychology was born and developed in an era of intergroup conflicts (Siem et al., 2016). The field was created during the first half of the 20th century, a period shadowed by the First and Second World Wars, and developed in the second half of the 20th century, which was dominated by the looming clouds of the cold war and the threat of a nuclear holocaust. In addition to the international tensions that dominated much of the 20th century, its second half was a time of social change and intergroup conflict *within* societies. The civil rights movement in the United States, the social strife around the Vietnam war, and social movements that challenged the then prevailing social values (e.g., the students' movements in the 1960s) contributed to viewing intergroup relations as competitive and conflictual. This social reality led social scientists, and social psychologists among them, to regard the study of intergroup conflicts and ways to end them as most urgent problems. The titles and content of the seminal contributions of the founding fathers of social psychology conveys the field's responsiveness to this call (e.g., resolving social conflict, Lewin, 1948; prejudice, Allport, 1954). Within this context, the study of intergroup relations sought to accomplish two goals: Broaden our basic understanding of phenomena such as prejudice, discrimination, and intergroup conflicts, and offer insights that will make intergroup relations within and between societies more harmonious.

The present shift onto more positive aspects of intergroup relations corresponds to recent trends in the study of ending intergroup conflict. In the last two decades, the social psychological study on ending intergroup conflict has moved from the traditional emphasis on resolving *conflicting interests* as the king's road to end conflict, to explore psychological mechanisms that promote enduring and positive intergroup relations (Nadler, 2012a). The increasing attention to processes that promote reconciliation, as distinct from settlement or resolution of conflicts (Kelman, 2008), represents this recent interest (Shnabel & Nadler, 2015). This shift in emphasis corresponds to changes in the practices that are used to end intergroup conflicts in the "real world." Practices such as public apologies (Blatz, Schumann, & Ross, 2009), truth committees (Hughes, Scabas, & Thakur, 2007), and peace-building projects (Lederach, 1997) reflect this change in the zeitgeist regarding intergroup conflicts: from ending them to building a solid base for enduring positive intergroup relations.


*Research on Prosocial Behavior*


The other foot of social psychological research on which the present volume stands is the study of prosocial behavior. This field of research shares a common outlook with the present volume in its emphasis on benevolent aspects of social behavior, but departs from it by its attention to *interpersonal* prosocial behavior. Research on prosocial behavior gained momentum during the 1960s and 1970s that evidenced a change from an emphasis on the old values of conformity and obedience to authority, to new values that emphasized spontaneity, emotional expressiveness, and compassion in social relations. Affected by this cultural change social psychologists extended their emphasis on negative aspects of social behaviors (e.g., aggression, obedience, and conformity), to more benevolent aspects of social relations (e.g., helping, attraction, and love). The study of prosocial behavior continues to be a central area of research in social psychology (Keltner, Kogan, Piff, & Saturn, 2014; Nadler, 2012a) and has gained impetus with the advent of "positive psychology" in the discipline of psychology (Lopez & Snyder, 2009). Here too, the extension of the field's perspective from a focus on negative to positive social behaviors has been driven by two complementary goals: to gain a better basic understanding of social behavior, and to contribute to more care and compassion in social life.

In recent years, the exclusive interpersonal emphasis in the field of prosocial behavior has been extended to research on intergroup helping relations (Nadler, 2016; Stürmer & Snyder, 2010). This is attributable to developments within and outside our field. Within our field, the shift from the interpersonal to the intergroup level was affected by the advent of the social identity perspective that has told us that when individuals' group affiliations are psychologically salient helping interactions between two people are experienced and need to be analyzed as intergroup interactions (Turner & Reynolds, 2001). Outside our field, societal changes such as globalization, progress in information technologies, and immigration from less to more economically developed countries have made interactions across group boundaries more common than they had been in previous decades. Although the present volume shares a common interest with this line of research on intergroup helping, it does not share its perspective on the underlying motivations of intergroup helping. The present volume conceptualizes positive behaviors across group boundaries (e.g., interest in, liking and helping) as reflecting group members' motivation to approach the out-group. In contrast, research on intergroup helping has viewed the readiness to give and receive assistance across group boundaries as reflecting power- and prestige-related motivations (Nadler & Halabi, 2015). Thus, for example, giving and receiving help between groups has been regarded as subtle mechanisms through which groups maintain or challenge hierarchical relations between them (Nadler, 2015), and giving across group boundaries as a strategy used by the in-group to cope with threats to its relative prestige (van Leeuwen & Täuber, 2009).

The present volume represents a departure from these research traditions by its focus on allophilia-related or xenophile behaviors. Allophilia represents a general positive behavioral orientation toward an out-group and its operational definition consists of feelings of liking and kinship toward the out-group, sense of comfort, and a wish to engage with it, and positive impressions of and enthusiasm toward the out-group (Pittinsky, Rosenthal, & Montoya, 2011). Xenophilia can be seen as an attraction to foreign cultures or people that manifests itself in curiosity and benevolent cross-cultural exploration (e.g., Stürmer et al., 2013). The measures that are used in the contributions in the present volume reflect this view of positive intergroup behaviors. They include measures of interest in the out-group (i.e., Barbarino & Stürmer, 2016; Livert, 2016) liking and friendship (i.e., Davies & Aron, 2016) empathic joy when the out-group's succeeds (i.e., Pittinisky & Montoya, 2016), and making contact with the out-group (i.e., Paolini, Wright, Dys-Steenbergen, & Favara, 2016; Rosenthal & Levy, 2016).

While all these developments are reflected in the emphasis of the present volume on positive intergroup helping behaviors, an important issue that is not addressed systematically by the present volume concerns the effects the intergroup relational contexts on the meaning of positive cross-group behaviors. I turn to discuss this aspect of positive behaviors across group boundaries in the next sections.

## The Meaning of Positive Intergroup Behaviors in Different Relational Contexts

The present volume represents a wide spectrum of contexts within which groups interact. Some are relatively neutral (e.g., orientation toward a generalized out-group, Barbarino & Stürmer, 2016), others consist of relations between more and less advantaged groups (e.g., ethnic/racial groups, Pittinksy & Montoya, 2016; natives and immigrants, Burhan & van Leeuwen, 2016), and some study-protracted intergroup conflict (e.g., Shnabel, SimanTov-Nachlieli, & Halabi, 2016). Although all contributions center on positive intergroup behaviors, *the meaning of what is a relevant positive behavior* depends on the particular intergroup relational within which it occurs. Thus, for example, while curiosity toward other societies may be a relevant when the relational context is relatively neutral, behaviors that promote intergroup equality are more relevant in an interactional context between advantaged and disadvantaged groups, and healing conflict-related psychological scars in contexts of protracted conflicts.

From a broad perspective, one can distinguish between *positive, neutral,* and *negative* intergroup relational contexts. A positive relational context is characterized by positive perceptions of and feelings toward the out-group and may be associated with the perception that there are elements of shared identity between the groups (e.g., common language, perceived common ancestry). During times of common threat (e.g., a common enemy, economic threats), the general positive orientation is transformed into a *cooperative alliance* and the shared elements of identity are transcended into a sense of common identity that unites the two groups. Positive behaviors across group boundaries in these contexts include the cognitive and affective elements of *allophilia* (e.g., feelings of liking/kinship and positive attitudes) and behavioral expressions of intergroup *solidarity* (i.e., concern for the out-group and out-group helping). In the international arena relationships between the United States and the United Kingdom before and during the Second World War constitutes an example of such a positive relational intergroup context.

A neutral relational intergroup context is one in which the groups coexist next to each other. The prevailing attitude in such intergroup contexts is one of "live and let live." Although our attention tends to focus on affectively loaded intergroup relational contexts, positive or negative, the number of groups that simply coexist is higher than the number of groups we "love" or "hate." In this context, meaningful and relevant positive behaviors across group boundaries consist of *changing relative indifference toward the out-group to expressions of positive interest* in it (e.g., liking, respect, interest, and curiosity to and about the out-group).

Galtung's (1969) distinction between intergroup relations that involve *direct violence*, and those that involve *structural violence* suggest two categories of *negative intergroup relational contexts*. Meaningful and relevant positive cross-group behaviors are different in each of these two relational contexts. An example of intergroup relations characterized by direct violence is open war, within or between nations, where groups inflict physical suffering in the form of death, injury, and destruction on the out-group. Structural violence represents negative perceptions and behaviors toward the out-group than emanate from the social structure within which the groups interact. Prime examples are prejudice and discrimination toward the disadvantaged group that are common in structurally unequal contexts.

In contexts of structural violence, behaviors that contribute to the elimination, or decrement, in prejudice and discrimination are relevant and meaningful positive cross-group behaviors. Research conducted within the broad context of the contact hypothesis has provided insights on these behaviors and the conditions under which they bring about positive change in intergroup relations (Pettigrew & Tropp, 2006). Other theoretical and empirical developments have added to the these (e.g., induction of common identity, Gaertner & Dovidio, 2000), and the present volume suggests other, meaningful positive cross-group behaviors that may contribute to lesser prejudice and discrimination. Yet, in contexts of structural violence, psychological changes are not enough and *structural change* needs to also occur to promote intergroup equality that will allow the existence of enduring positive intergroup relations (Wright & Lubensky, 2009).

One important antecedent of such a structural change is the readiness of members of the disadvantaged group to embark on the road of collective action to achieve greater equality. An important determinant of their willingness to take such a collective action is the perception that they are efficacious enough to produce a structural change through collective action (Van Zomeren, Postmes, & Spears, 2008). Yet, a positive cross-group behavior in the form of giving by the advantaged to the disadvantaged may undermine these perceptions. In fact, assistance directed at the disadvantaged group that underscores its dependence on the advantaged group highlights its lack of efficacy and its need to be dependent on more resourceful and powerful out-groups. To avert this danger, assistance given by the advantaged group must be directed at promoting future independence rather than eliminate present difficulties (autonomy- and dependency-oriented help, respectively, Nadler & Chernyak-Hai, 2014; Nadler, Gorodeisky-Harpaz, & Ben David, 2009). Such autonomy-oriented assistance will have positive impact on the disadvantaged group's perceptions of efficacy and encourage collective action toward greater equality. This is therefore a meaningful and relevant positive cross-group behavior in relational contexts that are marked by structural violence. In the same vein, the joining of the privileged group with the less privileged in a *joint collective action* to affect a structural change is an especially meaningful positive cross-group behavior. Because such a joint collective action undermines the advantaged group's privileged position, it constitutes a particularly costly cross-group positive behavior. It is likely to be evidenced when advantaged group members experience moral outrage at the prevailing injustice that the current unequal structure represents (Thomas, McGarty, & Mavor, 2009). Therefore, behaviors that amplify the immorality of the existing unjust social structure and allow feelings of moral outrage to emerge are positive intergroup behaviors in these relational contexts.

In intergroup relational contexts that are characterized by direct violence, another kind of positive cross-group behaviors is relevant and meaningful. In these contexts, intergroup relations are dominated by emotions, cognitions, and motivations that emanate from the pain and suffering that the group had inflicted on its adversary. Thus, members of one group are motivated to dissociate themselves from feelings of guilt over wrongdoings through processes of moral disengagement (Bandura, 1999; e.g., blaming the "other") that prepares the ground for more violence against the adversary. Members of the other group may feel that they had been wrongly victimized by the out-group and motivated to take revenge that takes the form of further aggression against the adversary. These psychological processes work to deepen cycles of violence and threaten to transform an intergroup conflict into a protracted conflict.

In such relational intergroup contexts, meaningful and relevant positive behaviors are those that help diffuse these destructive emotions and motivations and promote the possibility of intergroup reconciliation. These behaviors include accepting responsibility for past wrongdoings, offering reparations, acknowledging the other's victimhood, granting forgiveness in exchange for genuine apologies, and accepting the validity of the out-group's conflict-related narrative. Space limitations prevent a more detailed discussion of these cross-group positive behaviors and their consequences in contexts of direct violence (cf., Nadler, 2012b). Yet, the different nature of these positive cross-group behaviors from those discussed in the previous relational contexts illustrates the importance of considering the relational context when determining what is a relevant and meaningful positive behavior across group boundaries.

Although this discussion has highlighted the need to consider positive cross-group behaviors within the context in which they occur, it should not be taken to mean that a certain kind of positive behavior is relevant and meaningful *only* in a particular relational context. Thus, for example, cross-group friendships that contribute to more positive perceptions of the out-group in contexts of structural violence (Pettigrew & Tropp, 2006) also increase group members' readiness to forgive the out-group for past wrongdoings, which is meaningful and relevant positive behavior in contexts of direct violence (Tam, Hewstone, Kenworthy, & Cairns, 2008). Also, although general allophilia-related or xenophile behaviors (e.g., showing an interest in the other's culture) are not likely to promote greater equality in contexts of structural violence or reconciliation in contexts of direct violence, they may create a more favorable background for more context-relevant behaviors to occur (e.g., joint collective action and apologizing, respectively). I turn to this issue again in the concluding part of this article.

## Possible Future Research Directions: Motivations, Identities, and Web-Based Relationships

*The Motivational Bases of Positive Behaviors across Group Boundaries*

The present volume illuminates variables that predict the occurrence of positive cross-group behaviors and their consequences but pays a somewhat lesser attention to the motivation that drives them. Positive behaviors are not always driven by benevolent motivations toward the recipient. To illustrate, in unequal social structures, displaying liking and interest to the out-group may reflect different motivations when the acting group is high or low status. The low-status group may show an interest in the high-status group, and even try to emulate it, as an expression of its motivation to ingratiate itself to the more powerful. Such ingratiation-based positive cross-group behavior is more likely when the structural inequality is perceived as stable, legitimate, and relatively unchangeable. When, however, structural inequality is viewed as illegitimate, unstable and changeable ingratiation-based positive behaviors are less likely. Here, the low-status group will actively resist the display of positive behaviors toward the more advantaged out-group. This reluctance may not represent the low-status group's animosity toward the high-status group, but its motivation to separate from it, gain independence, and promote greater structural equality. Positive cross-group behaviors by the high-status group may be guided by a paternalistic motivation that takes the form of showing interest and liking, and providing assistance to the lower status group (Shnabel, Bar-Anan, Kende, Bareket, & Lazar, 2016). This behavior may be a façade for the deeper seated motivation to "pacify" the low-status group and maintain the unequal structure from which the in-group benefits. Such paternalistically based positive cross-group behaviors are especially likely when the social structure is perceived as illegitimate, unstable, and therefore threatening from the privileged group's perspective.

These different motivations that underlie positive intergroup behaviors of high- and low-status groups are likely to result in misunderstandings between the groups that worsen rather than benefit intergroup relations (Nadler, Halabi, & Harpaz-Gorodeisky, 2009). The investigation of these, and related, possibilities represents an important avenue for future research that will deepen our understanding of the meaning and consequences of positive behaviors across group boundaries in contexts of structural inequality.

Another avenue of future research concerns the links between the characteristics of the in-group's collective identity and positive behaviors across group boundaries.

*Collective Identities and Positive Behaviors across Group Boundaries*

Will group members who identify highly with their group be more or less likely to engage in positive behaviors toward the out-group? The answer to this question is not clear-cut. One possibility is that because high identifiers care strongly about their group's image, they will be readier to behave positively toward the out-group than will low identifiers, especially when this behavior is in line with their in-group's central norms (see Montoya & Pinter, 2016). Yet, it may also be that high identifiers care less about out-groups than low identifiers, which will make them less likely to behave positively across group boundaries. A conceptual distinction that is relevant to answering this question is between "glorification-based" and "attachment-based" identification (Roccas, Klar, & Liviatan, 2006). Glorification-based identification is based on viewing the in-group as superior to out-groups, and attachment-based identification expresses group members' genuine attachment to their group. Positive behavior across group boundaries by glorification-based high identifiers is likely to be motivated by the desire to present the in-group positively and not by a genuine benevolent interest in the out-group. As research on the links between giving and prestige suggests, glorification-based high identifiers will be especially likely to behave positively toward the out-group when these intergroup interactions are public (Nadler & Halabi, 2015). Attachment-based high identifiers are not expected to behave differently toward the out-group in public than in private conditions (van Vugt & Park, 2010). The study of the effects of the level, and kind, of in-group identification on the kind and amount of positive behaviors toward out-group members is an important avenue for future research.

*Internet Technologies and Positive Behaviors across Group Boundaries*

A research question that has not been addressed in the present volume but is of an increasing interest in today's world concerns positive cross-group boundaries behaviors as they occur on the Internet web. New information technologies render such behaviors easier than they had been in previous times. In fact, expressing an interest in another culture and indicating "liking" toward an out-group member are a computer click away in "Facebook"-dominated cross-group interactions. How do these technologies affect in-group members' willingness to invest efforts in positive behaviors toward others? Because Internet-based interactions are easier to initiate, group members may show greater readiness to behave positively toward out-groups. Yet, the ease of emitting positive behaviors on the web is also true for negative behaviors (e.g., making slanderous comments about other groups) and web-based intergroup interactions may reflect an increase in positive and negative behaviors across group boundaries.

Of even greater interest is the possibility that the web encourages "shallower" positive cross-group behaviors (e.g., liking, interest) at the expanse of "deeper" and commitment-based positive behaviors (e.g., joint collective action). People may feel that by expressing liking on "Facebook" for out-group members, or visiting a website that tells about the out-group's culture, they had done enough and are exempt from committing to more costly cross-boundaries positive behaviors (e.g., actively assisting the out-group). Another question in this regard concerns the meaning and impact of positive web-based behaviors. For example, although it may be easier to apologize through an impersonal channel such as the web, the value of a web-based apology may be regarded as lesser than the value of the same apology made in a nontechnologically mediated interaction. These and similar questions are increasingly important in a world that is characterized by an ever increasing pace of technological change.

## Concluding Comments

In conclusion, I propose to revisit the issue of what are "positive behaviors across group boundaries." A distinction may be drawn between three categories of positive intergroup behaviors: behaviors that *ameliorate negative intergroup phenomena* (e.g., prejudice), behaviors that express *a positive orientation* toward the out-group (i.e., allophilia-related or xenophile behaviors), and behaviors that aim to produce a change in the social structure within which the groups interact (e.g., joint collective action). These distinctions do not imply that the three categories are mutually exclusive. The present focus on allophilia-related behaviors gives rise to a central question that has implications for many applied contexts: What are the effects of xenophilia (e.g., expressed interest in the out-group's culture) on other kinds of positive intergroup positive behaviors?

In answering this question, it is important to note that the positive behaviors in the present volume apply to all intergroup contexts. One can express an interest in the culture of a group toward which one is prejudicial, locked into a protracted conflict with, or coexists with. From this perspective, xenophilia-related behaviors constitute a general category of positive behaviors that may facilitate other more context-specific intergroup behaviors. Groups that are locked into a conflict of direct violence may be more willing to embark on the road for dealing with the conflict-related psychological scars (e.g., apology, forgiveness, etc.) after they had learned that their rival is interested in learning about their culture. Similarly, a reciprocal expression of liking and respect by the advantaged and disadvantaged groups is likely to facilitate their readiness for joint collective action. Viewed in this manner allophilia-related behaviors and xenophilia can be a prelude to the initiation of behaviors that reduce negative intergroup phenomena, promote a positive structural change, or facilitate intergroup reconciliation.

The present volume's emphasis on positive behaviors across group boundaries is important and timely. Due to advances in transportation and information technologies, the world is getting psychologically smaller and people have encounters with more diverse cultures and societies than in previous times in history. While this makes for a more complex world, it also presents an opportunity as far as intergroup relations are concerned. Educational programs, cross-cultural exploration, and web-based encounters may shift the focus from suspicious and potentially prejudicial view of out-groups, to a positive appreciation of the differences between them. This is likely to promote people's tolerance of out-groups that will translate into equal and mutually respectful intergroup relations. As a final note, although expressions of allophilia-related behaviors are important in their own right, they have an additional importance in today's world that continues to be plagued by direct or structural violence in intergroup relations. Specifically, the positive behaviors discussed in the present volume may open the door to other behaviors that will transform negative intergroup relationships through psychological and structural changes. This amplifies the importance of the findings and issues that are raised by the present volume.

# References


Allport, G. (1954). *The nature of prejudice*. Reading, MA: Addison Wesley.

Bandura, A. (1999). Moral disengagement in the perpetration of inhumanities. *Personality and Social Psychology Review, 3*, 193–209. doi: 10.1207/s15327957pspr0303_3

Barbarino, M.-L., & Stürmer, S. (2016). Different origins of xenophile and xenophobic orientations in human personality structure: A theoretical perspective and some preliminary findings. *Journal of Social Issues, 72*, 432–449.

Blatz, C. W., Schumann, K., & Ross, M. (2009). Government apologies for historical injustices. *Political Psychology, 30*, 219–241. doi: 10.1111/j.1467-9221.2008.00689.x

Burhan, O. K., & van Leeuwen, E. (2016). Altering perceived cultural and economic threats can increase immigrant helping. *Journal of Social Issues, 72*, 548–565.

Davies, K., & Aron, A. (2016). Friendship development and intergroup attitudes: The role of interpersonal and intergroup friendship processes. *Journal of Social Issues, 72*, 489–510.

Gaertner, S. L., & Dovidio, J. F. (2000). *Reducing intergroup bias: The Common Ingroup Identity Model*. Philadelphia: Psychology Press.

Galtung, J. (1969). Violence, peace, and peace research. *Journal of Peace Research, 6*, 167–191.

Hughes, E., Scabas, W. A., & Thakur, R. (Eds.) (2007). *Atrocities and international accountability: Beyond transitional justice*. New York: United Nations University.

Kelman, H. C. (2008). Reconciliation from a social-psychological perspective. In A. Nadler, T. Malloy, & J. D. Fisher (Eds.), *Social psychology of intergroup reconciliation* (pp. 15–32). New York: Oxford University Press.

Keltner, D., Kogan, A., Piff, P. K., & Saturn, S. R. (2014). The sociocultural appraisals, values and emotions (SAVE) framework of prosociality: Core processes from Gene to Meme. *Annual Review of Psychology, 65*, 425–460. doi: 10.1146/annurev-psych-010213-115054

Lederach, J. P. (1997). *Building Peace: Sustainable reconciliation in divided societies*. Washington, DC: U.S. Institute of Peace.

Lewin, K. (1948). *Resolving social conflict*. Washington, DC: American Psychological Association.

Livert, D. (2016). A cook's tour abroad: Long term effects of intergroup contact on positive outgroup attitudes. *Journal of Social Issues, 72*, 524–547.

Lopez, S. J., & Snyder, C. R. (2009). *Oxford handbook of positive psychology* (2nd ed.). New York: Oxford University Press. doi: 10.1093/oxfordhb/9780195187243.001.0001

Montoya, R. M., & Pinter, B. (2016). A model for understanding positive intergroup relations using the ingroup-favoring norm. *Journal of Social Issues, 72*, 584–600.

Nadler, A. (2012a). From help-giving to helping relations: Belongingness and independence in social interaction. In K. Deaux & M. Snyder (Eds.), *The Oxford handbook of personality and social psychology* (pp. 394–419). New York: Oxford University Press. doi: 10.1093/oxfordhb/9780195398991.013.0016

Nadler, A. (2012b). Intergroup reconciliation: Definition, processes and dilemmas. In L. Tropp (Ed.), *Oxford handbook of conflict* (pp. 291–308). NY: Oxford University Press. doi: 10.1093/oxfordhb/9780199747672.013.0017

Nadler, A. (2015). The other side of helping: Seeking and receiving help. In D. Schroeder & W. Graziano (Eds.), *The Oxford handbook of prosocial behavior*. New York: Oxford University Press. doi: 10.1093/oxfordhb/9780195399813.013.004

Nadler, A. (in press). Intergroup helping relations. *Current Opinion in Psychology*.

Nadler, A., & Chernyak-Hai, L. (2014). Helping them stay where they are: Status effects on dependence/autonomy-oriented helping. *Journal of Personality and Social Psychology, 106*, 58–72. doi: 10.1037/a0034152

Nadler, A., & Halabi, S. (2015). Helping relations and inequality between individuals and groups. In M. Mikulincer, P. R. Shaver, J. F. Dovidio & J. A. Simpson (Eds.), *The APA handbook of personality and social psychology, volume 2, group processes* (pp. 371–393). Washington, DC: APA Press.

Nadler, A., Halabi, S., & Harpaz-Gorodeisky, G. (2009). Intergroup helping as status organizing processes: Creating, maintaining and challenging status relations through giving, seeking and receiving help. In S. Demoulin, J. P. Leyens, & J. F. Dovidio (Eds.), *Intergroup misunderstandings: Impact of divergent social realities* (pp. 311–331). Washington, DC: Psychology Press.

Nadler, A., Harpaz-Gorodeisky, G., & Ben-David, Y. (2009). Defensive helping: Threat to group identity, ingroup identification, status stability and common group identity as determinants of intergroup helping, *Journal of Personality and Social Psychology, 97*, 823–834. doi: 10.1037/a0015968

Paolini, S., Wright, S., Dys-Steenbergen, O., & Favara, I. (2016). Self-expansion and intergroup contact: Expectancies and motives to self-expand lead to greater interest in outgroup contact and more positive intergroup relations. *Journal of Social Issues, 72*, 450–471.

Pettigrew, T. F., & Tropp, L. R. (2006). Meta-analytic test of intergroup contact theory. *Journal of Personality and Social Psychology, 90*, 751–783. doi: 10.1037/0022-3514.90.5.751

Pittinsky, T. L., & Montoya, R. M. (2016). Empathic joy in positive intergroup relations. *Journal of Social Issues, 72*, 511–523.

Pittinsky, T. L., Rosenthal, S. A., & Montoya, R. M. (2011). Liking is not the opposite of disliking: The functional separability of positive and negative attitudes toward minority groups. *Cultural Diversity and Ethnic Minority Psychology, 17*, 134–143. doi: 10.1037/a0023806

Roccas, S., Klar, Y., & Liviatan, I. (2006). The paradox of group-based guilt: Modes of national identification, conflict vehemence, and reactions to the in-group's moral violations. *Journal of Personality and Social Psychology, 91*, 698–711. doi: 10.1037/0022-3514.91.4.698

Rosenthal, L., & Levy, S. R. (2016). Endorsement of polyculturalism predicts increased positive intergroup contact and friendship across the beginning of college. *Journal of Social Issues, 72*, 472–488.

Shnabel, N., Bar-Anan, Y., Kende, A., Bareket, O., & Lazar, Y. (2016). How to perpetuate traditional gender roles: Benevolent sexism increases engagement in dependence-oriented cross-gender helping. *Journal of Personality and Social Psychology, 110*, 55–75. doi: 10.1037/pspi0000037

Shnabel, N., & Nadler, A. (2015). The role of agency and morality in reconciliation processes: The perspective of the needs-based model. *Current Directions in Psychological Science, 24,* 477–483. doi: 10.1177/0963721415601625

Shnabel, N., SimanTov-Nachlieli, I., & Halabi, S. (2016). The power to be moral: Affirming Israelis' and Palestinians' agency promotes prosocial tendencies across group memberships. *Journal of Social Issues, 72,* 566–583.

Siem, B., Stürmer, S., & Pittinisky, T. L. (2016). The psychological study of positive behavior across group boundaries: An overview. *Journal of Social Issues, 72,* 419–431.

Stürmer, S., Benbow, A. E. F., Siem, B., Barth, M., Bodansky, A. N., & Lotz-Schmitt, K. (2013). Psychological foundations of xenophilia: The role of major personality traits in predicting favorable attitudes toward cross-cultural contact and exploration. *Journal of Personality and Social Psychology, 105,* 832–851. doi: 10.1037/a0033488

Stürmer, S., & Snyder, M. (Eds.). (2010). *The psychology of prosocial behavior: Group processes, intergroup relations, and helping.* Oxford: Wiley & Blackwell.

Tam, T., Hewstone, M., Kenworthy, J. B., & Cairns, E. (2008). Postconflict reconciliation: Intergroup forgiveness and implicit biases in Northern Ireland. *Journal of Social Issues, 64,* 303–320. doi: 10.1111/j.1540-4560.2008.00563.x

Thomas, E. F., McGarty, C., & Mavor, K. I. (2009). Transforming "apathy into movement": The role of prosocial emotions in motivating action for social change. *Personality and Social Psychology Review, 13,* 310–333. doi: 10.1177/1088868309343290

Turner, J. C., & Reynolds, K. J. (2001). The social identity perspective in inter-group relations: Theories, themes and controversies. In R. Brown & S. Gaertner (Eds.), *Intergroup processes* (pp. 133–153). Oxford, England: Blackwell. doi: 10.1002/9780470693421.ch7

van Leeuwen, E., & Täuber, S. (2009). The strategic side of out-group helping. In S. Stürmer & M. Snyder (Eds.), *The psychology of prosocial behavior: Group processes, intergroup relations, and helping* (pp. 81–99). Oxford, England: Wiley-Blackwell.

van Vugt, M., & Park, J. H. (2010). The tribal instinct hypothesis: Evolution and the social psychology of intergroup relations. In S. Stürmer & M. Snyder (Eds.), *The psychology of prosocial behavior: Group processes, intergroup relations, and helping* (pp. 13–32). Oxford, England: Wiley-Blackwell.

Van Zomeren, M., Postmes, T., & Spears, R. (2008). Toward an integrative social identity model of collective action: A quantitative synthesis of three socio-psychological properties. *Psychological Bulletin, 134,* 504–535. doi: 10.1037/0033-2909.134.4.504

Wright, S. C., & Lubensky, M. E. (2009). The struggle for social equality: Collective action versus prejudice reduction. In S. Demoulin, J. P. Leyens, & J. F. Dovidio (Eds.), *Intergroup misunderstandings: Impact of divergent social realities* (pp. 291–310). Washington, DC: Psychology Press.


ARIE NADLER is a Professor Emeritus at Tel Aviv University (Israel). His major research interests center on intergroup and interpersonal helping relations, and social psychological processes in reconciliation.

*Journal of Social Issues, Vol. 72, No. 3, 2016, p. 614*
*doi: 10.1111/josi.12185*

# Corrigendum to "This Old Stereotype: The Pervasiveness and Persistence of the Elderly Stereotype"

**Amy J. C. Cuddy**
*Princeton University*

**Michael I. Norton**
*Massachusetts Institute of Technology*

**Susan T. Fiske**
*Princeton University*

The content of this article has been changed on September 6, 2016 after the first publication on May 16, 2005.

The Results on p. 275 should read (changes in bold):

"A one-way ANOVA revealed the predicted main effect on this score, $F(2,52) = 3.93$, $p < .03$, such that participants rated the high-incompetence elderly person as warmer ($M = 7.47$, $SD = .73$) than the low-incompetence ($M = 6.85$, $SD = 1.28$) and control ($M = 6.59$, $SD = .87$) elderly targets. Paired comparisons supported these findings, that the high-incompetence elderly person was rated as warmer than both the low-incompetence **elderly target (marginally)** and control **elderly target (significantly)**, $t(35) = \mathbf{1.79}$, $\mathbf{p = .08,}$ and $t(34) = \mathbf{3.29}$, $\mathbf{p < .01}$, respectively."

This correction does not change the conclusions of the article.